The Creation of the Boer Identity

THE TRUTH ABOUT THE BOER HERITAGE

Wiets J Buys

Copyright

The Creation of the Boer Identity

Copyright 2024 © Wiets J. Buys

All Rights Reserved

No part of this publication may be reproduced, stored in a retrieval system, or transmitted in any form or by any means, electronic, mechanical, photocopying, recording or otherwise, without the prior written permission of the author.

First Edition: 19 February 2024

Written by: Wiets J Buys

ISBN: 978-0-9756467-0-0

WIETS BUYS

Dedication

Christian, Vaughn, Yoné, Anya, Larissa.

To the descendants of the Boers

Table of Contents

Preface v

Chapter 1: The Origin of the Boers 1
Chapter 2: The Boers Get Colonised 39
Chapter 3: The Boers under British Rule 72
Chapter 4: The Boers Trek 113
Chapter 5: The Boer Republics 209

Epilogue 325
Bibliography 327

Maps:
Map 1: Borders of the Cape in 1795 35
Map 2: The Zuurveld Region 40
Map 3: The Migration Routes of the Boers 181
Map 4: The United Boer Republic 257
Map 5: The Boer Republics 323

Preface

Objective historiography, the impartial and unbiased recording of history, is an unattainable ideal. It does not exist because history is written from specific perspectives. Historians carefully select and interpret facts to advance their chosen narrative. This book is no exception – it deliberately places its narrative within the Boer identity. The purpose of the book is to present the history of the creation and development of the Boer identity.

The status of white Afrikaans-speaking South Africans changed significantly after 1994 when democracy was extended to all South Africans. This change in status is evident in the altered narrative of the country's history. The focus now is on the achievement of democracy for all population groups, with specific emphasis on the role played by the black population. The history of the Afrikaans-speaking population is sometimes marginalised, and their positive contributions to the country's development are overlooked. The result is that many Afrikaans individuals either developed a sense of guilt or lost interest in their history, leading to a loss of knowledge about their collective past. History is crucial as a people are defined by their knowledge of their collective history.

Before 1994, the situation was reversed. The historical narrative in South Africa largely revolved around the white Afrikaans-speaking population, often neglecting the history of other groups. Throughout the 20th century, presenting history was a significant undertaking for successive Afrikaans governments. Much attention was given to history, and its importance was widely proclaimed among children and their parents. The government, educational institutions, churches, cultural institutions, and the media all played their part in ensuring that the Afrikaans child knew his/her history.

However, this historical presentation was primarily shaped by the ideology of Afrikaner nationalism. The story of the Boers was not told as their own. In presenting the history of the Afrikaans population of South Africa, Afrikaner nationalism never focused on the creation and development of the Boer identity, as if it never happened – as if such an epic shared history and shared trauma did not affect the formation of cultural identity. All of this was at the expense of the Boer identity.

Outside South Africa, the history of the Boers was mainly written by British authors. Some British authors were sympathetic to the Boers and portrayed them in a positive light, while others, mostly to justify their conflicts with the Boers, depicted them negatively. However, most did more to present the Boers as a cultural entity than Afrikaner nationalist historians ever did. The history of the Boers cannot be told without involving the British, as they had a massive influence on the development of the Boers as a cultural group. Afrikaner nationalist historians of the 20th century tended to avoid criticism of Britain. This work focuses on the creation and development of the Boer identity but must also tell inconvenient truths about the British governments of the time.

This book aims to free the presentation of the history of the Boers from the constraints of Afrikaner nationalism. It seeks to empower readers to decide for themselves whether the Boer identity truly developed into a unique and independent cultural identity.

NOTE: It is important to acknowledge that some historical figures used language that is considered offensive today. In the context of a history book, it is necessary to use the language that was used at the time to accurately represent the historical events and people. The author does not endorse or condone the use of such language but rather uses it to provide an accurate portrayal of the past.

Chapter 1:
The Origin of the Boers

The Cape of Good Hope, located at the southernmost point of Africa, was occupied by a private company, the Dutch United East India Company (VOC), for 143 years. During this time, the VOC's influence and character were reflected in the Cape's governance and overall identity, which continues to impact South Africa today. The VOC, which was established in 1602, was the first multinational company to offer shares to obtain capital, laying the origin of the global capitalist system. The trade area of the VOC extended from southeast Asia, Ceylon, India, and Persia to Cape Town.[1] The VOC was a capital-intensive company comparable to present-day companies like Apple and Google. Despite its high operating costs, the VOC consistently paid out excellent dividends of at least 12% to its shareholders during its entire existence.[2] In Asia, the VOC employed almost a million Europeans, using

---

[1] Ploeger, J. (2012). In diens van die Kompanjie. Scientia Militaria - South African Journal of Military Studies, 20(3), p5
[2] Schutte, G.J., (2002) Neerlands India. De wereld van de VOC: calvinistisch en multi-cultureel, Historia 47(1), Mei 2002, p159.

its 4,785 ships to transport over 2.5 million tons of stock to European markets. In comparison, its rival, the British East India Company, with 2,690 ships, could only transport one-fifth of the VOC's stock.[3] In 1602 the VOC was founded at a time when the Dutch were amid an 80-year revolt against Spain leading to their independence in 1648. As Protestants, the Dutch were seeking to protect their rights, freedoms, and religious beliefs. The VOC had to function as both a commercial and political-military entity. The States-General, the government of the Republic of the Seven United Netherlands, granted the VOC political and military powers in their mandate on 20 March 1602. The private company now had the powers of a state. It could establish colonies, appoint soldiers, and wage wars in the name of the government.[4]

When gaining its independence in 1648, the Republic of the United Netherlands became a Calvinist Reformed theocracy.[5] While the country allowed freedom of religion, only the Reformed Church could conduct public religious exercises and was supported by the state. The VOC then also had to be a Christian organisation and settle its colonies according to its Calvinist Protestant faith. However, as Dr Schutte put it, it also prioritised profit, and its directors "apparently believed that God, gold, and glory were a natural

---

[3] Van Boven, M. W. (2006). "Memory of the World - Archives of the Dutch East India Company: Nomination Form - VOC Archives Appendix 2".
[4] Schutte, G.J., (2002) Neerlands India. De wereld van de VOC: calvinistisch en multi-cultureel, Historia 47(1), Mei 2002, p164.
[5] Schutte, G.J., (2002) Neerlands India. De wereld van de VOC: calvinistisch en multi-cultureel, Historia 47(1), Mei 2002, p165.

combination."[6] In 1796, the National Assembly of the Batavian Republic nationalised the VOC and by the end of 1799 abolished it due to material bankruptcy as well as "moral bankruptcy".[7] The VOC was not only plagued with corruption and nepotism, but it was also involved in the slave trade, it mistreated its staff, forcefully relocated people, and traded in opium. Complaints by the Cape Patriots about the corruption of VOC officials "filled four volumes in 1784".[8]

Life on a VOC ship from the Netherlands to Batavia in the 1600s was extremely harsh and hazardous for ordinary sailors and soldiers. The crew faced cramped and uncomfortable living conditions, harsh weather, and strict discipline. Breaches of rules or disobedience resulted in severe punishment, including flogging, imprisonment, or even death. Inadequate nutrition was a significant challenge for the crew, as the food provided was often rotten and lacked necessary nutrients, leading to high mortality rates. Scurvy, caused by a deficiency of vitamin C due to a lack of fresh vegetables and meat, claimed the lives of about a third of the crew per ship, with another third falling ill.[9] To address the issue of scurvy during long sea voyages, the VOC decided to establish a refreshment station at the Cape of Good Hope in 1652. The outpost was intended to provide

---

[6] Schutte, G.J., (2002) Neerlands India. De wereld van de VOC: calvinistisch en multi-cultureel, Historia 47(1), Mei 2002, p163.
[7] Schutte, G.J., (2002) Neerlands India. De wereld van de VOC: calvinistisch en multi-cultureel, Historia 47(1), Mei 2002, p161.
[8] Schutte, G.J., (2002) Neerlands India. De wereld van de VOC: calvinistisch en multi-cultureel, Historia 47(1), Mei 2002, p160.
[9] Theal, G. M. (1916). The story of Nations - South Africa (8th ed., p. 24). T. Fisher Unwin Ltd., p23

passing fleets with fresh water, vegetables, meat, and medical care to combat the effects of scurvy. The refreshment station was to be administratively limited to keep costs low.[10] The VOC planned to cultivate gardens for fruit and vegetables but aimed to trade with the Khoi-Khoi people for cattle, which would provide a source of fresh meat for the crews. The refreshment outpost's primary goal was to increase the efficiency of the VOC's operations, as the Cape would never contribute much to the VOC's profits.

The VOC chose Jan van Riebeeck to establish the refreshment station at the Cape of Good Hope in 1652. Before this appointment, Van Riebeeck had worked for the VOC and was considered a talented individual who had advanced through the ranks. However, he had been dismissed from the VOC in December 1647 due to his involvement in private trading, which was a serious offence.[11] Despite his dismissal, Van Riebeeck hoped to return to the VOC's service. When he was sent to the Cape, he did not want to be there, but he saw it as a stepping stone to a better position in the East. Just eleven days after his arrival, he requested in a letter to be "liberated" from the Cape.[12] He didn't want to be based at the Cape because, in contrast to "Dutch India," at the Cape individuals could not become wealthy through trading

---

[10] Du Toit, A., & Giliomee, H. (1983). Afrikaner Political Thought. Volume 1: 1780-1850. University of California Press, p1
[11] Du Plessis, J. S. (1952) Jan Van Riebeeck — 'N Biografiese Skets En Enkele Karaktereienskappe. Koers, vol. 19, no. 4, 1952, pp. 129-143., p133
[12] Du Plessis, J. S. (1952) Jan Van Riebeeck — 'N Biografiese Skets En Enkele Karaktereienskappe. Koers, vol. 19, no. 4, 1952, pp. 129-143., p138

or speculating in commodities.[13] Despite his reluctance, Van Riebeeck realised that the better and sooner he completed his task at the Cape, the quicker he could receive a promotion to India. He ultimately succeeded in establishing the refreshment station, but he remained eager to leave the Cape and return to the East. He repeatedly requested to serve in India for a few more years, and his requests were finally granted on 12 August 1660. He was allowed to leave the Cape on 7 May 1662.[14] In the end, the VOC required him to stay in the Cape for ten years.

In 1652, the indigenous people of the land that is now South Africa, an estimated 100,000 Khoi-Khoi and 10,000 San lived throughout the land. To ensure a supply of fresh meat for passing fleets, the VOC decided not to raise cattle but instead to trade with the pastoral Khoi-Khoi. Van Riebeeck emphasised the importance of maintaining good relations with the Khoi-Khoi to secure the cattle trade. He ordered his men to show kindness and friendship to them, punishing anyone who mistreated them "in their presence with fifty lashes."[15] Van Riebeeck personally conducted trading with the Khoi-Khoi.

---

[13] Heese, H. F. (2019). Cape Melting Pot, the role and status of the mixed population at the Cape 1652-1795, as translated by Delia Robertson from Groep Sonder Grense, p46.
[14] Du Plessis, J. S. (1952) Jan Van Riebeeck — 'N Biografiese Skets En Enkele Karaktereienskappe. Koers, vol. 19, no. 4, 1952, pp. 129-143., p138
[15] Leftwich, A. (1976). Colonialism and the constitution of Cape society under the Dutch East India Company [Doctoral dissertation, University of York]., p4

THE CREATION OF THE BOER IDENTITY

Between 1652 and 1699, the Dutch exchanged 36,000 sheep and 16,000 cattle from the Khoi-Khoi for items such as beads, copper, tobacco, and alcohol.[16] These exchanges were highly unequal which devastated the Khoi-Khoi people. The cattle they bartered away were the core of their socioeconomic systems, and without them, their clan autonomy was destroyed.[17] The Dutch gave almost nothing in return. The Khoi-Khoi were unable to replenish their stocks of cattle and sheep, destroying their economy. Social upheavals led to internal conflict and wars between the Khoi-Khoi clans. The conflicts left them with no cattle to trade and resulted in a decline in the VOC's supplies. In 1672, the VOC expressed concern that the wealthiest cattle owners in the east were not visiting the fort due to fear of being robbed by their enemies, while those nearest to the fort were ruined by internal conflicts with neighbouring tribes.[18] Then, in 1779, the VOC decided to begin breeding cattle. Even still in March 1699, in a letter to Amsterdam, the Cape lamented the ongoing mutual wars and thefts that continued to impact the VOC's supplies.[19]

After a few difficult years, Jan van Riebeeck made good progress towards achieving the objectives of

---

[16] Steyn, J. C. (2016). Afrikanerjoernaal. FAK., P29
[17] Leftwich, A. (1976). Colonialism and the constitution of Cape society under the Dutch East India Company [Doctoral dissertation, University of York]., p316
[18] Leftwich, A. (1976). Colonialism and the constitution of Cape society under the Dutch East India Company [Doctoral dissertation, University of York]., p334
[19] Leftwich, A. (1976). Colonialism and the constitution of Cape society under the Dutch East India Company [Doctoral dissertation, University of York]., p335

establishing the refreshment station. A basic hospital with 200-300 beds was constructed, a large garden was cultivated, and various animals such as horses, pigs, sheep, dogs, rabbits, and poultry were introduced to the Cape from Java and Europe.[20] However, Van Riebeeck realised that the current production was inadequate to support the outpost and provide supplies for the fleet. They needed a significant increase in the production of grains and wheat.[21] He was also under pressure from his superiors at the VOC to reduce costs. To address this, he developed a strategy to increase production and cut costs by introducing a "Vryburger"(free citizen farmer) population in the Cape. During his presentation to the Heeren XVII (the board of directors of the VOC), Van Riebeeck outlined several advantages that the VOC could gain by settling Vryburgers in the Cape. First, he argued that these farmers could provide ships with more refreshments at a lower cost to the VOC. Additionally, as most Vryburgers would be former soldiers, a Civil Guard could protect the fort, which would enable the VOC to employ fewer soldiers and reduce defence expenditures. Property taxes enforced on the Vryburgers would also generate additional income for the VOC, and supplies could be sold to them at a profit. Van Riebeeck also suggested that VOC officials and their families would be able to receive lodging fees from the Vryburgers, which would relieve the

---

[20] Theal, G. M. (1916). The story of Nations - South Africa (8th ed., p. 24). T. Fisher Unwin Ltd., p23, p31
[21] Fourie, Johan and Uys, Jolandi, (2011), A survey and comparison of luxury item ownership in the eighteenth century Dutch Cape Colony, No. 14/2011, Working Papers, Stellenbosch University, Department of Economics, p4.

VOC's responsibility to provide them with food.[22] In February 1657, nine VOC employees were given "vrybriewe" (letters releasing them from the VOC's service and allowing them to start working as Vryburgers) and granted small plots of land in Rondebosch.[23]

The open exploitation on which Van Riebeeck's "Free Citizen" (Vryburger) plan was based was revealing of the type of government that the Vryburgers would suffer under. He implemented a unique market system in the Cape where the VOC dictated production decisions by prohibiting free trade and mandating that all goods be sold to the VOC at a fixed price.[24] There was a clear separation between the VOC-government and the citizens. The VOC transformed from the employer to, not only the government but also the only market. The Vryburgers had no political rights, and they were firmly under VOC jurisdiction. The Vryburgers would be caught in a mercantile system where the VOC utilised monopolies and manipulation to exert complete control over its subjects' lives. As a result, achieving financial independence was incredibly challenging for them.[25] As the sole buyer, the VOC not only aimed to set the prices as low as possible but all public trade could only be done by the

---

[22] Olivier, G. C. (1968). Die vestiging van die eerste vryburgers aan die Kaap die Goeie Hoop. Historia, 13(3), 146-175., p150

[23] Olivier, G. C. (1968). Die vestiging van die eerste vryburgers aan die Kaap die Goeie Hoop. Historia, 13(3), 146-175., p150

[24] Dieter and Johan Fourie, (2010), A history with evidence: Income inequality in the Dutch Cape Colony, No. 184, Working Papers, Economic Research Southern Africa, p4.

[25] Heese, H. F. (2019). Cape Melting Pot, The role and status of the mixed population at the Cape 1652-1795, as translated by Delia Robertson from Groep Sonder Grense, p48.

VOC. In addition, the VOC also awarded monopoly contracts, known as "pachts," through a tender process, for nearly every type of produce which allowed the wealthiest farmers to obtain the right to supply to the VOC.[26] This practice opened the door for wide-scale corruption and a vibrant smuggling trade.

Most of the initial Vryburgers were individuals who arrived at the Cape by chance as soldiers or sailors.[27] Most had no significant formal education. When they presented the Petition of 1658 to Jan van Riebeeck, seven of the fourteen could only sign with a mark.[28] They struggled due to their lack of knowledge about agriculture and the challenging weather conditions, compounded by the low prices offered by the VOC. Many of them became impoverished. In some cases, the church had to intervene by raising funds to support needy farmers whose "naked children had to sleep with animals in the hay".[29] Some had to resort to hunting and pastoral farming while others became stowaways on ships

---

[26] Fourie, Johan and van Zanden, Jan Luiten, (2012), GDP in the Dutch Cape Colony: The national accounts of a slave-based society, No. 04/2012, Working Papers, Stellenbosch University, Department of Economics, p468.

[27] Heese, H. F. (2019). Cape Melting Pot, The role and status of the mixed population at the Cape 1652-1795, as translated by Delia Robertson from Groep Sonder Grense, p46.

[28] Olivier, G. C. (1968). Die vestiging van die eerste vryburgers aan die Kaap die Goeie Hoop. *Historia*,), VI p176.

[29] Johan Fourie and Dieter von Fintel, (2010), *The dynamics of inequality in a newly settled, pre-industrial society: the case of the Cape Colony, Cliometrica, Journal of Historical Economics and Econometric History,* 4, (3), 229-267, p.8

heading back to Europe.³⁰ The appointment of the Vryburgers seemed like a process of selection, with only the hardworking and most reliable individuals succeeding. Once a man proved he could support himself, he could request that his wife and children be sent from Europe.³¹ Soon after the farmers, other professions also received their "vrybriewe" from the VOC: tailors, hunters, fishermen, sawyers, carpenters, general workmen, doctors, surveyors, millers, builders, tappers and gardeners.³² Due to the Vryburgers' inability to produce sufficiently the VOC was reluctant to encourage further expansion.³³ Europeans, therefore, did not move to the Cape in large numbers.

During most of the eighteenth century, the Cape was a society that relied heavily on slave labour. The first slaves arrived in the Cape in 1658 from a captured Portuguese slave ship that was on its way from Angola to Brazil.³⁴ However, it was only at the beginning of the eighteenth century that slave imports became preferred over European immigrants. European servants called Knechts were employed, but the

---

³⁰ Fourie, Johan and van Zanden, Jan Luiten, (2012), GDP in the Dutch Cape Colony: The national accounts of a slave-based society, No. 04/2012, Working Papers, Stellenbosch University, Department of Economics, p481.
³¹ Theal, G. M. (1916). The story of Nations - South Africa (8th ed., p. 24). T. Fisher Unwin Ltd., p33
³² Olivier, G. C. (1968). Die vestiging van die eerste vryburgers aan die Kaap die Goeie Hoop. *Historia*, VI p24
³³ Vrey, W.J.H., (1968), Blanke besetting en bevolkingsgroei van die Republiek van Suid-Afrika vanaf 1652 tot 1960, [Doctoral dissertation, University of the Orange Free State, Bloemfontein]., p163.
³⁴ Hattingh, J. L. (1988). Kaapse Notariële stukke waarin slawe van Vryburgers en amptenare vermeld word (1658 - 1730). *Kronos: Journal of Cape History*, *14*(1), 43-65., p49

VOC soon preferred to import slaves to keep input costs low so they could get the produce at low prices from the farmers. The slaves came primarily from four main destinations: the Indonesian archipelago, India (and Ceylon), Madagascar (and Mauritius), and Mozambique through the Dutch network in the East Indies.[35] The indigenous inhabitants were never to be enslaved.

At the start of the eighteenth century, viticulture moved towards economies of scale which demanded increasing amounts of cheap labour.[36] This prompted the VOC's involvement in the slave trade, resulting in over 60,000 slaves being brought to the Cape between 1652 and 1808.[37] Slaves soon became ubiquitous in the Cape, with 65% of settlers who left probate inventories owning at least one slave, mostly concentrated on the wheat and wine farms near Cape Town.[38] In 1706, the Heeren XVII revoked a decision made in 1700 to encourage European immigration to the Cape in favour of importing slaves. In 1716, the Heeren

---

[35] Fourie, Johan and van Zanden, Jan Luiten, (2012), GDP in the Dutch Cape Colony: The national accounts of a slave-based society, No. 04/2012, Working Papers, Stellenbosch University, Department of Economics, p470.
[36] Fourie, Johan, (2011), Slaves as capital investment in the Dutch Cape Colony, 1652-1795, No 21/2011, Working Papers, Stellenbosch University, Department of Economics, p13.
[37] Baten, Joerg and Fourie, Johan, (2015), Numeracy of Africans, Asians, and Europeans during the early modern period: new evidence from Cape Colony court registers, Economic History Review, 68, issue 2, p. 632-656, p8
[38] Fourie, Johan and van Zanden, Jan Luiten, (2012), GDP in the Dutch Cape Colony: The national accounts of a slave-based society, No. 04/2012, Working Papers, Stellenbosch University, Department of Economics, p470.

XVII again inquired whether the Cape Officials wanted European labourers or slaves to be imported in the future. By that time, there were around 2000 Vryburgers and 744 VOC officials compared to almost the same number of slaves, slightly more than 2700. The Cape Policy Council, which was entirely made up of VOC officials, decided in favour of importing slaves. [39]

The VOC's decision to import slaves proved to be a significant setback for the Vryburgers. The increased production resulting from the introduction of slave labour caused the small market to quickly saturate. The presence of slaves also brought about a shift in racial thinking, with skin colour becoming a differentiating factor between classes. The Vryburgers started to consider manual labour beneath them, leading to the widespread use of slave labour for both skilled and unskilled tasks. This reliance on slaves stunted the development of the Vryburgers.[40] Because of the high fertility of the Vryburgers, each generation more than replacing themselves, many as soon as they became adults had to get their own farms and raise cattle to sustain themselves. Many turned to subsistence cattle farming.[41]

The VOC could not have anticipated that assembling a limited refreshment station at the Cape would create an

---

[39] Steyn, J. C. (2016). Afrikanerjoernaal. FAK., P42
[40] Du Toit, A., & Giliomee, H. (1983). *Afrikaner Political Thought. Volume 1: 1780-1850.* University of California Press., p2
[41] Du Toit, A., & Giliomee, H. (1983). *Afrikaner Political Thought. Volume 1: 1780-1850.* University of California Press., p2

entirely new ethnicity.[42] Within the first fifty years of the existence of the refreshment outpost, a complex mixture of European, Asian, and African population groups was assembled in the Cape, and the consequence was the emergence of a new ethnicity. This new ethnicity cannot be found outside of Africa. It cannot be classified as Dutch, German, French, Khoi-Khoi, San, or Asian. A new African ethnicity was born.

Commissioner Rijckloff van Goens, who was present at van Riebeeck's initial Vryburgers settlement, specified certain criteria for becoming Vryburgers. These criteria included being of Dutch or German origin, married, and possessing a reputation of unimpeachable character.[43] Additionally, he stipulated that Catholics were ineligible probably due to the war with Catholic Spain, and English

---

[42] During that time, a second new ethnicity had been created in the Cape. Today in South Africa they self-identify as Coloured. Compared to the ethnicity under discussion in this book, the Coloured population has more diverse origins. The Cape Coloured population from Wellington (within the region of the original Cape colony): 30.1% Khoe-San, 24% European, 10.5% East Asian, 19.7% South Asian, 15.6% West/East African and 0.2% Native American. The Coloured populations living further from the original Cape colony had different admixture patterns with less Asian and more Khoe-San contribution: Colesberg Coloured (48.6% Khoe-San, 20% European, 2.9% East Asian, 6.7% South Asian, 21.6% West/East African, 0.2% Native American) and Askham Coloured (76.9% Khoe-San, 11.1% European, 0.9% East Asian, 3.9% South Asian, 7.2% West/East African, 0% Native American). Hollfelder, N., Erasmus, J.C., Hammaren, R. et al. Patterns of African and Asian admixture in the Afrikaner population of South Africa. BMC Biol 18, 16 (2020)., p5

[43] Vrey, W.J.H., (1968), Blanke besetting en bevolkingsgroei van die Republiek van Suid-Afrika vanaf 1652 tot 1960, [Doctoral dissertation, University of the Orange Free State, Bloemfontein]., p27

were deemed untrustworthy and dangerous.[44] The majority of Vryburgers were appointed from the ranks of soldiers, most of whom were not of Dutch origin, but were Germans.[45] The majority of them who arrived at the Cape were between the ages of twenty and twenty-three.[46] Some Germans moved to the Netherlands to escape poverty and displacement after the Thirty Years' War, where they were then recruited by the VOC and sent to the Cape. Others migrated directly from Germany.[47] Before 1800, nearly 15,000 men and women from German-speaking parts of Europe made their way to the Cape.[48] In total, three times more "vrybriewe" would be issued to Germans than to Dutch people.[49] In addition to Germans, Vryburgers were also recruited from other seafaring European countries such as Sweden and even some Poles.[50]

---

[44] Vrey, W.J.H., (1968), Blanke besetting en bevolkingsgroei van die Republiek van Suid-Afrika vanaf 1652 tot 1960, [Doctoral dissertation, University of the Orange Free State, Bloemfontein]., p42

[45] Ploeger, J. (2012). In diens van die Kompanjie. Scientia Militaria - South African Journal of Military Studies, 20(3)., p24

[46] Olga Witmer, "Germans, the Dutch East India Company, and Early Colonial South Africa," in German Historical Institute London Blog, 15/09/2020, https://ghil.hypotheses.org/23. P1

[47] Vrey, W.J.H., (1968), Blanke besetting en bevolkingsgroei van die Republiek van Suid-Afrika vanaf 1652 tot 1960, [Doctoral dissertation, University of the Orange Free State, Bloemfontein]., p29

[48] Olga Witmer, "Germans, the Dutch East India Company, and Early Colonial South Africa," in German Historical Institute London Blog, 15/09/2020, https://ghil.hypotheses.org/23. P1

[49] Vrey, W.J.H., (1968), Blanke besetting en bevolkingsgroei van die Republiek van Suid-Afrika vanaf 1652 tot 1960, [Doctoral dissertation, University of the Orange Free State, Bloemfontein]., p39

[50] Zukowski, A. (1992). Polish relations with and settlement in South Africa (circa 1500-1835). Historia, 37(1)., p4

THE ORIGIN OF THE BOERS

In 1688, a group of French Huguenot immigrants settled in the Cape after fleeing their homeland in search of religious freedom.[51] The gender imbalance in the Vryburger population resulted in mixed-ancestry relationships with slave or Khoi-Khoi women with the offspring frequently absorbed into the Vryburger population or the Coloured populations.[52] The church recorded marriages between Vryburgers and manumitted slaves.[53] Vryburger men sometimes had a "voorkind" (a child born before marriage) with slaves before marrying women arriving from Europe. These children were sometimes absorbed into the Vryburger population.[54] Later, in the 18th century, 167 women who were wedded to men who received 'vrybriewe', were either slaves or Khoi-Khoi women.[55] Following the introduction of the loan system for land allocation in the interior in 1717, it is highly probable that all these farmers, along with their families, trekked into the interior and were accepted into the Boer community. A gradual shift towards negative attitudes about mixed-race relationships developed later.[56] The

---

[51] Theal, G. M. (1916). The story of Nations - South Africa (8th ed., p. 24). T. Fisher Unwin Ltd., p51

[52] Hollfelder, N., Erasmus, J.C., Hammaren, R. et al. Patterns of African and Asian admixture in the Afrikaner population of South Africa. BMC Biol 18, 16 (2020)., p1

[53] Hollfelder, N., Erasmus, J.C., Hammaren, R. et al. Patterns of African and Asian admixture in the Afrikaner population of South Africa. BMC Biol 18, 16 (2020)., p2

[54] Hollfelder, N., Erasmus, J.C., Hammaren, R. et al. Patterns of African and Asian admixture in the Afrikaner population of South Africa. BMC Biol 18, 16 (2020)., p2

[55] Vrey, W.J.H., (1968), Blanke besetting en bevolkingsgroei van die Republiek van Suid-Afrika vanaf 1652 tot 1960, [Doctoral dissertation, University of the Orange Free State, Bloemfontein]., p39

[56] Steyn, J. C. (2016). *Afrikanerjoernaal*. FAK., p47

Vryburger population continued to grow due to high birth rates of almost 3% per year and immigration.[57]

Genealogical and genetic studies into the make-up of the new ethnicity created by the Vryburger population in the Cape in the late 1600s show remarkably similar results. The genetic analysis of the descendants of this new ethnicity, today referred to as Afrikaners, shows that 95.3% of its ancestry came from European populations, mostly coming from Dutch and German (61–and 71%), French (13–26%), with smaller fractions from other European groups.[58] Noticeable levels were shown from South Asians (1.7%), Khoe-San (1.3%), East Asians (0.9%), West/East Africans (0.8%), and Native Americans (0.1%).[59] Despite having originated from a small population, the ethnicity does not exhibit genetic bottlenecking when compared to European groups. This may be due to their diverse European ancestry and interbreeding, which has prevented alleles from becoming concentrated, resulting in low inbreeding coefficients even with 125 common ancestors traced.[60]

---

[57] Hollfelder, N., Erasmus, J.C., Hammaren, R. et al. Patterns of African and Asian admixture in the Afrikaner population of South Africa. BMC Biol 18, 16 (2020)., p2
[58] Hollfelder, N., Erasmus, J.C., Hammaren, R. et al. Patterns of African and Asian admixture in the Afrikaner population of South Africa. BMC Biol 18, 16 (2020)., p7
[59] Hollfelder, N., Erasmus, J.C., Hammaren, R. et al. Patterns of African and Asian admixture in the Afrikaner population of South Africa. BMC Biol 18, 16 (2020)., p3
[60] Hollfelder, N., Erasmus, J.C., Hammaren, R. et al. Patterns of African and Asian admixture in the Afrikaner population of South Africa. BMC Biol 18, 16 (2020)., p9

The genetic analysis of the ethnicity is an intriguing subject. The ethnicity displays marked genetic differences from European groups. They exhibit a marker linked to a testes gene that engages in sperm function, indicating potential adaptation to their environment and the development of unique reproductive characteristics.[61] Genetic analysis of the ethnicity also revealed the presence of diet-related genes that impact intestinal function, fat, and sugar processing. These findings suggest adaptation to new or diverse food sources over time.[62] Furthermore, the ethnicity has West African genes, primarily from West African slaves, rather than Southern African Bantu speakers. When looking at their genes, Boers and Afrikaners are more similar to the Yoruba people from Nigeria than to Bantu speakers from south-eastern Africa. This is because the southern and eastern Bantu speakers were not living in the Cape region when the ethnicity was being formed.[63] Despite being a British colony since 1806, genetic analysis supports genealogical records confirming that British individuals did not significantly contribute to the Boer or the Afrikaner population.[64]

---

[61] Hollfelder, N., Erasmus, J.C., Hammaren, R. et al. Patterns of African and Asian admixture in the Afrikaner population of South Africa. BMC Biol 18, 16 (2020)., p8
[62] Hollfelder, N., Erasmus, J.C., Hammaren, R. et al. Patterns of African and Asian admixture in the Afrikaner population of South Africa. BMC Biol 18, 16 (2020)., p8
[63] Hollfelder, N., Erasmus, J.C., Hammaren, R. et al. Patterns of African and Asian admixture in the Afrikaner population of South Africa. BMC Biol 18, 16 (2020)., p8
[64] Hollfelder, N., Erasmus, J.C., Hammaren, R. et al. Patterns of African and Asian admixture in the Afrikaner population of South Africa. BMC Biol 18, 16 (2020)., p7

THE CREATION OF THE BOER IDENTITY

By 1730, the Cape had, in a "series of personal struggles", assimilated various identities into a Dutch-oriented society.[65] The Germans were almost as numerous as the Dutch, but they assimilated quickly. Not even the approval of a Lutheran church in the Cape in 1780 could prevent them from assimilating fast.[66] The reason for that is probably because they were young men aged twenty to twenty-three who, almost without exception, married Dutch women.[67] Around 200 French Huguenots arrived at the Cape between 1688 and 1689. The VOC implemented a policy of enforced cultural assimilation towards the Huguenots. Simon van der Stel settled most of the Huguenots in Franschhoek and Drakenstein, among Dutch-speaking citizens to facilitate rapid assimilation. Additionally, the Heeren XVII, the VOC's governing body, instructed that appropriate actions be taken to gradually eliminate the French language.[68] The VOC's aggressive policy of assimilation succeeded because despite their best efforts to preserve their French identity and language, by 1780 the Huguenots were already fully assimilated into the Dutch-oriented community.[69]

---

[65] Kapp, P. (2002). Die VOC-tydperk en die ontwikkeling van identiteitsbewussyne aan die Kaap. *Historia, 47*(2), 709-738., p720 (Prof. Kapp refers to a statement in his doctoral thesis by A. Biewenga)
[66] Giliomee, Hermann. Die Afrikaners (Afrikaans Edition). Tafelberg. Kindle Edition. P28
[67] Theal, G. M. (1916). The story of Nations - South Africa (8th ed., p. 24). T. Fisher Unwin Ltd., p52
[68] Giliomee, Hermann. Die Afrikaners (Afrikaans Edition). Tafelberg. Kindle Edition. P28-29
[69] Vrey, W.J.H., (1968), Blanke besetting en bevolkingsgroei van die Republiek van Suid-Afrika vanaf 1652 tot 1960, [Doctoral dissertation, University of the Orange Free State,Bloemfontein]., p31

When the French Huguenots arrived at the Cape, some of them came from wine-making regions in France and had expertise in both vine cultivation and the production of brandy and vinegar. Their knowledge and skills in winemaking brought changes to production methods which significantly increased production and led to economies of scale. Some wheat farms also applied these changes in production.[70] As a result, with the improvement in market conditions from the 1730s, the Cape became relatively wealthy. The economies of scale and scope were achieved through slavery after the VOC discouraged the immigration of Europeans to keep labour costs down.[71] Cape Town was the central point of economic activity in the Cape. Alcohol played a significant role in the economy of 18th-century Cape Town, as evidenced by the fact that a substantial proportion of the population was not engaged in agricultural activity. The town was known as the "tavern of the seas," with nearly every house providing some form of public entertainment or lodging.[72] Alcohol monopolists (pachters) who had exclusive rights to sell alcohol to the public made substantial profits from their business, as indicated by the

---

[70] Fourie, J. & von Fintel, D. (2010) The Fruit of the Vine? An Augmented Endowments-Inequality Hypothesis and the Rise of an Elite in the Cape Colony. WIDER Working Paper 2010/112. Helsinki: UNU-WIDER., p2

[71] Fourie, Johan, (2011), Slaves as capital investment in the Dutch Cape Colony, 1652-1795, No 21/2011, Working Papers, Stellenbosch University, Department of Economics, p1

[72] *Dieter* and *Johan Fourie*, (2010), A history with evidence: Income inequality in the Dutch Cape Colony, No 184, Working Papers, Economic Research Southern Africa, p7

fact that the gross profits were 247% of the initial monopolist fee paid.[73]

In the eighteenth century, the Cape was one of the most prosperous regions in the world.[74] The Cape inhabitants of the 18th century were remarkably wealthy compared to their European and North American counterparts. They owned more assets, including luxury items such as books, paintings, and timepieces, than people in other regions.[75] Sumptuary laws were issued in 1755 to limit the number of possessions that an individual could own due to the excessive display of wealth by some inhabitants.[76] Visitors noted the affluence of farmers and their expensive taste.[77] The Cape citizenry had high levels of literacy and owned more books and pictures per household than citizens in most regions of England.[78] The Cape was a prosperous society, even for

---

[73] *Dieter* and *Johan Fourie*, (2010), A history with evidence: Income inequality in the Dutch Cape Colony, No 184, Working Papers, Economic Research Southern Africa, p7

[74] Fourie, Johan, (2011), Slaves as capital investment in the Dutch Cape Colony, 1652-1795, No 21/2011, Working Papers, Stellenbosch University, Department of Economics, p1

[75] Fourie, Johan, (2013), The quantitative Cape: Notes from a new Histriography of the Dutch Cape Colony, No 371, Working Papers, Economic Research Southern Africa, p14

[76] Fourie, J., The remarkable wealth of the Dutch Cape Colony: measurements from eighteenth-century probate inventories, Economic History Review, 66, 2 (2013), pp. 419–448, p421

[77] Fourie, J. & von Fintel, D. (2010) The Fruit of the Vine? An Augmented Endowments-Inequality Hypothesis and the Rise of an Elite in the Cape Colony. WIDER Working Paper 2010/112. Helsinki: UNU-WIDER., p7

[78] Fourie, J., The remarkable wealth of the Dutch Cape Colony: measurements from eighteenth-century probate inventories, Economic History Review, 66, 2 (2013), pp. 419–448, p441

those in the bottom quintile, with a strong link between art and economic performance.[79] Overall, the average Cape citizen had a high standard of living, comparable to some of the most prosperous regions of England and Holland, and there is no evidence to suggest a decline in living standards over the course of the century.[80] However, the wealth was not distributed equally, and the growth of the wine industry led to the formation of elites over time.

The attainment of economies of scale in wine production, and to a lesser extent in wheat production, using low-cost slave labour, resulted in an elite that dominated the economy, generating significant inequalities among the Vryburgers.[81] The pacht-system of the VOC excessively favoured the elite even further, as they were able to sell their extensive wine and wheat harvests to the VOC at monopolistic profits.[82] Many farmers were faced with a lack of opportunities because the VOC imposed high trade barriers, while low-cost land was available in abundance in the interior. Therefore, these farmers, especially the younger ones, had no alternative but to embrace cattle farming in the

---

[79] Fourie, J., The remarkable wealth of the Dutch Cape Colony: measurements from eighteenth-century probate inventories, Economic History Review, 66, 2 (2013), pp. 419–448, p444

[80] Fourie, J., The remarkable wealth of the Dutch Cape Colony: measurements from eighteenth-century probate inventories, Economic History Review, 66, 2 (2013), pp. 419–448, p444

[81] Fourie, J. & von Fintel, D. (2010) The Fruit of the Vine? An Augmented Endowments-Inequality Hypothesis and the Rise of an Elite in the Cape Colony. WIDER Working Paper 2010/112. Helsinki: UNU-WIDER., p3

[82] *Dieter* and *Johan Fourie*, (2010), A history with evidence: Income inequality in the Dutch Cape Colony, No 184, Working Papers, Economic Research Southern Africa,

interior.[83] The transition to cattle farming in the interior, forced by economic necessity, was a decisive factor in the rise of the Boer people.

The Vryburger population who inhabited the Cape in the early 18th century were not Dutch. Due to their Dutch orientation, they can be identified as Cape Dutch, but despite their Dutch orientation, they were different from the Dutch in the Netherlands both in terms of genetics and culture. These differences were due to the assimilation of people from diverse ethnic backgrounds into the community, as well as mixing and contact with other groups, such as the Khoi-Khoi, San, and slaves with diverse identities. Their ethnic makeup cannot be found outside of Africa. Despite their Dutch influence, the Cape Dutch was therefore an African ethnicity and not European. However, cultural identity is not a static or unchanging concept - it is a fluid and dynamic concept that adapts to new circumstances.[84] During the 1700s, a significant portion of this population would experience profound changes and intense experiences that would fundamentally alter their shared outlook on life, way of living, and cultural identity.

The first thirty years of the 18th century were a period of economic hardship in the Cape due to stagnant demand from ships, the price ceilings imposed by the VOC and, for

---

[83] Fourie, J. & von Fintel, D. (2010) The Fruit of the Vine? An Augmented Endowments-Inequality Hypothesis and the Rise of an Elite in the Cape Colony. WIDER Working Paper 2010/112. Helsinki: UNU-WIDER.

[84] Kapp, P. (2002). *Die VOC-tydperk en die ontwikkeling van identiteitsbewussyne aan die Kaap. Historia*, 47(2), 709-738., p712

the first time, an oversupply in production.[85] The VOC did not allow a free market and free trade. The wheat, wine, and meat markets were all controlled by wealthy merchants, who were given monopoly rights to sell their products to the VOC. Governor W.A. van der Stel's flock of 18,000 sheep and 1,000 cattle could supply all of the VOC's ships on its own even though, by their own laws, VOC officials were not permitted to farm.[86] Additionally, the VOC also had a ban on any form of manufacturing and prevented private traders from exporting Cape goods.[87] For the "surplus" Vryburgers – the young people, the poor, and the landless[88] – there were no other opportunities available. Many had to turn to subsistence cattle farming, pastoral farming, and hunting as their primary sources of income.[89] That, however, could not be done within the borders of the territory the VOC occupied at the time.

To survive, they had to take control of their own destiny instead of relying on the VOC. They could not survive within the confines of the VOC's territory and had to transform into true frontiersmen and make Africa their own.

---

[85] Fourie, J., *The remarkable wealth of the Dutch Cape Colony: measurements from eighteenth-century probate inventories, Economic History Review*, 66, 2 (2013), pp. 419–448, p438

[86] Giliomee, Hermann. Die Afrikaners (Afrikaans Edition) (p. 37). Tafelberg. Kindle Edition.

[87] Fourie, Johan, (2011), Slaves as capital investment in the Dutch Cape Colony, 1652-1795, No 21/2011, Working Papers, Stellenbosch University, Department of Economics, p12

[88] Du Toit, A., & Giliomee, H. (1983). *Afrikaner Political Thought. Volume 1: 1780-1850*. University of California Press., p.3

[89] Fourie, Johan and van Zanden, Jan Luiten, (2012), GDP in the Dutch Cape Colony: The national accounts of a slave-based society, No 04/2012, Working Papers, Stellenbosch University, Department of Economics, p481

The shift to livestock farming was now irreversible. With their wagons, they trekked into the arid and dangerous interior with the sole purpose of surviving. They bartered cattle with the Khoi-Khoi, grazed their cattle and they hunted. This marked the beginning of the Trekboer era, laying the foundation for the Boer cultural identity. As De Kiewiet put it: "In the long quietude of the eighteenth century, the Boer race was formed."[90]

The early Boers, the Trekboers of the 1700s, were nomadic livestock farmers and their production was primarily self-sustaining. In contrast to the Khoi-Khoi and Xhosa, whom they would later encounter, the Boers practised individual ownership rather than communal ownership of resources. The pastoral production of the Boers revolved around the family, which was patriarchal with the father as the authoritative figure, and included his wife, unmarried children, and also his workers. The family could also include an extended family of up to three generations.[91] The family was of utmost importance. The condition of a man's family and family size was closely related to the number and condition of cattle or sheep he could own and control because the family was largely the labour force that had to manage and maintain the livestock. Pastoral people used kinship and alliances to ensure reproduction at the household level. They often connected the household group with other household

---

[90] De Kiewiet, C. W. (1957). *A History of South Africa, Social & Economic.* Oxford University Press., p17
[91] Penn, N. (1995). The Northern Cape frontier zone, 1700 - c.1815. (Doctoral thesis). University of Cape Town, Faculty of Humanities, Department of Historical Studies., p214

groups through marriage, thus connecting the entire community. While the Boers were extremely individualistic, the community played an important role in acquiring natural resources that were essential for the entire community's reproduction. The community was necessary for the individual's reproduction and expansion. Therefore, the expansion of the community was led by sons who had to leave the parental home due to declining resources, increasing livestock, or their desire for independence.[92] Warfare and raids were critical to the survival of any nomadic pastoral society, as several communities competed for resources. The Boers developed their own military organisation, the commando, which was strongly based on kinship structures inherited from household groups. The commando was the most important institution in the frontier region.[93]

In the early 1700s, cattle farmers moved northwards and started to settle between the west coast and the mountain range. They were unable to move eastward because the governor occupied the land in that direction. It was only after the recall of W.A. van der Stel in 1708 that the Trekboers were able to commence their eastward trek.[94] During March

---

[92] Penn, N. (1995). The Northern Cape frontier zone, 1700 - c.1815. (Doctoral thesis). University of Cape Town, Faculty of Humanities, Department of Historical Studies., p214
[93] Penn, N. (1995). The Northern Cape frontier zone, 1700 - c.1815. (Doctoral thesis). University of Cape Town, Faculty of Humanities, Department of Historical Studies., p211
[94] Van der Merwe, P. J. (1937). *Die Noordwaartse beweging van die Boere voor die Groot Trek (1770-1842)* [Doctoral dissertation, Rijksuniversiteit, Leyden]., p1

of 1713, an outbreak of smallpox occurred in the Cape, resulting in the death of almost a quarter of the Vryburger inhabitants of Cape Town.[95] However, the Khoi-Khoi people suffered the most devastating losses. Reports suggest that up to 90% of the western Khoi-Khoi population around the area of Cape Town died because of the outbreak.[96] Entire kraals of the western Khoi-Khoi were wiped out.[97] This tragic event resulted in opening up land for the cattle farmers' inland trek. The Trekboers began their new lives in the interior on a positive note. They found the Khoi-Khoi to be friendly towards them because they paid better prices for cattle than the VOC's servants did. Wildlife was in abundance and the Trekboers had the freedom to acquire farmland wherever they desired.[98] In the beginning, the Trekboers constantly wandered in search of new grazing lands and usually did not build proper houses on their farms.[99] They hardly ever had any contact with officials from the VOC government and were not interested in the corruption that was happening in

---

[95] Theal, G. M. (1916). The story of Nations - South Africa (8th ed., p. 24). T. Fisher Unwin Ltd., p71

[96] Fourie, J. & von Fintel, D. (2010) The Fruit of the Vine? An Augmented Endowments-Inequality Hypothesis and the Rise of an Elite in the Cape Colony. WIDER Working Paper 2010/112. Helsinki: UNU-WIDER., p6

[97] Theal, G. M. (1916). The story of Nations - South Africa (8th ed., p. 24). T. Fisher Unwin Ltd., p72

[98] Roux, P. E. (1946). *Die geskiedenis van die burgerkommando's in die Kaapkolonie (1652-1878)* [Doctoral dissertation, Universiteit Stellenbosch]., p37

[99] Steyn, J. C. (2016). *Afrikanerjoernaal*. FAK., p46

THE ORIGIN OF THE BOERS

the western Cape.[100] Theal called it "the most perfect freedom".[101]

In 1714, the VOC established a system of loan farms that allowed Trekboers to rent large pieces of land, of at least 2420 hectares (6000 acres), for a small amount per year.[102] This allowed the Trekboers to obtain large farms without capital and encouraged them to spread quickly over an extensive area, making it difficult for the government to control them. However, the goal the VOC wanted to achieve with the loan system was to establish its ownership of the land that the Trekboers occupied by making them pay annual rent, called recognition fees.[103] Over time, the Trekboers began to see the loan farm system as a fundamental right and young Boers would leave their parents' homes to claim their own farms. The high birth rates among the Boers drastically expanded the boundaries of the Cape thanks to the loan farm system. As the Boers moved deeper into the interior, they increasingly identified themselves as independent people who belonged in Africa.[104] This was not what the VOC wanted because they had now lost control over them. The VOC government wanted to retain control over the Boers and prevent them from moving too far because that would

---

[100] Theal, G. M. (1916). The story of Nations - South Africa (8th ed., p. 24). T. Fisher Unwin Ltd., p86
[101] Theal, G. M. (1916). The story of Nations - South Africa (8th ed., p. 24). T. Fisher Unwin Ltd., p63
[102] Die Afrikaners (Afrikaans Edition). Tafelberg. Kindle Edition., pp34-35
[103] De Kiewiet, C. W. (1957). *A History of South Africa, Social & Economic*. Oxford University Press., p16
[104] Giliomee, Hermann. Die Afrikaners (Afrikaans Edition) (pp. 34-35). Tafelberg. Kindle Edition

increase their expenses to manage the area. All they could do now was follow the Trekboers and constantly shift the boundaries of the Cape as they moved further from the western Cape.

The Boers at the forefront were supposed to obtain government permission before occupying land, but they disregarded the VOC too much to comply.[105] The VOC established laws and regulations for the Boers, such as a ban on livestock trading with the Khoi-Khoi and the obligation of hunting licenses. These laws and regulations were largely ignored by the Boers. The VOC wanted to exercise control over the Boers and claim ownership of the land they occupied, but they did not want to incur the expenses associated with establishing structures for effective government service delivery. The VOC did not provide for the security needs of the Boers. For decades they did not provide a landrost (magistrate), a Church or a Dutch Reformed Minister to marry them or baptise their children. The Boers had to protect their own lives and property through their commandos. Nonetheless, the Boers still used the VOC's markets in the Cape to sell their cattle and other products, despite the great distances.

The life of the Trekboers, who led a nomadic lifestyle in the interior, was very difficult.[106] The Trekboers moved as grazing became depleted, which limited the accumulation of

---

[105] De Kiewiet, C. W. (1957). *A History of South Africa, Social & Economic.* Oxford University Press., p.16

[106] Fourie, Johan, (2013), The quantitative Cape: Notes from a new Historiography of the Dutch Cape Colony, No 371, Working Papers, Economic Research Southern Africa, p.421

capital to goods that could be transported by ox-wagon. When the Boers obtained suitable loan farms, however, they often inhabited them for the rest of their lives and formed stable communities.[107] The absence of property rights in the interior contributed to inequality in relation to the residents of the western Cape.[108] Despite this, most Boers maintained ties with the Cape Town market of the VOC. Even the poorest of the Boers owned luxury items, which proved that they had maintained contact with the market. This also suggests that most Boers lived better than just at survival levels of the economy. They had to produce a surplus to sell on the market.[109] By 1770, livestock farming represented two-thirds of all farmers in the Cape, compared to one-tenth in 1716.[110] The high levels of cattle and sheep ownership indicated in the inventories suggest that livestock was an important source of income.[111] Boers from the interior also obtained items such as weapons, ammunition, coffee, sugar, fine textiles, and tobacco from the markets in Cape Town in

---

[107] Markram, W. J. (2001). *Die lewe en werk van Petrus Lafras Uys, 1797-1838* [Doctoral dissertation, University of Stellenbosch]., p.11

[108] *Johan Fourie and Dieter von Fintel, (2010), The dynamics of inequality in a newly settled, pre-industrial society: the case of the Cape Colony, Cliometrica, Journal of Historical Economics and Econometric History, 4, (3), 229-267, p.7*

[109] Fourie, Johan, (2011), Slaves as capital investment in the Dutch Cape Colony, 1652-1795, No 21/2011, Working Papers, Stellenbosch University, Department of Economics, p.4

[110] *Johan Fourie and Dieter von Fintel, (2010), The dynamics of inequality in a newly settled, pre-industrial society: the case of the Cape Colony, Cliometrica, Journal of Historical Economics and Econometric History, 4, (3), 229-267, p7*

[111] Fourie, Johan, (2011), Slaves as capital investment in the Dutch Cape Colony, 1652-1795, No 21/2011, Working Papers, Stellenbosch University, Department of Economics, p4

exchange for their own products such as meat and wool, as well as other agricultural by-products such as butter, aloe, ivory, hides, tallow, candles, and rope.[112]

    Due to the long distances to the markets in the Cape, the Boers had to give up most luxuries and delicacies. There was no wheat for bread, and there was also no wine or beer. The Boer pioneers hunted every day for relaxation and for their food. Even the wealthy Boers hunted for their food to save their livestock for breeding. The Boers ate meat – mostly only meat - and drank water. They would treat themselves to milk on Sundays, which they exchanged with the Khoi-Khoi. The meat-based diet was very good for them, as they rarely fell ill.[113] They learned from the Khoi-Khoi to wear velskoene (leather shoes) and eat biltong (dried meat). They lived in an extremely widespread and isolated manner. The isolation they faced developed a strong sense of independence and individualism in their character that made it difficult for them to establish healthy connections with others. This individuality also contributed to a rebellious attitude towards those in authority whom they felt were indifferent to their needs.[114] Their isolation also resulted in them becoming disconnected from their community. They only interacted with their fellow Boers when crisis or danger necessitated it, and most only came out to the market or church once a year. Nevertheless, they had a strong sense of

---

[112] Fourie, Johan, (2013), The quantitative Cape: Notes from a new Histriography of the Dutch Cape Colony, No 371, Working Papers, Economic Research Southern Africa, p424
[113] Steyn, J. C. (2016). *Afrikanerjoernaal*. FAK., p45
[114] Steyn, J. C. (2016). *Afrikanerjoernaal*. FAK., p46

awareness of unity and loyalty with their own Boer people. De Kiewiet compared their social habits, which sometimes showed a lack of cooperation, to their commandos. When they were willing to work together, it performed excellently, but at other times, it fell apart.[115]

The early Boers faced a real risk of becoming untamed and uncivilised. In 1776, Hendrik Swellengrebel Jr., the son of the former governor at the Cape, observed that the Boers on the eastern border "lived not much better than the Hottentots".[116] They were less developed intellectually and culturally compared to the Cape Dutch (later the Cape Afrikaners) in the western Cape, and the vast distances hindered their social development. Consequently, they struggled to attend social activities like going to church regularly or sending their children to school. Despite these challenges, their simple religion prevented them from descending into barbarism. They developed a few basic cultural habits, such as starting and ending each day by reading a small portion from the large state bible and citing a prayer. These simple religious habits helped them approach life with a calm and open mind. For the Boers family worship was important. To educate their children, they employed travelling schoolteachers who taught the basics of mathematics, reading, writing, and religion.[117]

---

[115] De Kiewiet, C. W. (1957). *A History of South Africa, Social & Economic*. Oxford University Press., p19
[116] Giliomee, Hermann. Die Afrikaners (Afrikaans Edition). Tafelberg. Kindle Edition., p.45
[117] Steyn, J. C. (2016). *Afrikanerjoernaal*. FAK., p46

The San posed a serious threat to the Boers. The San's attacks were so intense that the Boers were almost forced to retreat to the Cape. North and eastward expansion was almost halted by the San's attacks. In the northwestern region, the trekboers encountered a series of conflicts with the San due to incidents of cattle theft by the San. After a few years, peace was eventually restored between the two groups, and the San behaved peacefully for a few years thereafter.[118] The San fought for their survival because the Boers wiped out wildlife everywhere they settled. The San also attacked the Khoi-Khoi and together with Khoi-Khoi and Basters[119], the Boers fought against the San and hundreds were killed. This only made the San fight harder.[120] It appears that the Boers in the eastern region faced fewer difficulties with the San compared to those in the northwest. However, in 1754, thefts along the northeastern border resumed. Entire herds of livestock were stolen, and guards were killed. In September of that year, Boers had to evacuate their farms due to the severity of the attacks, but the local commandos were eventually successful in apprehending the robbers.[121] Following earlier conflicts, formal peace was re-established with the San. However, in 1770, new reports of raids by the

---

[118] Van der Merwe, P. J. (1937). *Die Noordwaartse beweging van die Boere voor die Groot Trek (1770-1842)* [Doctoral dissertation, Rijksuniversiteit, Leyden]., p8

[119] Basters were persons of mixed-race descent who formed clans in the Cape. In the latter part of the 19th century, some migrated to Rehoboth in Namibia, where they are an ethnic minority.

[120] Theal, G. M. (1916). The story of Nations - South Africa (8th ed., p. 24). T. Fisher Unwin Ltd., p89

[121] Van der Merwe, P. J. (1937). *Die Noordwaartse beweging van die Boere voor die Groot Trek (1770-1842)* [Doctoral dissertation, Rijksuniversiteit, Leyden]., p9

San began to emerge.[122] The San became a significant threat along the northeastern border, and in 1771, Boers were again forced to evacuate their farms due to the intensity of the situation. It has been estimated that during the two years from 1786 to 1788, the San killed 107 herdsmen and stole or killed 99 horses, 6,299 cattle, and 17,970 small livestock.[123] Despite the deployment of regular commando units against the San, lasting peace was not achieved for the next thirty years, and the Boers continued to face ongoing security difficulties.[124] Further expansion to the north has been temporarily halted due to the threat posed by the San.

The Boers, thanks to their rapid population growth and the loan farm system, significantly expanded the Cape's borders. A small group of farmers occupied a vast area. Whenever a farm was depleted due to overgrazing, the Boer farmer would either relocate or send his sons to explore the inland regions in search of fresh land to farm.[125] The Swellendam district was established in 1743 after many Boers had already settled there for some time. By the second half of the 1700s, Boers had already established themselves as far as the Great Fish River, and a new district named

---

[122] Van der Merwe, P. J. (1937). *Die Noordwaartse beweging van die Boere voor die Groot Trek (1770-1842)* [Doctoral dissertation, Rijksuniversiteit, Leyden]., p10
[123] Botha, J. P. (2008). *Ons Geskiedenis* (1st ed.). J.P. Botha., p45
[124] Van der Merwe, P. J. (1937). *Die Noordwaartse beweging van die Boere voor die Groot Trek (1770-1842)* [Doctoral dissertation, Rijksuniversiteit, Leyden]., p11
[125] Giliomee, Hermann. Die Afrikaners (Afrikaans Edition). Tafelberg. Kindle Edition, pp.39-40

THE CREATION OF THE BOER IDENTITY

Graaff-Reinet was formed in 1786.[126] Boers had already settled on the banks of the Fish River by the time Governor van Plettenberg made his famous journey through the Colony in 1778.[127] Further expansion to the east was halted when they met up with the Xhosas who were engaged in their own migration to the south as well as by the VOC's desperate attempts to maintain peace.[128] By following the Boers and expanding their borders to wherever the Boers settled, the area occupied by the VOC expanded by 500 kilometres to the northwest and 800 kilometres to the east of the Cape. The four districts of the Cape, namely Cape Town, Stellenbosch, Swellendam and Graaff-Reinet now encompass 110,000 square miles (286,000 square kilometres).[129]

---

[126] Fourie, Johan, (2013), The quantitative Cape: Notes from a new Histriography of the Dutch Cape Colony, No 371, Working Papers, Economic Research Southern Africa, p426

[127] Van der Merwe, P. J. (1937). *Die Noordwaartse beweging van die Boere voor die Groot Trek (1770-1842)* [Doctoral dissertation, Rijksuniversiteit, Leyden]., p3

[128] Van der Merwe, P. J. (1937). *Die Noordwaartse beweging van die Boere voor die Groot Trek (1770-1842)* [Doctoral dissertation, Rijksuniversiteit, Leyden]., p3

[129] Giliomee, Hermann. Die Afrikaners (Afrikaans Edition). Tafelberg. Kindle Edition., pp39-40

THE ORIGIN OF THE BOERS

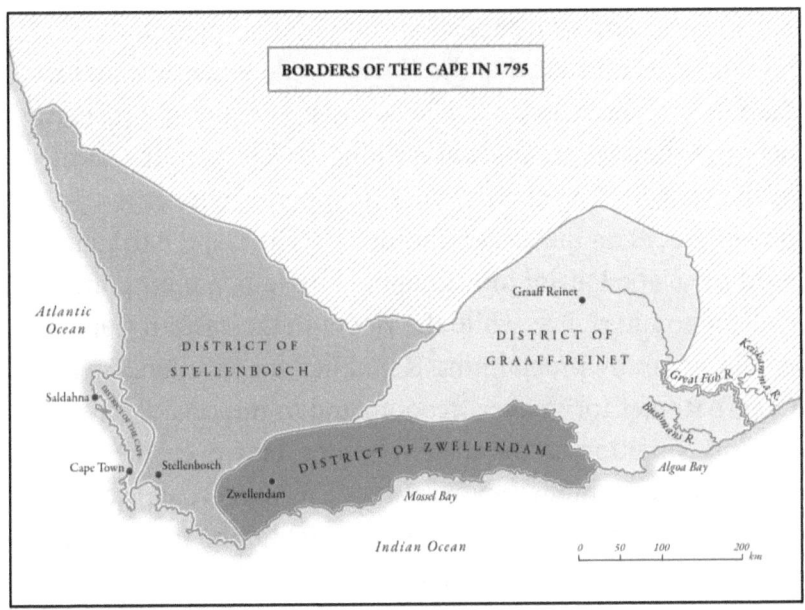

Map 1: Borders of the Cape in 1795

Over almost a century, due to the large distances and extremely different circumstances and experiences, the Boers in the eastern districts drifted away culturally from the Cape Afrikaners in the western Cape. According to the historian, Hermann Giliomee, the two groups could not form a "spiritual bond" because they did not have contact, and the significant difference in development level that had arisen between the two groups worked against a sense of unity and the development of a common consciousness.[130] The Cape Afrikaners, regardless of their own differences in spiritual development and material prosperity, formed a group that differed from the Boers on the eastern border. The Cape

---

[130]Giliomee, H. B. (1973). Die Kaapse samelewing teen die einde van die kompanjiesbewind. *Historia, 18*(1), 2-17., p16

Afrikaners were an established and orderly community without the conflicts that the Boers would experience with the San and the Xhosa.[131] The contrast in material prosperity between the two groups was striking.[132] The wealthy farmers of the western Cape had a sense of superiority over the poorer Boers on the eastern border.[133] The Cape Afrikaners used the Cape Patriot movement to strengthen their political and economic rights, while the Boers in the eastern Cape would revolt by proclaiming Republics for Swellendam and Graaff-Reinet for greater freedom and to improve their security situation on the eastern border. However, the Cape Afrikaners, although they were twice as numerous, would never rise for their political freedom, while the Boers would, through extreme struggles and hardship, create their freedom in several Boer Republics in Natalia and the interior.

The two groups have even developed different language variants. The Boers developed their own distinct dialect of language, which was initially referred to as Boerhollands (Boer Dutch) by Van Rijn, C.J., and later as Oosgrensafrikaans (Eastern Border Afrikaans) by Van Rensburg, M.C.J.[134] This dialect differed from the form of Dutch spoken in the western Cape, known as Burgerhollands (Citizen Dutch) or Kaapse Afrikaans (Cape Afrikaans).

---

[131] Giliomee, H. B. (1973). Die Kaapse samelewing teen die einde van die kompanjiesbewind. *Historia*, *18*(1), 2-17., p14
[132] Fourie, Johan, (2013), The quantitative Cape: Notes from a new Histriography of the Dutch Cape Colony, No 371, Working Papers, Economic Research Southern Africa, p421
[133] Giliomee, H. B. (1973). Die Kaapse samelewing teen die einde van die kompanjiesbewind. *Historia*, *18*(1), 2-17., p16
[134] Grebe, H. P. (1999). Oosgrensafrikaans: 'n te eksklusiewe begrip? *Literator*, *Vol. 20*(no.1), pp.51-66.

THE ORIGIN OF THE BOERS

Boerhollands or Oosgrensafrikaans was a simplified form of Dutch that had naturally evolved due to isolation. According to Van Rensburg, Oosgrensafrikaans was primarily spoken in rural areas between 1770 and 1840 along the Eastern frontier. This linguistic variant was later taken inland by the Great Trek.[135] When modern Afrikaans (Standard Afrikaans) was developed in the early 20th century, it was according to Van Rensburg as well as F.A. Ponelis, based on Boerhollands.[136] The grammatical structure of Boerhollands, as it was used from the mid-1700s onwards, was already the same as that of modern Afrikaans.[137]

The story of the Trekboers is a success story. From an economic situation of depression and corrupt oppression by the VOC, they achieved much more than just survival in extremely difficult and dangerous circumstances. De Kiewiet compared the Trekboers' migration to the biblical Exodus, but with the difference that the migration of the Boers covered a much more extensive area and lasted much longer than 40 years.[138] The more the VOC government tried to prevent them from moving further, the more their numbers grew. While there was a net loss of people due to migration

---

[135] Grebe, H. P. (1999). Oosgrensafrikaans: 'n te eksklusiewe begrip? *Literator, Vol. 20*(no.1), pp.51-66.
[136] Grebe, H. P. (1999). Oosgrensafrikaans: 'n te eksklusiewe begrip? Literator, Vol. 20(no.1), pp.51-66, p.61
[137] Giliomee, Hermann. Die Afrikaners (Afrikaans Edition) Tafelberg. Kindle Edition, p63
[138] De Kiewiet, C. W. (1957). *A History of South Africa, Social & Economic*. Oxford University Press., p15

that was greater than immigration in that period,[139] their population, thanks to their high natural birthrate, rose from 1308 in the year 1700 to 14952 in 1795.[140] They expanded the territory of the Cape to 110 000 square miles to the Great Fish River in the Eastern Cape.[141] They overcame droughts, wild animals, hostility by the San, natural obstacles, great distances, and isolation with determination and resourcefulness. Most of all, this migration of almost a century had such a significant impact on the Trekboers that they developed a unique communal character known as the Boer cultural identity.

---

[139] Vrey, W.J.H., (1968), Blanke besetting en bevolkingsgroei van die Republiek van Suid-Afrika vanaf 1652 tot 1960, [Doctoral dissertation, University of the Orange Free State, Bloemfontein]., p37
[140] Vrey, W.J.H., (1968), Blanke besetting en bevolkingsgroei van die Republiek van Suid-Afrika vanaf 1652 tot 1960, [Doctoral dissertation, University of the Orange Free State, Bloemfontein]. P131
[141] Giliomee, H. B. (1973). Die Kaapse samelewing teen die einde van die kompanjiesbewind. *Historia, 18*(1), 2-17., p2

Chapter 2:
The Boers get Colonised

In 1770, the last clans of the aboriginal Khoi-Khoi in the Zuurveld region, between the Fish- and Bushman's rivers, were about to get colonised - either by the Boers who migrated into that area from the west or by the Xhosa who migrated there from the northeast. The southern migration of the Xhosa resulted in the domination of the Khoi-Khoi tribes, who were placed in a subordinate position to the Xhosa leaders. Some Khoi-Khoi and San groups were incorporated into Xhosa tribes and assimilated into their tribal structures. In the 18th century, the Gonaqua Khoi-Khoi residing in the region between the Kei and Keiskamma rivers were conquered by Xhosa chiefs. As a result, they became subordinates of the Xhosa and worked as cattle herders and servants for them.[1] Some of the Gonaqua also provided military and administrative services to Xhosa tribal leaders and were highly respected by the Xhosa.[2] The

---

[1] De Klerk, P. (2002). 1652 - Die begin van kolonialisme in Suid-Afrika? *Historia, 47*(2), 739-764, p755
[2] De Klerk, P. (2002). 1652 - Die begin van kolonialisme in Suid-Afrika? *Historia, 47*(2), 739-764, p755

THE CREATION OF THE BOER IDENTITY

Khoi-Khoi clans in the western Cape lost their tribal structure and economy due to unequal livestock trading with the Dutch East India Company. They intermixed with Cape slaves and Vryburgers. Some were absorbed into the Cape economy as farm labourers, while others broke away and migrated northwards, settling outside of the Cape territory. These migrations led to the emergence of significant cultural groups, like the Afrikaner Basters, the Griquas and the Korannas. These tribes assimilated Western culture and adopted the Afrikaans language, clothing, guns, and horses, which enabled them to hold their own against the San and other Bantu tribes in the north.[3]

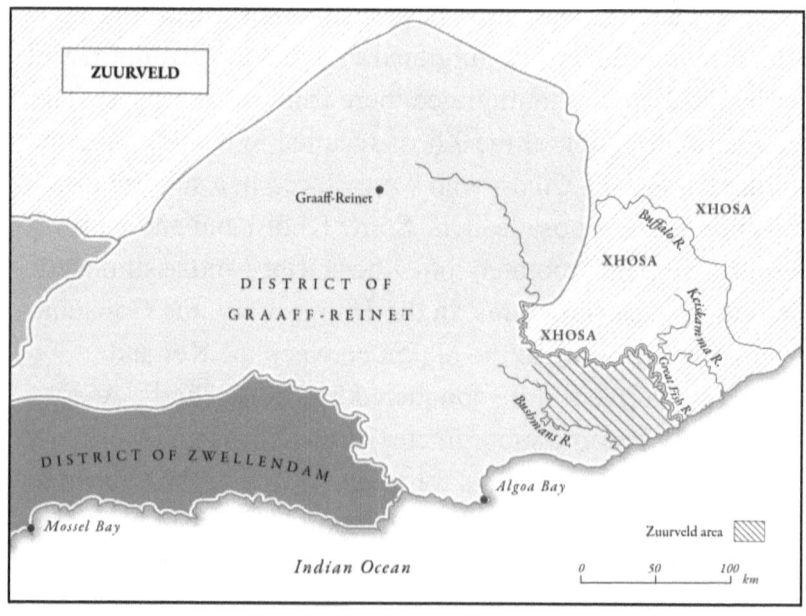

Map 2: The Zuurveld Region

---

[3] Miller, C. F. (1981). *500 Years - A History of South Africa* (3rd ed.). Academica, p91

THE BOERS GET COLONISED

During the 1770s, the Boers arrived at the Fish River and encountered the Xhosa people. They lived in a cordial relationship in close proximity to each other west of the Fish River, in a region known as the Zuurveld, for a considerable time.[4] However, as the number of migrants increased, cultural differences and competition for resources would set the stage for future conflicts. By the time Governor van Plettenberg undertook his journey through the colony when he delimited the eastern border of the Cape in 1778, conflict between the Boers and Xhosas was already looming.[5] It would have been a formidable task for the people of that era to overcome the cultural divide between the Boers and Xhosa regarding land ownership. The Boers, who held individualistic beliefs, subscribed to the notion of private ownership of land and resources, whereas the Xhosa favoured a communal approach to land usage. Additionally, the Xhosa people had a tradition of exchanging gifts and food with visitors to show friendliness. As part of this custom, they would visit Boer farms in groups, expecting to receive gifts and food. These visits could last for days, but unfortunately, some of them would escalate into situations where the Boer farmer felt threatened or imposed upon. In some cases, the Xhosa visitors would make veiled threats and taunts, which made the Boers, living in solitude with their families on remote farms, feel uneasy and fear for their safety.[6]

---

[4] Van der Merwe, P. J. (1995). *The Migrant Farmer in the History of the Cape Colony 1657-1842*. Ohio University Press, p213
[5] Van der Merwe, P. J. (1995). The Migrant Farmer in the History of the Cape Colony 1657-1842. Ohio University Press, p125
[6] Du Toit, A., & Giliomee, H. (1983). Afrikaner Political Thought. Volume 1: 1780-1850. University of California Press, p129

THE CREATION OF THE BOER IDENTITY

The Boer farmers, who were already paying recognition fees (property taxes) to the VOC, were distressed to see the Xhosa destroying their grazing lands with their large herds of cattle. The presence of a large number of Xhosa made the isolated frontier farmers feel insecure, leading some to abandon their farms along the Fish River. From June to October 1779, the Xhosa attacked several farms and carried off at least 21 000 livestock from the farmers living along the Bushman's River.[7] The Xhosa alleged that they were motivated by the fact that the Gonaqua Khoi-Khoi, whom they alleged acted as the Boers' henchmen, stole their livestock.[8] Despite efforts to persuade the Xhosa to move back east of the Fish River, discussions failed. The Boers were left with two choices: abandon the fertile land of the Zuurveld or force the Xhosa back to "their country" by force. In early 1780, a strong, well-armed commando comprising 92 Boers and 40 Khoi-Khoi,[9] led by Adriaan van Jaarsveld, drove several Xhosa captains and their people across the government-proclaimed border and confiscated around 5,000 heads of livestock.[10] This event marked the end of the First Border War (1779-1781). The frontier would remain relatively peaceful for almost the next decade.

---

[7] Giliomee, Hermann. Die Afrikaners (Afrikaans Edition), Tafelberg. Kindle Edition, p72
[8] Van der Merwe, P. J. (1995). The Migrant Farmer in the History of the Cape Colony 1657-1842. Ohio University Press, p216
[9] Van der Merwe, P. J. (1995). The Migrant Farmer in the History of the Cape Colony 1657-1842. Ohio University Press, p228
[10] Van der Merwe, P. J. (1995). The Migrant Farmer in the History of the Cape Colony 1657-1842. Ohio University Press, p216

The Boers have cultivated a strong sense of independence and individualism. They would resist authority that did not serve their interests.[11] From their point of view, they only needed a government to legitimise the claims of their farms and to provide them with a church and a minister - which was regarded as a function of government at the time. They were used to handling local government and military affairs on their own, and the only requirement they had from the government, was for officials to provide the required ammunition in times of conflict.[12] When the Boers in the Camdeboo (Graaff-Reinett) area requested the VOC government for a drostdy (a local administrative unit) and a clergyman in 1778, that was all they required from them. By the time the Boers occupied the eastern frontier, the administration of the VOC government remained unchanged for the last 100 years.[13] By 1790 there were still less than 10 clergymen in the entire Cape.[14] Up to then, some Boers had to travel distances of up to 800 kilometres to Cape Town to marry, have their children baptised or if they had any business to do with the government like paying their recognition fees. That would mean they had to leave their farms unattended for long periods. The drostdy of Graaff-Reinett was established in 1786 with M. H. O. Woeke as

---

[11] Giliomee, H. B. (1973). Die Kaapse samelewing teen die einde van die kompanjiesbewind. Historia, 18(1), 2-17., p15
[12] Miller, C. F. (1981). *500 Years - A History of South Africa* (3rd ed.). Academica, p82
[13] Du Toit, A., & Giliomee, H. (1983). *Afrikaner Political Thought. Volume 1: 1780-1850.* University of California Press, p3
[14] Du Toit, A., & Giliomee, H. (1983). *Afrikaner Political Thought. Volume 1: 1780-1850.* University of California Press, p10

THE CREATION OF THE BOER IDENTITY

landrost and only in 1792 the first minister, Reverend J. H. von Manger, arrived there.[15]

Soon after the Graaff-Reinet drostdy was established, actions of the VOC officials would reduce the power of Boers to defend themselves.[16] In the late 1780s, political unrest within Xhosaland caused a large number of Xhosa people to migrate to the Zuurveld. Some resorted to small-scale theft of cattle from colonists seemingly to compensate for losses suffered in battles with other Xhosa.[17] According to the Boers, only 493 heads of cattle were stolen from January 1790 to 15 May 1793.[18] Although the Xhosa did not intend to harm the Boers, their vast herds of up to 16,000 cattle depleted the Boers' grazing lands,[19] and their hunting caused the wild game to disappear, putting the Boers' livelihoods and lives in danger. Even though the isolated Boer families lived in fear of Xhosa attacks, the new landrost, Maynier ruthlessly demanded that they do not leave their farms[20] and he refused to call the commandos together to expel the Xhosa from their land. Maynier was a typical VOC official looking to save the VOC any potential

---

[15] Miller, C. F. (1981). *500 Years - A History of South Africa* (3rd ed.). Academica, p93
[16] Miller, C. F. (1981). *500 Years - A History of South Africa* (3rd ed.). Academica. P93
[17] Du Toit, A., & Giliomee, H. (1983). *Afrikaner Political Thought. Volume 1: 1780-1850*. University of California Press, p14
[18] Smith, K. W. (1974). From frontier to midlands - A history of the Graaff-Reinet District, 1786-1910 [Doctoral dissertation, Rhodes University], p47
[19] Van der Merwe, P. J. (1995). *The Migrant Farmer in the History of the Cape Colony 1657-1842*. Ohio University Press, p235
[20] Giliomee, Hermann. Die Afrikaners (Afrikaans Edition). Tafelberg. Kindle Edition, p74

expenses by trying to avoid conflict at all costs.[21] He would rather try to appease the Xhosa with smooth words and gifts, but he failed to grasp the situation the Boers and the Xhosa found themselves in. During discussions, the Xhosa revealed the reason why they could not move back to the eastern side of the Fish River which was also the reason for the conflict on the eastern frontier that would last almost another 100 years. They could not exist without the land they occupied west of the Fish River, as this was the only place where they could graze their livestock and obtain hides for clothing.[22] They offered to pay for the land, but the landdrost had to refuse.

Meanwhile, some Boers in the Zuurveld became frustrated with the landdrost's refusal to mobilise the district and, under the command of Field Cornet Barend Lindeque, allied with Xhosa chief Ndlambe to attack the Xhosas who had settled west of the Fish River.[23] The plan failed, and the Xhosa launched a massive counterattack, burning down almost all the farmhouses in the Zuurveld and taking over 50,000 cattle, 11,000 sheep, and 2,000 horses.[24] The Boers fled and set up laagers.[25] Maynier forbade any additional

---

[21] Giliomee, Hermann. Die Afrikaners (Afrikaans Edition). Tafelberg. Kindle Edition, p74
[22] Van der Merwe, P. J. (1995). *The Migrant Farmer in the History of the Cape Colony 1657-1842*. Ohio University Press, p238
[23] Smith, K. W. (1974). From frontier to midlands - A history of the Graaff-Reinet District, 1786-1910 [Doctoral dissertation, Rhodes University], p48
[24] Giliomee, Hermann. The Afrikaners (Afrikaans Edition). Table Mountain. Kindle Edition. P73
[25] The Boers used the laager as a military stronghold. It was formed by arranging fifty or more heavy wagons in a circular formation, with thorn

commando attacks on the Xhosa and attempted, unsuccessfully, to convince them to return to their side of the border and return the stolen cattle. Later, with an insufficient force, Maynier again tried and failed to remove the Xhosa from the area.[26] A commando from Graaff-Reinet and Swellendam then retaliated and forced a considerable number of Xhosas to retreat across the Fish River. They could only recover around 8,000 cattle. Maynier and Landdrost Faure of Swellendam decided to conclude an insecure peace with the Xhosa.[27] However, many Xhosas and their cattle remained in the Zuurveld, and the Boers blamed Landdrost Maynier for their heavy losses and failure to recover all their livestock.[28] Now the Boers realised that the Dutch East India Company would never rule in their interests and embarked on a quest for self-determination.

In the final year of the 143 years of VOC rule, the Boers revolted against the VOC to fight for their freedom and right to self-government.[29] On 4 February 1795, Adriaan van Jaarsveld and two Tregard brothers (the father and uncle of

---

tree branches placed between the wagon wheels. At the laager's centre were four wagons positioned in a square, covered by boards and animal skins to provide shelter for women, the elderly, and children. Giliomee, Hermann. The Afrikaners (Afrikaans Edition). Table Mountain. Kindle Edition, p. 73

[26] Miller, C. F. (1981). *500 Years - A History of South Africa* (3rd ed.). Academica, p95

[27] Smith, K. W. (1974). From frontier to midlands - A history of the Graaff-Reinet District, 1786-1910 [Doctoral dissertation, Rhodes University], p49

[28] Giliomee, Hermann. The Afrikaners (Afrikaans Edition). Table Mountain. Kindle Edition, pp. 73-74

[29] Miller, C. F. (1981). *500 Years - A History of South Africa* (3rd ed.). Academica, p80

the later Voortrekker leader Louis Trichardt), on behalf of a group of Boers, called a meeting of officials, ex-officials, and military officers. Two days later, when the meeting took place, a document called the "Tesamenstemming" was presented and signed by forty-three Boers. Maynier was instructed to leave the district of Graaff-Reinet.[30] These "people's representatives" took over the district and displayed the tricolour of the French Revolution, calling the form of government they introduced a "National Convention."[31] They also refused to pay taxes to the VOC or obey its laws.[32] The Swellendam district was also taken over by Boer rebels in June 1795. The "Nationals" established their own "national landdrost" and governing body called the "National Convention." They too protested the taxes and ousted Landdrost A.A. Faure, who had led the unsuccessful 1793 commando with Maynier.[33]

Some VOC government officials started to fear what they called "Jacobin mania" when a rumour circulated among the Swellendammers that a list was being circulated with the names of government officials, who were to be beheaded or banished.[34] The Dutch Reformed Church viewed the Boers as

---

[30] Smith, K. W. (1974). From frontier to midlands - A history of the Graaff-Reinet District, 1786-1910 [Doctoral dissertation, Rhodes University], p49
[31] Giliomee, Hermann. The Afrikaners (Afrikaans Edition). Table Mountain. Kindle Edition, p. 74
[32] Giliomee, Hermann. The Afrikaners (Afrikaans Edition). Table Mountain. Kindle Edition, p. 74
[33] Giliomee, Hermann. The Afrikaners (Afrikaans Edition). Table Mountain. Kindle Edition, p. 74
[34] Giliomee, H. B. (1971). Die Kaap tydens die eerste Britse bewind, 1795-1803 [Doctoral dissertation, Stellenbosch University], p29

"uncivilised," which contributed to the development of "ridiculous ideas of political freedom" in their minds.[35] The Church also believed that a "fortune-seeking Italian" (Napoleon) had incited simple people to rebel against the government.[36] Meanwhile, in the western districts of the Cape, the Cape Afrikaners attempted to improve their political, economic, and social status through the Cape Patriot Movement.[37] Even though there wasn't much shared interest between the Patriots and the Boers, the concept that an unpopular government should be opposed spread to the eastern districts where it moved the Boers to take action on their dissatisfaction with the VOC government.[38] It appears that the Boers did not agree on their future system of freedom. Although they still wanted to remain under the Dutch government, a VOC official at the Cape, J.F. Kirsten, pointed out in a letter to the British authorities in 1795 that the American Revolution had inspired the Boers of the Graaff-Reinet district to declare their independence.[39] All of

---

[35] De Wet, J. (1888). *Beknopte geschiedenis van de Nederduitsche Hervormde Kerk van de Kaap de Goede Hoop sedert de stichting der volkplanting in 1652 tot 1804.* J.C. Juta & Co., p79

[36] De Wet, J. (1888). *Beknopte geschiedenis van de Nederduitsche Hervormde Kerk van de Kaap de Goede Hoop sedert de stichting der volkplanting in 1652 tot 1804.* J.C. Juta & Co., p79

[37] Giliomee, H. B. (1971). Die Kaap tydens die eerste Britse bewind, 1795-1803 [Doctoral dissertation, Stellenbosch University], p17

[38] Smith, K. W. (1974). From frontier to midlands - A history of the Graaff-Reinet District, 1786-1910 [Doctoral dissertation, Rhodes University], p3

[39] Nel, H. F. (1967). *Die Britse verowering van die Kaap in 1795* [Masters' Thesis, University of Cape Town], p9

their plans would, however, come to nothing when the British occupied the Cape in September 1795.[40]

As a result of European conflicts, the Cape of Good Hope would change hands several times from 1795. The French Revolutionary Wars (1792-1802) was a series of wars fought between France and a coalition of European powers.[41] The British were initially neutral in this war, but they became involved in 1793 after France declared war on Britain. On 16 May 1795, the Netherlands surrendered and became a vassal state of France, with the name Batavian Republic. The British feared that France could seize the strategically important Cape, and to prevent that from happening, they occupied the Cape in 1795.[42] The Treaty of Amiens was a peace treaty signed in 1802 between France and Britain. The treaty ended the French Revolutionary Wars and restored the Cape of Good Hope to the Dutch. Merely three months after the Dutch flag was hoisted in the Cape on 21 February 1803,[43] the Napoleonic Wars started on 18 May 1803. When Napoleon achieved significant successes in the war, in 1806, the British again became concerned that the French might occupy the Cape and use it as a base to attack British shipping in the Indian Ocean and again occupied the Cape.

---

[40] Giliomee, Hermann. *The Afrikaners* (Afrikaans Edition). Table Mountain. Kindle Edition, p. 74
[41] Britannica, T. Editors of Encyclopaedia (2017, Februarie 14). Franse Rewolusionêre oorloë. Encyclopedia Britannica.
https://www.britannica.com/event/French-revolutionary-wars
[42] Nel, H. F. (1967). *Die Britse verowering van die Kaap in 1795* [Masters' Thesis, University of Cape Town], p.38
[43] Giliomee, H. B. (1971). *Die Kaap tydens die Eerste Britse Bewind, 1795-1803* [Doctoral dissertation, University of Stellenbosch], p.393

The Treaty of Paris was a peace treaty signed in 1814 between France and Britain.[44] The treaty ended the Napoleonic Wars and permanently ceded the Cape of Good Hope to the British.

The spirit of liberation ignited by the American and French revolutions also led to uprisings in the Netherlands. The Patriots, who aimed to implement the principles of the French Revolution in the Netherlands with the support of France, clashed with the Orange party, which backed Prince Willem of Orange as a monarch. Prince Willem aligned himself with Britain.[45] This same political division occurred in the Cape. The officials of the Dutch East India Company in the Cape supported the Orange party in the Netherlands and were pro-Britain, while the Cape Patriots were pro-France and protested for economic and political rights. The Boers in the eastern Cape generally showed little interest in the concerns raised by the Cape Afrikaner Patriots closer to the capital.[46] In the volatile eastern frontier, their issues were more serious than the economic freedom the Cape Afrikaners in the west were striving for. They were more interested in freedom through self-determination and declared independence through the Republics of Graaff-Reinet and Swellendam. Their "freedom" was very short-lived. When the French captured Utrecht in January 1795, Prince Willem

---

[44] Britannica, T. Editors of Encyclopaedia (2022, Oktober 3). Napoleontiese Oorloë. Encyclopedia Britannica. (https://www.britannica.com/event/Napoleonic-Wars
[45] Nel, H. F. (1967). *Die Britse verowering van die Kaap in 1795* [Masters' Thesis, University of Cape Town], p3
[46] Smith, K. W. (1974). From frontier to midlands - A history of the Graaff-Reinet District, 1786-1910 [Doctoral dissertation, Rhodes University], p51

fled to Britain. According to an agreement signed in 1788 between the Netherlands, Britain, and Prussia, Prince Willem requested the British to protect the Cape against a possible invasion by France. Britain occupied the Cape on 16 September 1795, based on this agreement.[47]

The Dutch VOC officials who were supposed to defend the Cape were supporters of the House of Orange and pro-British, which is why the British conquered the Cape with little resistance. General Craig, commander of the conquering British forces, handed a letter from Prince Willem of Orange to the VOC officials, commanding them to surrender the Cape to him. They seemingly decided to obey the command of the exiled Stadtholder.[48] Lieutenant Colonel C. de Lille made a half-hearted attempt to defend the Cape but he ordered his men to lay down their weapons on 16 September 1795, and Craig took possession of the Cape.[49] The Cape districts of Cape Town, Stellenbosch, and even Swellendam, except for Commandant Petrus Delport, who was later banished from the Cape without trial, surrendered quickly, but Graaff-Reinet refused to submit to British rule.[50]

---

[47] Nel, H. F. (1967). *Die Britse verowering van die Kaap in 1795* [Masters' Thesis, University of Cape Town], p4
[48] Voigt, J. C. (1969). *Fifty years of the history of the Republic in South Africa 1795 - 1845, Volume 1*. New York, Negro Universities Press, p48
[49] Voigt, J. C. (1969). *Fifty years of the history of the Republic in South Africa 1795 - 1845, Volume 1*. New York, Negro Universities Press, p49
[50] Giliomee, H. B. (1971). *Die Kaap tydens die Eerste Britse Bewind, 1795-1803* [Doctoral dissertation, University of Stellenbosch], p43

Craig sent a VOC officer, Frans Bresler, to Graaff-Reinet with a proclamation appointing him as Magistrate there.[51] Bressler arrived in Graaff-Reinet on 9 February 1796, but the Boers denied him access to the courthouse and official documents.[52] On 22 February Bressler hoisted the British flag, which was immediately pulled down by three Boers, Jan Kruger, Jacobus Joubert, and Jan Groning, after which Bressler returned to Cape Town.[53] In response to the Boers' refusal to accept British authority, General Craig imposed a ban on the shipment of ammunition to Graaff-Reinet and sent 300 soldiers there to establish British rule by force.[54] The Boers had already experienced a shortage of ammunition after the VOC government cut off their supply when they removed the hated Landdrost Maynier from his position earlier. They would not be able to offer effective resistance against the British, and in the frontier area, which remained volatile after the 1793 unrest, sufficient supplies of gunpowder and bullets were vital. After exchanging letters with General Craig, the last Boers of Graaff-Reinet surrendered in a letter dated 14 January 1797 and pledged loyalty to the British government.[55]

---

[51] Voigt, J. C. (1969). *Fifty years of the history of the Republic in South Africa 1795 - 1845, Volume 1*. New York, Negro Universities Press, p56
[52] Cory, G. E. (1921). The Rise of South Africa. Longmans, Green & Co., p66
[53] Voigt, J. C. (1969). Fifty years of the history of the Republic in South Africa 1795 - 1845, Volume 1. New York, Negro Universities Press, p57
[54] Voigt, J. C. (1969). Fifty years of the history of the Republic in South Africa 1795 - 1845, Volume 1. New York, Negro Universities Press, p59
[55] Giliomee, H. B. (1971). Die Kaap tydens die Eerste Britse Bewind, 1795-1803 [Doctoral dissertation, University of Stellenbosch], p59

THE BOERS GET COLONISED

The First British occupation of the Cape from 1795 to 1803 laid the foundation for Anglo-Boer relations, which would culminate in the Anglo-Boer War from 1899 to 1902. The Boers were first ruled by an oppressive, profit-seeking private company and now they are being colonised by a foreign imperial power. During the first British occupation of the Cape, unlike in other British colonies, the Cape colony's government was deliberately designed as an autocracy. All civil and military power rested solely with the governor, ensuring direct and absolute control by the imperial authority over the Cape colony.[56] Criticising the British government in the Cape was a punishable crime. Giliomee quoted General Dundas, who once stated that the administration was purely military, and criticism was "seditious and inflammatory and therefore incompatible with public peace".[57] Theal described the British government in the Cape as despotism.[58]

The British takeover in 1795 resulted in the loss of citizenship status of the Boers and the Cape Afrikaner burghers.[59] The British government imposed distinct obligations and responsibilities on them which they would not impose on other population groups in the Cape. Only they were compelled to swear allegiance to the British crown and only they were prohibited from leaving the Cape Colony

---

[56] Du Toit, A., & Giliomee, H. (1983). Afrikaner Political Thought. Volume 1: 1780-1850. University of California Press, p11
[57] Giliomee, H. B. (1971). Die Kaap tydens die Eerste Britse Bewind, 1795-1803 [Doctoral dissertation, University of Stellenbosch], p82
[58] Cilliers, D. H. (1951). Die Eerste Verhoudinge Tussen Boer en Brit. Koersjoernaal, 19(3), p96
[59] Giliomee, Hermann. Die Afrikaners (Afrikaans Edition) (p. 77). Tafelberg. Kindle Edition.

without special permission. Only they were expected to do military service and only they were obliged to pay taxes. Soon, they would also become the only cultural group who were forcibly denied the freedom to exercise self-determination in their own states beyond British colonial territory. John Barrow, the British Private Secretary to Governor Lord George Macartney, who had a wide influence on policy on the Boers, held strong prejudices against the Boers. He dismissed the Boers as savages who, according to Dr Henry Lichtenstein, he "regarded as turbulent, seditious and a disturber of the public peace, ... and with whom it was scarcely worth any man's while to make a further acquaintance" before he ever knew the Boer's way of life and before he even knew where Graaff-Reinet was located.[60]

Influenced by the philanthropists and evangelical Christians, and without determining the true causes of the conflicts on the eastern frontier, the British authorities decided that, despite evidence to the contrary, the Boers were the aggressors and that the way to achieve peace was to eliminate any military action by the Boers.[61] This policy, based on prejudice and ignorance, posed an existential threat to the Boers as it "almost made Boer self-preservation in the eastern districts a crime."[62] The British attitude towards the Boers was most clearly demonstrated by General Francis Dundas, the acting governor, in his letter to the British State

---

[60] Cory, G. E. (1921). The Rise of South Africa. Longmans, Green & Co., p74
[61] Cory, G. E. (1921). The Rise of South Africa. Longmans, Green & Co., p72
[62] Cory, G. E. (1921). The Rise of South Africa. Longmans, Green & Co., p72

Secretary for War and the Colonies. In this letter, General Dundas stated his intention to send troops to Graaff-Reinet to suppress a Boer rebellion against Manyier. He explicitly mentioned that he planned to attack the Boers and, if they refused to cease their rebellion, eradicate them entirely (wipe them all out).[63] Considering the difficulty and expense of establishing effective systems for protection and governance for the seemingly valueless territory, this policy of containment of the Boers, however, was a convenient and cheap policy to uphold.[64]

The following discussion of the Third Xhosa War is mainly based on information obtained from the doctoral dissertation of H.B. Giliomee. However, while Giliomee used terms like "Whites" and "Colonists," this work uses the correct identity of the people on the eastern border, namely Boers.

In 1797, a large-scale migration of Xhosa people took place across the Fish River due to an internal tribal conflict.[65] This migration worsened an already tense situation on the eastern border since the Xhosas involved in the 1793 war had not been expelled from the area. There were now several Xhosa chiefs, along with their followers and cattle, in the Zuurveld region. The large number of Xhosa cattle would

---

[63] Giliomee, H. B. (1971). Die Kaap tydens die Eerste Britse Bewind, 1795-1803 [Doctoral dissertation, University of Stellenbosch], p367
[64] Cory, G. E. (1921). The Rise of South Africa. Longmans, Green & Co., p43
[65] Giliomee, H. B. (1971). Die Kaap tydens die Eerste Britse Bewind, 1795-1803 [Doctoral dissertation, University of Stellenbosch], p313

devastate the Boers' grazing lands.[66] Large groups of Xhosas began visiting the farms of the Boers, seeking "gifts," which posed a significant threat to the safety of the Boers.[67] The sheer number of Xhosas caused great concern among the Boers, who feared potential attacks on their farms and harm to their families. The British authority prohibited the Boers from acting against the Xhosas, and due to the government's ban, the Boers faced a severe shortage of ammunition. Many Boers saw no alternative but to abandon their farms.[68] By the beginning of 1798, according to Bresler, the area between the Fish River and the Sundays River was completely vacated by the Boers.[69] The Xhosas in the Zuurveld now had to be convinced by non-violent means to leave the colony. Bresler and Barrow arrived in Graaff-Reinet on 30 July 1797, to negotiate with Xhosa chiefs from both sides of the Fish River. After discussions with the Xhosa chiefs, they believed they had resolved the situation, but they were mistaken.[70] In 1798, Macartney made it clear that he had no intention of compelling the Xhosas to return across the Fish River, despite the evident difficulty in persuading them to do so. The British government attributed the failure of the negotiation policy to the Boers who prevented the Xhosas

---

[66] Giliomee, H. B. (1971). Die Kaap tydens die Eerste Britse Bewind, 1795-1803 [Doctoral dissertation, University of Stellenbosch], p320
[67] Giliomee, H. B. (1971). Die Kaap tydens die Eerste Britse Bewind, 1795-1803 [Doctoral dissertation, University of Stellenbosch], p321
[68] Giliomee, H. B. (1971). Die Kaap tydens die Eerste Britse Bewind, 1795-1803 [Doctoral dissertation, University of Stellenbosch], p318
[69] Giliomee, H. B. (1971). Die Kaap tydens die Eerste Britse Bewind, 1795-1803 [Doctoral dissertation, University of Stellenbosch], p318
[70] Giliomee, H. B. (1971). Die Kaap tydens die Eerste Britse Bewind, 1795-1803 [Doctoral dissertation, University of Stellenbosch], p316

from migrating back to Xhosaland.[71] Nonetheless, the policy of conciliation was continued.

Adriaan van Jaarsveld, the leader of the 1795 uprising in Graaff-Reinet against the VOC, was arrested by the British authorities on 17 January 1799, on charges of tampering with a receipt. Allegedly, the date on the receipt had been altered from 1791 to 1794, a few years before the Cape fell under British control. However, on 21 January during his transfer to Cape Town under guard, he was freed by a group of 40 armed Boers led by Marthinus Prinsloo.[72] When the news of Van Jaarsveld's escape reached Cape Town on 16 February 1799, General Dundas decided to take immediate action to punish the rebels. General Vandeleur arrived in Graaff-Reinet via Algoa Bay with troops and apprehended both Van Jaarsveld and Prinsloo.[73] The British Imperial Government in London insisted on a death sentence for them,[74] but, because they didn't resist Vandeleur, it was commuted to life imprisonment. Van Jaarsveld passed away while incarcerated at the Castle, and Marthinus Prinsloo was later released by the Batavian government.[75]

---

[71] Giliomee, H. B. (1971). Die Kaap tydens die Eerste Britse Bewind, 1795-1803 [Doctoral dissertation, University of Stellenbosch], p321
[72] Smith, K. W. (1974). From frontier to midlands - A history of the Graaff-Reinet District, 1786-1910 [Doctoral dissertation, Rhodes University], p57
[73] Giliomee, H. B. (1971). Die Kaap tydens die Eerste Britse Bewind, 1795-1803 [Doctoral dissertation, University of Stellenbosch], p78
[74] Giliomee, H. B. (1971). Die Kaap tydens die Eerste Britse Bewind, 1795-1803 [Doctoral dissertation, University of Stellenbosch], p80
[75] Smith, K. W. (1974). From frontier to midlands - A history of the Graaff-Reinet District, 1786-1910 [Doctoral dissertation, Rhodes University], p58

THE CREATION OF THE BOER IDENTITY

On their way from Algoa Bay to Graaff-Reinet, General Vandeleur and his soldiers encountered a large group of armed Khoi-Khoi who had been engaging in acts of raiding, plundering farms, and stealing weapons and clothing from the Boers. These Khoi-Khoi were probably under the impression that they could join forces with Vandeleur. Their leader, Klaas Stuurman, explained that the Khoi-Khoi needed to regain the land that had been taken from them by the Boers.[76] In response, General Vandeleur persuaded them to relinquish their weapons and to accompany the troops temporarily, while they worked out further arrangements. At another point in their journey, General Vandeleur crossed paths with a contingent of Xhosas led by Cunwa, whom he ordered to withdraw across the Fish River. While on their return journey to Algoa Bay, General Vandeleur's forces were attacked by this very group of Xhosas. This assault claimed the lives of 16 British soldiers and a lieutenant.[77] A considerable number of Khoi-Khoi then joined forces with the Xhosas in the Zuurveld region. Together, as a combined force of Xhosa and Khoi-Khoi, they embarked on a campaign of widespread looting and the destruction of farms and homesteads in the district of Graaff-Reinet.[78] These actions marked the commencement of the Third Xhosa War.

The joint forces of the Khoi-Khoi and Xhosas conducted devastating raids that sparked fear and chaos

---

[76] Giliomee, H. B. (1971). Die Kaap tydens die Eerste Britse Bewind, 1795-1803 [Doctoral dissertation, University of Stellenbosch], p322
[77] Giliomee, H. B. (1971). Die Kaap tydens die Eerste Britse Bewind, 1795-1803 [Doctoral dissertation, University of Stellenbosch]. P323
[78] Giliomee, H. B. (1971). Die Kaap tydens die Eerste Britse Bewind, 1795-1803 [Doctoral dissertation, University of Stellenbosch], p324

among the Boers in the region. With many Boers lacking ammunition, they were forced to flee towards the west, seeking safety. Adding to their predicament, the Boers were unable to get ammunition from the magistrate's office, rendering it impossible for their commandos to act.[79] On 24 May 1799, General Vandeleur urgently called upon field commander Hendrik Jansen van Rensburg to assemble a commando to push the Xhosas across the Fish River. Boers who still possessed ammunition promptly joined the commando and started to systematically drive the Xhosas away.[80] Despite the Boers' desperate need, Dundas adamantly refused to distribute any ammunition, but he instructed Vandeleur to provide ammunition to "deserving cases". In June 1799 Van Rensburg's commando suffered a defeat at the hands of a force consisting of Xhosas and Khoi-Khoi after a surprise night attack.[81] Motivated by their successes, the Xhosas and Khoi-Khoi embarked on a rampant campaign of looting and pillaging, confiscating livestock, and setting farmsteads ablaze. Due to the scarcity of ammunition, the Boers and their families were compelled to seek refuge by setting up laagers.[82] Vandeleur himself was trapped in Algoa Bay with approximately 200 troops. The Xhosas and Khoi-Khoi then launched incursions into the eastern region of

---

[79] Giliomee, H. B. (1971). Die Kaap tydens die Eerste Britse Bewind, 1795-1803 [Doctoral dissertation, University of Stellenbosch], p329
[80] Giliomee, H. B. (1971). Die Kaap tydens die Eerste Britse Bewind, 1795-1803 [Doctoral dissertation, University of Stellenbosch], p329
[81] Giliomee, H. B. (1971). Die Kaap tydens die Eerste Britse Bewind, 1795-1803 [Doctoral dissertation, University of Stellenbosch], p330
[82] Giliomee, H. B. (1971). Die Kaap tydens die Eerste Britse Bewind, 1795-1803 [Doctoral dissertation, University of Stellenbosch], p330

Swellendam, killing several Boers and capturing women and children.[83]

During August 1799, the Boers displayed their first signs of effective resistance.[84] Boer women and children had to remain in the fields in poverty and discomfort while their husbands were on commando.[85] While Field Cornet S. de Beer was away on commando, his brave wife wrote him: "I don't rest a single hour during the night. The enemy is on our heels."[86] Dundas and Vandeleur held a strong disdain for what they perceived as the Boers' cowardly resistance and their subsequent flight.[87] The basis for such judgment remains unclear. Vandeleur, according to himself, was in a "state of siege" in Algoa Bay with 200 armed troops. Despite having a sizable and well-equipped force at his disposal, Dundas saw no viable possibility of a successful attack against the opposing forces. It was only in August that Dundas, in Cape Town, grasped the gravity of the situation. He now issued orders to dispatch 1,600 pounds of gunpowder to Graaff-Reinet and Swellendam. On 6 August 1799, in command of a force comprising of approximately 500 men, he headed towards the eastern border. Simultaneously,

---

[83] Giliomee, H. B. (1971). Die Kaap tydens die Eerste Britse Bewind, 1795-1803 [Doctoral dissertation, University of Stellenbosch], p331
[84] Giliomee, H. B. (1971). Die Kaap tydens die Eerste Britse Bewind, 1795-1803 [Doctoral dissertation, University of Stellenbosch], p332
[85] Giliomee, Hermann. Die Afrikaners (Afrikaans Edition). Tafelberg. Kindle Edition., p.117
[86] Giliomee, Hermann. Die Afrikaners (Afrikaans Edition). Tafelberg. Kindle Edition., p.119
[87] Giliomee, H. B. (1971). Die Kaap tydens die Eerste Britse Bewind, 1795-1803 [Doctoral dissertation, University of Stellenbosch], p333

Vandeleur received reinforcement via Algoa Bay as additional troops arrived by ship.[88]

On 9 August 1799, Dundas requested that former Landdrost Maynier join him to negotiate a peace agreement with the Xhosas. Although Dundas now had Maynier with him, he still wanted a strong Boer commando to be present in case the friendly measures failed. Therefore, by mid-August, he issued orders for the formation of Boer commandos to act in conjunction with the troops under his command.[89] After the arrival of ammunition at the beginning of September 1799, more Boers from Graaff-Reinet joined Tjaart van der Walt and his Swellendam commando. Due to immediate threats on their farms, many Boers from the southeastern part of Graaff-Reinet could not join the commandos. In other areas, Boers joined their commandos in greater numbers.[90] Dundas's impression regarding the reason why the Graaff-Reineters did not immediately join the commandos was that they "resisted any measures taken by the government for the district's defence".[91] While Dundas and his troops were still en route to Graaff-Reinet, the threat posed by the Khoi-Khois and Xhosas, particularly in the Swellendam district, began to diminish.

---

[88] Giliomee, H. B. (1971). Die Kaap tydens die Eerste Britse Bewind, 1795-1803 [Doctoral dissertation, University of Stellenbosch], p334
[89] Giliomee, H. B. (1971). Die Kaap tydens die Eerste Britse Bewind, 1795-1803 [Doctoral dissertation, University of Stellenbosch], p335
[90] Giliomee, H. B. (1971). Die Kaap tydens die Eerste Britse Bewind, 1795-1803 [Doctoral dissertation, University of Stellenbosch], p337
[91] Giliomee, H. B. (1971). Die Kaap tydens die Eerste Britse Bewind, 1795-1803 [Doctoral dissertation, University of Stellenbosch], p338

THE CREATION OF THE BOER IDENTITY

In Algoa Bay, Vandeleur and Dundas held contrasting views on how to end the war. Vandeleur argued against ending the war through negotiations, fearing that it would be perceived as a sign of weakness. However, Dundas held a different perspective. In early October 1799, he issued an order to cease all hostilities, ordering that the Xhosas and Khoi-Khois should not be attacked under any circumstances. He believed that the combined forces of the Khoi-Khois and Xhosas would be too strong for the Boers and his soldiers.[92] However, on 21 September 1799, Dundas wrote from Algoa Bay: "I believe the intention of the Caffers and the Hottentots is merely to possess themselves of as many cattle and destroy as many habitations as possible."[93] Through Maynier's negotiations, Dundas concluded peace with the Xhosas as well as the Khoi-Khoi. On 16 October 1799, the cessation of hostilities was officially announced. In November 1799, Maynier visited the Xhosa chief Ngqika on the eastern side of the Fish River. However, he achieved no success and was almost killed by Ngqika.[94] Interestingly, the Boers' relationship with Xhosa chief Ngqika east of the Fish River was much better than with the Xhosa captains in the Zuurveld. In 1799, Ngqika extended an offer to the Boers, granting them a piece of land between the Kacha Mountains and the Koonap River. Ngqika said he desired to coexist

---

[92] Giliomee, H. B. (1971). Die Kaap tydens die Eerste Britse Bewind, 1795-1803 [Doctoral dissertation, University of Stellenbosch], p339
[93] Giliomee, H. B. (1971). Die Kaap tydens die Eerste Britse Bewind, 1795-1803 [Doctoral dissertation, University of Stellenbosch], p340
[94] Giliomee, H. B. (1971). Die Kaap tydens die Eerste Britse Bewind, 1795-1803 [Doctoral dissertation, University of Stellenbosch], p341

THE BOERS GET COLONISED

peacefully with the Boers and wanted to provide them protection.[95]

The peace concluded in 1799 was merely a temporary cessation of hostilities in the conflict between the various population groups on the eastern frontier. It essentially resulted in the surrender of the Zuurveld, which was initially inhabited by Boers, to the Xhosa people.[96] In the war, the Khoi-Khoi and Xhosa inflicted significant losses on the Boers before peace was established with them. With the peace, they were also allowed to retain everything they had plundered from the Boers. When only two-thirds of the Boers had declared their losses, 858 horses, 4,475 oxen, 35,474 cattle, 34,023 sheep, and 2,480 goats were lost. 470 farms in Graaff-Reinet and Swellendam were plundered and abandoned.[97] Dundas himself acknowledged that the garrison at Algoa Bay would provide little or no protection in the event of an invasion. Dundas was primarily interested in, as he put it, keeping the "troublesome, unfaithful, and licentious Boers" under control.[98] As a reward for his services, Maynier was appointed as Resident Commissioner, the highest office, for the Graaff-Reinet and Swellendam districts on 25 December 1799. The first British occupation of the Cape was the darkest period for the Boers on the eastern frontier.

---

[95] Giliomee, H. B. (1971). Die Kaap tydens die Eerste Britse Bewind, 1795-1803 [Doctoral dissertation, University of Stellenbosch], p74
[96] Giliomee, H. B. (1971). Die Kaap tydens die Eerste Britse Bewind, 1795-1803 [Doctoral dissertation, University of Stellenbosch], p343
[97] Giliomee, Hermann. Die Afrikaners (Afrikaans Edition) (p. 119). Tafelberg. Kindle Edition.
[98] Giliomee, H. B. (1971). Die Kaap tydens die Eerste Britse Bewind, 1795-1803 [Doctoral dissertation, University of Stellenbosch], p343

THE CREATION OF THE BOER IDENTITY

The history of South Africa could have been much different if the British as the colonial authority and the world's mightiest empire made more effort to understand the situation in the eastern Cape frontier. They should have understood that the Xhosa were in a process of migration to the south and that the Xhosas who moved into the areas west of the Fish River were driven by internal struggles with enemies on the east of the river far more dangerous than the Boers to the west. They should have realised that the Boers were not Europeans but pre-industrial African frontier cattle farmers who, for their survival, had no option but to protect their grazing lands from getting destroyed by large Xhosa herds and that, if they moved back west would only destroy the grazing lands and impoverish the Boers behind them. They should have known that the last free Khoi-Khoi, as the true aboriginal people of southern Africa, were making a last stand, fighting for their land and their right to exist and that they did not deserve to be moved to missionary settlement camps. Above all, the gravest mistake the British colonial authority made regarding the Boers was, as De Kiewiet stated, "its refusal to respect the self-rule of the Boers which the neglect of the VOC had enabled them to develop".[99]

Napoleon achieved a significant milestone with the Peace of Amiens which was concluded on 25 March 1802 between France and Britain. This treaty not only brought an end to the French Revolutionary Wars, but France's territorial gains were now also accepted and recognised by its greatest

---

[99] De Kiewiet, C. W. (1957). A History of South Africa, Social & Economic. Oxford University Press, p33

rival, Great Britain.[100] For its support to the French, the Batavian government in the Netherlands received ownership of the Cape of Good Hope through this treaty. Commissioner-General Jacob Abraham Uitenhage de Mist was dispatched by the government of the Batavian Republic to assume control of the Cape from the English and to establish a government and administration. He was accompanied by Lieutenant-General Jan Willem Janssens who would be the first governor.[101] Despite the Boers having little in common with the progressive Netherlands of that era, the majority of Boers held emotional loyalty towards the Netherlands and embraced the new government warmly.[102] Interestingly, as early as 1801, even before ever setting foot in the Cape, de Mist had prepared a detailed report for the Batavian government outlining his principles for governing the Cape.[103] His research for his "Memorie" heavily relied on information gathered from oral accounts and writings of John Barrow, the former British private secretary in the Cape - the same John Barrow who believed that the Boers were barbaric because they did not eat bread.[104] In his "Memorie," de Mist described his intentions for the administration of the Cape: "The inhabitants have the right to demand a government over themselves that does not always and exclusively rule for the

---

[100] Erasmus, L. J. (1972). Die Tweede Britse Verowering van die Kaap, 1806 [Master's Thesis, Potchefstroomse Universiteit vir Christelike Hoer Onderwys], p5
[101] Botha, J. P. (2008). Ons Geskiedenis (1st ed.). J.P. Botha., p67
[102] Voigt, J. C. (1899). Fifty Years of the History of the Republic in South Africa 1795-1845 - Vol 1. E. O. Dutton & Co., p92
[103] Gie, S. F. (1932). Geskiedenis vir Suid-Afrika, II (2nd ed.). Pro Ecclesia-Drukkery., p96
[104] Van der Merwe, J. P. (1926). Die Kaap onder die Bataafse Republiek 1803-1806. Swets & Zeilinger, Amsterdam., p168

benefit of a third party but primarily and chiefly according to fixed, written, and just laws to promote their own welfare."[105] However, he planned comprehensive reforms so that the "strategically important Cape will become a bread basket and a source of wealth for the Motherland."[106]

The social reforms in De Mist's memorandum were based on the enlightened ideas of liberal humanitarianism prevailing in Holland at the time. It is against this backdrop that he developed strong prejudices against the Boers from sources such as Barrow's Travels.[107] According to De Mist, the provision of more churches and better schools for the Boers was necessary to gradually develop the "savage Boers" who treated the "natives so inhumanly cruel" into well-disposed, civilised individuals.[108] To his credit, De Mist, as well as Janssens, made a tour through the eastern frontier regions to gain a better understanding of the Boers and the situation there. They found the region devastated. Hundreds of farms and homesteads were burnt down, and large numbers of livestock were plundered by the Xhosas. The Xhosas moved uncontrollably through large parts of the district.[109] When most Boers requested an exemption from recognition fees due to their losses in the recent war, De Mist

---

[105] Gie, S. F. (1932). Geskiedenis vir Suid-Afrika, II (2nd ed.). Pro Ecclesia-Drukkery., p97
[106] Gie, S. F. (1932). Geskiedenis vir Suid-Afrika, II (2nd ed.). Pro Ecclesia-Drukkery. P100
[107] Van Zyl M.C., Edited by Muller, C. F. (1984). 500 Years, A History of South Africa (4th ed.). Academica, p110
[108] Gie, S. F. (1932). Geskiedenis vir Suid-Afrika, II (2nd ed.). Pro Ecclesia-Drukkery, p99
[109] Van der Merwe, J. P. (1926). Die Kaap onder die Bataafse Republiek 1803-1806. Swets & Zeilinger, Amsterdam, p165

was hesitant to grant it because he considered their "simplicity as pretence" and "greatly exaggerated."[110] He condescendingly referred to the requests of these Boers as an indication of what the future held for his government. He believed their requests were "complaints of vindictive people" who were looking to "get the Xhosas' oxen and cows through the government". He dismissed the unfortunate Boers as people "dissatisfied with anyone who achieved success", people who "hope that the new government will save everything." Later, Janssens wrote to De Mist that the men from Swellendam were "particularly attractive with good qualities", but some among them had hidden agendas that could "make life very dangerous for all of them". De Mist wrote that his "heart bled" for "his Africans", as he called the Boers, when he encountered "a few hundred beautiful young people of both sexes" on the eastern frontier, "to whom the generous nature has not denied anything," who, due to the "lack of opportunities," could hardly "reach the first stage of human civilisation".[111] He believed that "reasonably young men" become "harmful and unmanageable" due to their uncivilised nature. Therefore, according to De Mist's report to the Staatsbewind (Dutch Batavian Government), he urgently requested the provision of ministers and teachers "of impeccable morals."[112]

---

[110] Van der Merwe, J. P. (1926). Die Kaap onder die Bataafse Republiek 1803-1806. Swets & Zeilinger, Amsterdam, p166
[111] Van der Merwe, J. P. (1926). Die Kaap onder die Bataafse Republiek 1803-1806. Swets & Zeilinger, Amsterdam, p169/170
[112] Van der Merwe, J. P. (1926). Die Kaap onder die Bataafse Republiek 1803-1806. Swets & Zeilinger, Amsterdam, p.169/170

When Governor Janssens arrived at Algoa Bay, he encountered the evangelic Christian missionary Van der Kemp of the London Missionary Society, who had arrived there with the English in 1799.[113] Van der Kemp and his fellow missionary, Reid, were in charge of a group of several hundred Khoi-Khoi, most of whom had been involved in the attacks on the frontier during the previous British occupation.[114] Jansen granted Van der Kemp a farm of 7000 morgen for a mission station at Bethelsdorp.[115] The missionaries levelled several accusations of mistreatment against the Boers with Janssens on behalf of the Khoi-Khoi. Initially, these accusations disturbed Janssens, but as the allegations became more extravagant, he started to doubt their authenticity. One accusation made by a Khoi-Khoi against a Boer was that he had "cut the throat of a Khoi-Khoi woman and sliced her child into pieces while still alive".[116] After initially being convinced of the Boers' cruel treatment of the indigenous people, both Janssens and De Mist now, after their border visits, stopped taking the accusations against the Boers seriously.[117] When De Mist later visited the Mission Station of the London Missionary Society at Bethelsdorp, he found the place "disordered" and "impoverished". All the trees have been cut down for

---

[113] Voigt, J. C. (1899). Fifty Years of the History of the Republic in South Africa 1795-1845 - Vol 1. E. O. Dutton & Co, p93

[114] Voigt, J. C. (1899). Fifty Years of the History of the Republic in South Africa 1795-1845 - Vol 1. E. O. Dutton & Co, p93

[115] Van Zyl M.C., Edited by Muller, C. F. (1984). 500 Years, A History of South Africa (4th ed.). Academica., p114

[116] Gie, S. F. (1932). Geskiedenis vir Suid-Afrika, II (2nd ed.). Pro Ecclesia-Drukkery, p103

[117] Gie, S. F. (1932). Geskiedenis vir Suid-Afrika, II (2nd ed.). Pro Ecclesia-Drukkery, p103

THE BOERS GET COLONISED

firewood, and there is no shade on the bare ground. There is no sign that anyone is working, and the people are emaciated, covered with old rags or completely naked. Dr Lichtenstein, who accompanied De Mist on his journey, believed that Van der Kemp and Reid were not suitable for "working as missionaries to convert heathens".[118] Upon his return to Cape Town, De Mist made marginal notes in his Memorie on the Boers, confirming that his opinions about the Boers were formed before he visited the Cape and that they were primarily based on the authority of Barrow.[119] In his marginal note, he wrote about Barrow's writings on the Boers: "I did not then think it possible to spew so much slander out of national envy alone".[120]

De Mist implemented extensive reforms in the Cape, some of which would have been rejected by the Boers. These reforms included the establishment of a strong central government and a new local government system. He created two new districts. He divided the Graaff-Reinet district into two parts, with the second part, Uitenhage, named after himself.[121] De Mist announced significant economic reforms. Education was a priority, and De Mist reforms included a new educational order that established secular schools. Before this, all schools in the Cape were under the

---

[118] Gie, S. F. (1932). Geskiedenis vir Suid-Afrika, II (2nd ed.). Pro Ecclesia-Drukkery., p107
[119] Gie, S. F. (1932). Geskiedenis vir Suid-Afrika, II (2nd ed.). Pro Ecclesia-Drukkery, p104
[120] Gie, S. F. (1932). Geskiedenis vir Suid-Afrika, II (2nd ed.). Pro Ecclesia-Drukkery, p104
[121] Voigt, J. C. (1899). Fifty Years of the History of the Republic in South Africa 1795-1845 - Vol 1. E. O. Dutton & Co, p92

administration of the Dutch Reformed Church. He also founded the Educational College "Tot Nut Van't Algemeen", which later became known as the "South African College."[122] In his efforts towards equality, De Mist proclaimed a new church order that aimed to treat all churches and faiths equally. He also introduced a new marriage ordinance for the eastern border districts, mandating all marriage through the landrost (magistrate).[123] On 25 September 1804, De Mist resigned from his position as Commissioner-General at the Cape. They expected a British attack on the Cape at any day and De Mist wanted to allow General Janssens to prepare for the defence of the Cape. Janssens' troops were no match for General Baird's superior forces, resulting in their surrender to the British conquerors after the Battle of Blaauwberg on 18 January 1806.[124] The Dutch government in the Cape did not have sufficient time for their numerous reform programs to yield tangible results. The English replaced many of the enlightened and liberal Dutch policies with more conservative British ideas.[125]

The British became the owners of the Cape in 1806 through conquest. Thereafter, the Cape transferred into permanent British possession with the signing of the Treaty of Paris on 30 May 1814. After this agreement, in August

---

[122] Voigt, J. C. (1899). Fifty Years of the History of the Republic in South Africa 1795-1845 - Vol 1. E. O. Dutton & Co, p92
[123] Van der Merwe, J. P. (1926). Die Kaap onder die Bataafse Republiek 1803-1806. Swets & Zeilinger, Amsterdam, p157
[124] Van Zyl M.C., Edited by Muller, C. F. (1984). 500 Years, A History of South Africa (4th ed.). Academica, p116
[125] Van Zyl M.C., Edited by Muller, C. F. (1984). 500 Years, A History of South Africa (4th ed.). Academica, p116

1814, the British agreed to pay the Dutch £5 million in exchange for the Cape and other territories. The Boers were simply included in this transaction without their knowledge or consent and without any special consideration. The Boers had no rights. They were not citizens of any country and had no say in their destiny. The Dutch and British governments held unrestricted power over them, without any obligation to respect their rights or interests. As a result, the Boers were forced to become British subjects against their will. They could not resist the superior military forces of the British. Their only alternative to accepting permanent British rule was to leave the Cape, which was not a viable option at the time. During the handover of the Cape to British General Baird, the outgoing Dutch governor, General Janssens made a final plea to Baird. He urged Baird not to believe the disinformation that was spread about the Boers by their enemies, such as Barrow.[126]

---

[126] Erasmus, L. J. (1972). Die Tweede Britse Verowering van die Kaap, 1806 [Master's Thesis, Potchefstroomse Universiteit vir Christelike Hoer Onderwys], p181

Chapter 3:
The Boers under British Rule

During the time of the second British occupation of the Cape in 1806, the Boers had already developed into an independent and self-sustaining cultural group. In their first century of development, they had learned how to protect and govern themselves. All they desired from a government was to be left in peace.[1] However, the Cape had now become a permanent British possession, and they had long-term plans for it. The British implemented an extremely aggressive anglicisation policy in the Cape, surpassing their assimilation efforts on other peoples in their territories, such as the French in Canada. The British wanted to anglicise the Boer population to establish political control and culturally assimilate them to promote social cohesion within the British Empire. The British government not only wanted to teach the Boers to speak English but also to make them better people, according to the British Colonial Office: "gradually superseding the Dutch Schoolmasters by Englishmen of a superior class, as affording both the best means of making

---

[1] Kotze C.R., Edited by Muller, C. F. J.(1984). *500 Years, A History of South Africa* (4th ed.). Academica, p.125

the English language more general in the Colony & improving the manners & morals of the people."[2] They wanted to turn the Boers into Englishmen. An English settler from Uitenhage at the time wrote about the education of Boer children in the free English school: "And whether we hear the infant of three years old lisping his A, B, C, or the boy of eight fluently reading the English language, our hearts must overflow with gratitude, to that paternal Government which has thus planted seeds of knowledge upon the soil of ignorance and barbarism."[3] The English believed that they would uplift the Boers by anglicising them.[4] If the Boers became anglicised, they would be much more loyal to the British Crown.

The total size of the Boer population was comparable to towns like Exeter and Leicester at the time of the permanent British occupation of the Cape.[5] The British government could, therefore, believe that they didn't need to be cautious with the assimilation of the Boers. They did not consider the possibility that the Boers, as a small nation, would want to retain their cultural identity.[6] They established a strong, autocratic central government like their first

---

[2] Kotze, C. R. (2021). Reaksie van die Afrikaners op die owerheidsbeleid teenoor hulle, 1806-1828 : II. *Historia*, p.252
[3] Kotze, C. R. (2021). Reaksie van die Afrikaners op die owerheidsbeleid teenoor hulle, 1806-1828 : II. *Historia*, p.251
[4] Kotze, C. R. (2021). Reaksie van die Afrikaners op die owerheidsbeleid teenoor hulle, 1806-1828 : II. *Historia*, p.247
[5] Lambert, T. (2021, March 14). *A History of the Population of England*. Retrieved June 12, 2023, from https://localhistories.org/a-history-of-the-population-of-england/
[6] Kotze C.R., Edited by Muller, C. F. (1984). *500 Years, A History of South Africa* (4th ed.). Academica, p.125

occupation of the Cape. The independence of the high court, previously established by the Batavian government, was revoked and came under the control of the governor. The governor, along with a few assessors that he appointed, would serve as the highest appellate court in the Cape.[7] To exert greater control over the border districts, the British government in the Cape established two new districts, George, and Albany, and it established a circuit court. The circuit court was a high court consisting of two or three judges who periodically travelled the country to hear cases. The first circuit court began its journey in October 1811.[8]

Governor Cradock established English proficiency as a requirement for appointment in government institutions in 1813.[9] Education played a decisive role in promoting the anglicisation agenda, although attempts before 1820 to promote the English language in schools had limited success. From 1820, English and Scottish schoolmasters were introduced. A language proclamation in 1822 declared English as the exclusive official language in government offices from 1 January 1825, even though very few Boers could speak English at the time.[10] From 1 January 1827, court proceedings were also anglicised. The British administration at the Cape would also introduce a new legal

---

[7] Gie, S. F. (1932). *Geskiedenis vir Suid-Afrika, II* (2nd ed.). Pro Ecclesia-Drukkery, p.126
[8] Gie, S. F. (1932). *Geskiedenis vir Suid-Afrika, II* (2nd ed.). Pro Ecclesia-Drukkery, p.128
[9] Kotze, C. R. (2021). Reaksie van die Afrikaners op die owerheidsbeleid teenoor hulle, 1806-1828 : II. *Historia*, p.247
[10] Kotze C.R., Edited by Muller, C. F. (1984). *500 Years, A History of South Africa* (4th ed.). Academica, p.129

system, replacing the criminal law to follow the English legal system. Judges were appointed from the British bar and were required to hold degrees from England.[11] They also later established a jury system, and although very few Boers were proficient in English, the British colonial government made English a requirement to serve on the jury.[12]

The Dutch Reformed Church played a significant role as the primary cultural institution of the Boers. For this reason, the British authorities involved the Church in their anglicisation efforts. Governor Somerset implemented a plan to appoint Scottish ministers within the Dutch Reformed Church in Boer areas.[13] All these reforms were imposed on the Boers without any representation. Yet, the Boers did not resist the new British occupation and did not rebel against the changes and regulations imposed. They rarely criticised the British administration. On the contrary, in the early 1820s, the Boers, according to British civil servant and philanthropist Wilberforce Bird, were so "content to be quiet, and to obey" that it irritated the British settlers.[14] Many Britons believed that the Boers' "habitual submission" to their circumstances stemmed from their shared phlegmatic

---

[11] Giliomee, Hermann. Die Afrikaners (Afrikaans Edition). Tafelberg. Kindle Edition, p.89
[12] Giliomee, Hermann. Die Afrikaners (Afrikaans Edition). Tafelberg. Kindle Edition., p.196
[13] Gabriels, B. (1999). *'n Vergelyking tussen die verengelsingsbeleid na die Tweede Britse besetting van die Kaap aan die begin van die 19de eeu en die verengelsingsbeleid na die oorname van die ANC-regering in 1994 in Suid-Afrika* [Master's Thesis, Stellenbosch Universiteit]., p.7
[14] Kotze, C. R. (2021). Reaksie van die Afrikaners op die owerheidsbeleid teenoor hulle, 1806-1828 : II. *Historia*, p,246

character.¹⁵ But why was there no resistance and uprising against the anglicisation measures of the British government? One important reason was that, due to their isolated rural lifestyle, the Boers had little contact with the English authorities. However, the most important reason for the Boers' submissiveness to the British government and their lack of action and resistance against the British anglicisation attempts was the influence the Dutch Reformed Church had on them.

It was easy for the British authorities to involve the Church in their anglicisation program because the Church functioned as a state-controlled entity, with the governor as its head.¹⁶ All ministers were appointed and paid by the authorities, which made them fully subject to the governor's authority. As a result, the ministers, including the Scottish ministers, were servilely submissive to the government and preached it to the members as well.¹⁷ As an example of how British state authority was applied in the Dutch Reformed Church, Governor Cradock issued an order that a prayer for the British royal family and British victories in their wars had to be recited every Sunday.¹⁸ The church preached obedience to the government to its members and emphasised and

---

[15] Kotze, C. R. (2021). Reaksie van die Afrikaners op die owerheidsbeleid teenoor hulle, 1806-1828 : II. *Historia*, p.246
[16] Gabriels, B. (1999). *'n Vergelyking tussen die verengelsingsbeleid na die Tweede Britse besetting van die Kaap aan die begin van die 19de eeu en die verengelsingsbeleid na die oorname van die ANC-regering in 1994 in Suid-Afrika* [Master's Thesis, Stellenbosch Universiteit]., p.6
[17] Kotze, C. R. (2021). Reaksie van die Afrikaners op die owerheidsbeleid teenoor hulle, 1806-1828 : II. *Historia*, p.246
[18] Kotze C.R., Edited by Muller, C. F. (1984). *500 Years, A History of South Africa* (4th ed.). Academica, p.128

promoted the necessity of learning the English language. The synod adopted resolutions stating that religious instruction should be bilingual and that the Heidelberg Catechism should be made available in English. Dutch Reformed ministers made efforts to promote English-speaking schools on local school committees.[19] The Boers would later resist the British government, but it would be for reasons much greater than the British attempts to anglicise them.

Initially, it seemed as though the new British administration appreciated the interests of the Boers and genuinely sought to improve relations with them. They would take concrete steps to address and improve the Boers' security situation, leading to the establishment of positive relationships between the Boers and various British governors and military leaders over the subsequent decades. In his mandate from the Imperial government in London, the first British governor had to protect "our subjects in the inland part," referring to the Boers, "against attacks from the Xhosas and other wild tribes" by, among other things, establishing "forts and posts."[20] The British government's commitment to building strong ties with the Boers is evident in a letter from the new landdrost of Uitenhage, Cuyler, to the colonial secretary, Alexander. Cuyler expressed concerns about a law that prevented the Boers from acting against cattle theft, fearing that it could potentially alienate the

---

[19] Kotze, C. R. (2021). Reaksie van die Afrikaners op die owerheidsbeleid teenoor hulle, 1806-1828 : II. *Historia*, p.249
[20] Gie, S. F. (1932). *Geskiedenis vir Suid-Afrika, II* (2nd ed.). Pro Ecclesia-Drukkery, p.131

Boers.[21] In 1809, Governor Caledon dispatched Lieutenant Colonel Collins to investigate the situation in the borderlands. Collins discovered that the Boers residing on the northeastern border needed protection against San attacks. He recommended supplying the Boers with ammunition at reduced prices and deploying an approved Boer commando to counter the San threat.[22] Similar to Dr Lichtenstein's earlier observations, Collins, after visiting the mission station of Reid and Van der Kemp from the London Missionary Society in Bethelsdorp, concluded that they were unsuitable as missionaries.[23] Collins also commented on Barrow's propaganda against the Boers, stating that Barrow made great efforts to unfairly portray the Boers in a negative light with "convincing speeches and seemingly charitable intentions" and that his accusations against the Boers were "highly inaccurate."[24] On the eastern frontier, Collins, together with Landdrost Anders Stockenström, unsuccessfully tried to persuade several chiefs in Xhosaland not to cross the Fish River and urged those who were rebels in the Zuurveld to leave the colony. Upon his return, Collins submitted a report to the governor, recommending the forceful removal of the

---

[21] Gie, S. F. (1932). *Geskiedenis vir Suid-Afrika, II* (2nd ed.). Pro Ecclesia-Drukkery, p.133
[22] Gie, S. F. (1932). *Geskiedenis vir Suid-Afrika, II* (2nd ed.). Pro Ecclesia-Drukkery, p.132
[23] Gie, S. F. (1932). *Geskiedenis vir Suid-Afrika, II* (2nd ed.). Pro Ecclesia-Drukkery, p,130
[24] Gie, S. F. (1932). *Geskiedenis vir Suid-Afrika, II* (2nd ed.). Pro Ecclesia-Drukkery, p.132

Xhosas across the Fish River and the clearing of the Zuurveld.[25]

Even though the Fish River was considered the colonial boundary, by 1811, an estimated 20,000 Xhosas were roaming west of the Fish River boundary in the Zuurveld region and beyond.[26] Although Xhosa chiefs like Nhlambe and Chungwa had tried to maintain peace with the Boers, their large herds devastated the Boers' grazing lands. Smaller tribal leaders such as Habana, Galata, and Xasa, who functioned to a large extent independently from their superiors, occupied the fertile grazing lands around the Suurberg from where they launched attacks on Boer farms.[27] When Sir John Cradock arrived in the Cape as the new governor on 6 September 1811, reports from Caledon, and also Landrosts Stockenström and Cuyler made him decide to "to clear His Majesty's Territories from the Caffre nation or marauders of any description and that they be repelled permanently within their own boundaries".[28] Colonel John Graham was put in charge of the clearing operation against Nhlambe's forces. He requested the assistance of Field-Commandant Gabriel Stoltz and Fieldcornets Willem Grobler and Willem Nel to mobilise two Boer commandos, which

---

[25] Bezuidenhout, J. P. (1985). Forte en Verdedigingswerke op die Kaapse Oosgrens 1806-1836. *Scientia Militaria, South African Journal of Military Studies*, 15(4), 23-45, p.27

[26] De Villiers, J. (2012). Colonel John Graham of Fintry and the Fourth Cape Eastern Frontier War, 1811-1812. *Scientia Militaria - South African Journal of Military Studies*, 31(2)., p.3

[27] Markram, W. J. (2001). *Die lewe en werk van Petrus Lafras Uys, 1797-1838* [Doctoral dissertation, Universiteit van Stellenbosch]., p.72

[28] Gie, S. F. (1932). *Geskiedenis vir Suid-Afrika, II* (2nd ed.). Pro Ecclesia-Drukkery, p.135

would operate under the command of Landrost Cuyler of Uitenhage and Landrost Stockenström of Graaff-Reinet.[29] In December 1811, Colonel John Graham with a combined force consisting of 440 British troops, 431 Khoi-Khoi soldiers, and 450 Boers, embarked on a campaign against the Xhosa intruders.[30] On 29 December 2011, Landrost Anders Stockenström, accompanied by Fieldcornets Potgieter and Greyling, and several Boers were killed by imiDange warriors belonging to petty Chief Xasa in what would later become known as the massacre at Zuurberg.[31] Landrost Stockenström had approached the Xhosa leader unarmed in an attempt to negotiate peace.[32] When Cuyler approached Nhlambi, the Xhosa chief stated that he had acquired the Zuurveld through war and would not relinquish it.[33]

---

[29] De Villiers, J. (2012). Colonel John Graham of Fintry and the Fourth Cape Eastern Frontier War, 1811-1812. *Scientia Militaria - South African Journal of Military Studies, 31*(2)., p.7
[30] Giliomee, Hermann. Die Afrikaners (Afrikaans Edition). Tafelberg. Kindle Edition, P120
[31] In a letter composed by P. Mare, J.B. Rabie, W.S. Pretorius, and H.A. Meyntjes, addressed to Governor Cradock to inform him of the murders, the deaths of the following Boers were listed: Field Cornet Johan Christiaan Greyling, Field Cornet Jacobus Potgieter, Philip Botha, Piet Botha, Philip Buys (likely a son of Coenrad de Buys), Jacobus du Plessis, Michiel Hattingh, Willem Pretorius, and Isaac van Heerden. Cornelis Erasmus and Andries Krugel were wounded, while Christiaan Robberts and Paul du Plessis managed to escape. Source: Meintjes, K. (n.d.). The Massacre at Zuurberg. Eggsa.org. Retrieved September 17, 2023, from https://www.eggsa.org/articles/Zuurberg_intro.htm
[32] De Villiers, J. (2012). Colonel John Graham of Fintry and the Fourth Cape Eastern Frontier War, 1811-1812. *Scientia Militaria - South African Journal of Military Studies, 31*(2)., p.8
[33] Gie, S. F. (1932). *Geskiedenis vir Suid-Afrika, II* (2nd ed.). Pro Ecclesia-Drukkery, p.137

By the end of January, Nhlambe and his entire community, along with their cattle, had crossed the Fish River, abandoning the Zuurveld. This allowed Colonel Graham to redirect his efforts towards the Boesmansberg area. There, Xhosa attackers had murdered Mrs. van der Merwe, the wife of a Boer who was part of the commando, as well as several Khoi-Khoi farm workers. In response, Graham ordered his men to track down the stolen cattle and kill all male attackers indiscriminately.[34] Governor Cradock declared the official end of the fourth Xhosa war on 7 March 1812. In just two months, Graham successfully led the removal of approximately 20,000 Xhosa intruders from the Zuurveld region. Colonel Graham's exceptional military and organisational skills played a significant role in this achievement.[35]

In the decades before the British government took military control over the eastern border region, the Boers had a difficult relationship with the Xhosas. The Boers regularly traded with the Xhosas and sometimes even assisted them in factional battles with other tribes, and many Xhosas also worked for the Boers on their farms.[36] They also maintained good relations with the Xhosas in Xhosaland, east of the Fish River. Several Boers even lived there after the paramount

---

[34] De Villiers, J. (2012). Colonel John Graham of Fintry and the Fourth Cape Eastern Frontier War, 1811-1812. *Scientia Militaria - South African Journal of Military Studies, 31*(2)., p.9

[35] De Villiers, J. (2012). Colonel John Graham of Fintry and the Fourth Cape Eastern Frontier War, 1811-1812. *Scientia Militaria - South African Journal of Military Studies, 31*(2)., p.11

[36] Giliomee, Hermann. Die Afrikaners (Afrikaans Edition). Tafelberg. Kindle Edition, PP.120-121.

Xhosa chief, Ngqika, gave them a piece of land between the Kacha Mountains and the Koonap River and offered them protection.[37] West of the Fish River, however, the Xhosas' large herds of cattle devastated their grazing lands, and the Boers felt threatened by the persistent, uninvited visits to their farms by groups of Xhosas demanding gifts.[38] Before 1811, the Boers were constantly engaged in an extremely difficult struggle just to retain the Zuurveld region.[39] On the other hand, the British-controlled border war from 1811 to 1812 completely expelled the Xhosas from the area. The Xhosas were shocked. They could not believe that they could be crushed like this. For the first time in the border region, they experienced total war, with the tremendous losses it brought upon them.[40] Later, the British would drive the Xhosas further east beyond the Keiskamma River and declare the area between the Fish and Keiskamma Rivers as a neutral zone. The Boers simply did not have the military capacity to achieve such significant victories over the Xhosas.[41]

Meanwhile, missionaries Reid and Van der Kemp, stationed at Bethelsdorp, wrote to the London Missionary Society claiming that the Boers were cruelly mistreating the Khoi-Khoi, with "over a hundred murders reported to them in

---

[37] Giliomee, H. B. (1971). Die Kaap tydens die eerste Britse bewind, 1795-1803 [Doctoral dissertation, Stellenbosch University], p.74
[38] Giliomee, Hermann. Die Afrikaners (Afrikaans Edition). Tafelberg. Kindle Edition, p.120.
[39] Du Toit, A., & Giliomee, H. (1983). Afrikaner Political Thought. Volume 1: 1780-1850. University of California Press, p11
[40] Giliomee, Hermann. Die Afrikaners (Afrikaans Edition). Tafelberg. Kindle Edition, PP.120-121.
[41] Du Toit, A., & Giliomee, H. (1983). Afrikaner Political Thought. Volume 1: 1780-1850. University of California Press, p15

the Uitenhage district alone".[42] Due to the massive influence of the evangelistic philanthropists in London, the British Imperial government ordered Cape Governor Cradock on 9 August 1811 to investigate the allegations and to punish the perpetrators severely.[43] Cradock meticulously carried out this instruction and gave Read all possible assistance to collect evidence.[44] In September 1812, the second circuit court, or the "Black Circuit" as the Boers called it, set out to hear these complaints in George, Uitenhage, and Graaff-Reinet.[45] The four-month-long session of the court heard twenty-two cases of different types of complaints, some of which referred to apparent events from long ago, despite Reid's propaganda to London.[46] The court acquitted all the accused of murder charges and imposed some fines for lesser offences such as withholding workers' pay.[47] The judges' report criticised the missionaries for not verifying the charges, stating that many were mere fabrications.[48] The mission station at Bethelsdorp was described as a place of "laziness and idleness, and as a

---

[42] Kotze C.R., Edited by Muller, C. F. (1984). *500 Years, A History of South Africa* (4th ed.). Academica, p.135
[43] Gie, S. F. (1932). *Geskiedenis vir Suid-Afrika, II* (2nd ed.). Pro Ecclesia-Drukkery, p.142
[44] Kotze C.R., Edited by Muller, C. F. (1984). *500 Years, A History of South Africa* (4th ed.). Academica, p.135
[45] Gie, S. F. (1932). *Geskiedenis vir Suid-Afrika, II* (2nd ed.). Pro Ecclesia-Drukkery, p.143
[46] Patterson, S. (1957). The Last Trek: A study of the Boer people and the Afrikaner Nation. Routledge & Keagan Paul Ltd., London., p.15
[47] Kotze C.R., Edited by Muller, C. F. (1984). *500 Years, A History of South Africa* (4th ed.). Academica, p.135
[48] Gie, S. F. (1932). *Geskiedenis vir Suid-Afrika, II* (2nd ed.). Pro Ecclesia-Drukkery, p.144

result, dirt and filth thrive there to perfection".[49] The "Black Circuit" sparked outrage among the Boers, who felt that the false accusations besmirched their good name. Despite being exonerated by the court, they held distrust toward the British government. This would not be the last instance of enemies using faith as a pretext against the Boers.

Graham's removal of the Xhosa people from the Zuurveld region presented Cradock with a strategic opportunity to expropriate the farms that the Boers had abandoned in the face of Xhosa attacks, while also implementing a new form of land ownership.[50] After the Boers lived for a century under the loan farm system, Cradock introduced a new system known as "perpetual quitrent" on 6 August 1813.[51] This system, although more costly than the recognition fees previously paid on loan farms, offered greater security in land ownership due to the requirement for thorough land surveys and registration. For this reason, the Boers were initially eager to support the new quitrent system to thereby secure their property rights for their descendants. Under the new system, farmers not only had to pay significantly higher fees but were also responsible for covering the expenses associated with land surveying for registration.[52] Existing landowners could remain under the

---

[49] Gie, S. F. (1932). *Geskiedenis vir Suid-Afrika, II* (2nd ed.). Pro Ecclesia-Drukkery, p.144
[50] Cory, G. E. (1921). *The Rise of South Africa, Vol. 1.* Longmans. Green & Co., p.255
[51] Gie, S. F. (1932). *Geskiedenis vir Suid-Afrika, II* (2nd ed.). Pro Ecclesia-Drukkery, p.150
[52] Gie, S. F. (1932). *Geskiedenis vir Suid-Afrika, II* (2nd ed.). Pro Ecclesia-Drukkery, p.150

old system, which most did, but all new farms had to be registered under the new system. Due to the high prevalence of malpractices in the surveying of farms and the colonial government's inability to administer the quitrent system efficiently, by 1820, there was already a backlog of 5,000 land requests. This delay led to the inability to issue land deeds.[53] It was common for the government to take up to twenty years to issue registered land deeds.

In 1817, Jacobus Uys, the father of Voortrekker leader, Piet Uys, requested that his farms, Driefontein and Spitskop, be granted to him under perpetual quitrent. Despite that he reiterated this request on 3 April 1820, and 14 October 1822, the land deeds for the two farms were only granted to Nicolaas Barend Swart on 1 November 1838, after the deaths of Piet and Jacobus Uys in Natal. The land deed for Piet Uys' farm, Welbedagt, for which he applied for a lease on 2 March 1822, was only issued nineteen years later, long after his death.[54] The government's land administration was so inefficient that the Boers developed their own system of land ownership known as the "rekwes farm system."[55] This incompetence on the part of the government created a climate of uncertainty among the Boers in the following decades. The Boers not only faced uncertainty regarding property rights due to the ineffective administration of the new system, but they also suffered economic losses as a

---

[53] Markram, W. J. (2001). *Die lewe en werk van Petrus Lafras Uys, 1797-1838* [Doctoral dissertation, Universiteit van Stellenbosch]., p.61
[54] Markram, W. J. (2001). *Die lewe en werk van Petrus Lafras Uys, 1797-1838* [Doctoral dissertation, University of Stellenbosch]., p.60
[55] Markram, W. J. (2001). *Die lewe en werk van Petrus Lafras Uys, 1797-1838* [Doctoral dissertation, Universiteit van Stellenbosch]., p.58

result. In some areas, Boers lost almost entire herds to diseases like lame sickness due to the nature and quality of the grass and desperately needed the additional grazing land for their cattle.[56] The poor land administration by the British colonial government would contribute as a major catalyst for the Boers' quest for self-determination.

In 1815, Frederik Bezuidenhout, a Boer living on the eastern frontier, received a summons from Magistrate Andries Stockenström to appear in court in Graaff-Reinet on 5 October 1815. He was accused of assaulting a Khoi-Khoi worker. When Bezuidenhout failed to show up, a warrant for his arrest was issued. On 10 October 1815, Lieutenant H. Rousseau and fourteen Khoi-Khoi soldiers arrived at Bezuidenhout's farm to apprehend him. Bezuidenhout and a coloured worker sought refuge in a nearby cave and resisted arrest from there. The soldiers shot and killed Bezuidenhout and just left his body there. His older brother, Hans Bezuidenhout, discovered the body later that evening.[57] At Frederick's funeral two days later, Hans Bezuidenhout and a friend vowed revenge against the British government. Hans Bezuidenhout, together with Hendrik Prinsloo, the son of Marthiens Prinsloo who was involved in the Van Jaarsveld uprising during the first English occupation, recruited men for a rebellion. They sent Cornelis Faber and Frans Marais across the Fish River to negotiate with Xhosa chief Ngqika to

---

[56] Markram, W. J. (2001). *Die lewe en werk van Petrus Lafras Uys, 1797-1838* [Doctoral dissertation, Universiteit van Stellenbosch]., p.47
[57] Voigt, J. C. (1899). *Fifty Years of the History of the Republic in South Africa 1795-1845 - Vol 1*. E. O. Dutton & Co., p.130

THE BOERS UNDER BRITISH RULE

neutralize the Khoi-Khoi troops.[58] However, this decision proved to be a mistake as the Boers, although sympathetic, could not support a rebellion against the British with the assistance of the Xhosa chief. Despite this setback, approximately 60 Boers, including established families like Willem Krugel, acting Field Cornet of Baviaansriver, and others from his district, moved to support the Bezuidenhouts. The group was confronted by Magistrate JG Cuyler from Uitenhage, backed by a commando led by Commandant Nel and Khoi-Khoi troops. Commandant Nel convinced the rebels to surrender and lay down their weapons. Some escaped, but Hans Bezuidenhout was captured and killed, while Martha, his wife, and their 12-year-old son were wounded. The rest of the rebels were arrested.

The rebels faced trial in Uitenhage from 16 December 1815 to 22 January 1816, but the British government were determined to make an example of them. The two judges were appointed by the governor, and the prosecutor was both the military officer who arrested the rebels and the landrost of the Uitenhage district, Colonel Cuyler.[59] Despite the rebels having caused no harm or fatalities and their actions being limited to resisting arrest, the court exhibited extreme mercilessness towards the accused individuals. Hendrik Prinslo (32), Stephanus Bothma (43), Cornelis Faber (59), Theunis de Klerk (29), and Abraham Bothma (28) were sentenced to death. They would hang at Slagtersnek, where

---

[58] Giliomee, Hermann. Die Afrikaners (Afrikaans Edition). Tafelberg. Kindle Edition., p. 122
[59] Voigt, J. C. (1899). *Fifty Years of the History of the Republic in South Africa 1795-1845 - Vol 1*. E. O. Dutton & Co., p.144

they had vowed revenge against the English government.[60] Willem Krugel, initially sentenced to death, received a pardon due to his exceptional service in a recent border war. Instead, he was banished from the district. Martha Bezuidenhout was condemned to lifelong banishment from the eastern districts of the Colony. The remaining thirty-two rebels were compelled to witness the executions.[61] In a further act of humiliation, Frans Marais was bound by the neck to the gallows, forced to witness the execution and subsequently banished from the Cape Colony for life.

The men who had been condemned to death were hanged at Slagtersnek on 9 March 1816, under the vigilant watch of three hundred soldiers. The men faced their impending execution with calmness and acceptance.[62] However, during the execution, the ropes of four of the men broke. The family saw this as a sign by God that the men

---

[60] Voigt, J. C. (1899). *Fifty Years of the History of the Republic in South Africa 1795-1845 - Vol 1*. E. O. Dutton & Co., p.145

[61] David Malan, Nicolaas and Pieter Prinsloo, Andries Meyer, and Adriaan Engelbrecht were banished for life from the eastern districts of the Cape. The following persons were sentenced to imprisonment or fines: Hendrik Liebenberg, Abraham and Christoffel Botha, Andries van Dyk, Theunis Mulder, Pieter Delport, Barend de Lange, Gerrit Bezuidenhout, Adriaan and Leendert Labuschagne. The remaining sixteen men were sentenced to witness the execution of their comrades. They were Joachim Johannes Prinsloo, Nicolaas Prinsloo, Willem Jacobus Prinsloo, Jan Prinsloo, Pieter Laurens Erasmus, Andries Hendrik Klopper, Hendrik Petrus Klopper, Jacobus Marthinus Klopper, Thomas Andries Dreyer, Johannes Bronkhorst, Willem Adriaan Nel, Frans Johannes van Dyk, Johannes Frederik Botha, Philip Eudolf Botha, Hendrik van der Nest, Cornells van der Nest. Voigt, J. C. (1899). *Fifty Years of the History of the Republic in South Africa 1795-1845 - Vol 1*. E. O. Dutton & Co., p.145/146

[62] Voigt, J. C. (1899). *Fifty Years of the History of the Republic in South Africa 1795-1845 - Vol 1*. E. O. Dutton & Co., p.149

should be spared, and they made an impassioned plea for mercy. Cuyler, the authority in charge, was unable to grant their request. Consequently, once the condemned regained consciousness, they were hanged again.[63] The family's request to receive the bodies for a proper Christian burial was rejected. They had to be buried at the gallows.[64] The place at Slagtersnek where the gallows were erected was situated on the farm of a Boer named Van Aarde. The British authorities refused to dismantle the gallows after the hangings. The next morning, when Van Aarde's sons arrived to dismantle the structure, they found the hand and arm of Theuns de Klerk protruding from the ground. The men were buried in the same careless manner as in which they were hanged.

The cruelty and disrespect displayed by the British authorities towards the Boers of Slagtersnek stirred up bitterness within the Boer people. The events of Slagtersnek sparked a spirit of resistance among the Boers. When the Voortrekkers departed from the colony twenty years later, they took that beam from Slagtersnek with them. Later in Natal, the Boers told Commissioner Cloete that they would never forget Slagtersnek. When Shepstone annexed the South African Republic (ZAR) before the First Boer War in 1877, there were Boers who suggested that he should be hanged from that same beam.[65] The genealogist, J.A. Heese, showed in his book "Slagtersnek en sy mense" (Slagtersnek and his

---

[63] Steyn, J.C. 2016 Afrikanerjoernaal. 'n Vervolgverhaal in 365 episodes. Pretoria: FAK., p.87
[64] Voigt, J. C. (1899). *Fifty Years of the History of the Republic in South Africa 1795-1845 - Vol 1*. E. O. Dutton & Co., p.151
[65] Botha, J. P. (2008). Ons Geskiedenis (1st ed.). J.P. Botha., p.82

THE CREATION OF THE BOER IDENTITY

people), that people like General Louis Botha, General Koos de la Rey, and President M.T. Steyn, who would later play significant roles in the history of the Boer nation, were descendants of the people of Slagtersnek. The beam from Slagtersnek is currently housed in the basement of the State Archives in Pretoria.

Farm attacks did not cease after the Fourth Border War, but Graham took steps to address the issue. He increased the Khoi-Khoi regiment to 800 soldiers[66] and fortified the Fish River area with twenty-two military posts, permanently stationing the entire Khoi-Khoi Cape Regiment along the eastern border.[67] A tracking system was established for patrols to track stolen cattle twice a day from the military posts. Xhosa kraals, where the tracks of stolen cattle led to, were held accountable, and they had to return the stolen livestock or provide compensation.[68] The border patrols were highly effective due to the deterrent effect of the military posts. [69] On 30 March 1817, Governor Somerset visited Ngqika and arranged with the Xhosa chief to halt farm attacks in exchange for military assistance during times of

---

[66] Gie, S. F. (1932). *Geskiedenis vir Suid-Afrika, II* (2nd ed.). Pro Ecclesia-Drukkery, p.139

[67] Bezuidenhout, J. P. (1985). Forte en Verdedigingswerke op die Kaapse Oosgrens 1806-1836. *Scientia Militaria, South African Journal of Military Studies, 15*(4), 23-45., p.30

[68] Giliomee, Hermann. Die Afrikaners (Afrikaans Edition). Tafelberg. Kindle Edition., p.123

[69] Bezuidenhout, J. P. (1985). Forte en Verdedigingswerke op die Kaapse Oosgrens 1806-1836. *Scientia Militaria, South African Journal of Military Studies, 15*(4), 23-45., p.30

THE BOERS UNDER BRITISH RULE

war against Ngqika's enemies.[70] Although Ngqika was not the most powerful chief and had no control over the actions of his uncle, Nhlambe, he wanted to use Somerset's colonial forces as allies against Nhlambe. In 1818, with the help of his new colonial ally, Ngqika attacked Nhlambe, defeated him, and seized 23,000 cattle from Nhlambe and his people.[71] Somerset now intervened in the internal conflicts of the Xhosa, and in early 1819, driven by hunger and a desire for revenge, Nhlambe launched a massive force that took over the entire Zuurveld area. However, British troops and Boer commandos managed to drive the Xhosas back across the Kei River.[72] During a battle in the Fifth Xhosa War, 6,000 Xhosa soldiers, led by their medicine man Makanna, attacked military barracks in Grahamstown. This resulted in the deaths of thousands of Xhosas, while only three British soldiers were killed and five wounded. The courageous actions of Captain Trappes, who commanded the barracks with fewer than 100 men, not only saved Grahamstown but likely the entire Zuurveld area as well.[73]

In response to the Xhosa invasion of the Zuurveld during the Fifth Frontier War, Somerset decided to move all Xhosas, including Ngqika, further east, across the

---

[70] Bezuidenhout, J. P. (1985). Forte en Verdedigingswerke op die Kaapse Oosgrens 1806-1836. *Scientia Militaria, South African Journal of Military Studies*, *15*(4), 23-45., p.30
[71] Giliomee, Hermann. Die Afrikaners (Afrikaans Edition). Tafelberg. Kindle Edition., p.123
[72] Giliomee, Hermann. Die Afrikaners (Afrikaans Edition). Tafelberg. Kindle Edition,, p.123
[73] Bezuidenhout, J. P. (1985). Forte en Verdedigingswerke op die Kaapse Oosgrens 1806-1836. *Scientia Militaria, South African Journal of Military Studies*, *15*(4), 23-45., p.33

Keiskamma River. He declared the area between the Fish and Baviaans rivers, the existing colonial border on one side, and the Keiskamma and Lower Tyumie rivers further east, a neutral territory.[74] This measure by Somerset put tremendous pressure on the Xhosas as they now struggled with a severe shortage of grazing land for their cattle. Additionally, the Xhosas experienced significant disruption and loss of life due to the Mfecane from the opposite direction.[75] The policy regarding the neutral area was inconsistent which would later lead to more conflict with the Xhosa people. In 1822, Maqomo, the eldest son of Xhosa chief Ngqika, and his followers were initially permitted to settle there, but were later, in 1829, again forcibly expelled. In that same year, the Kat River Khoi-Khoi settlement was established in the area. British colonial Governor Lowry Cole then decided to settle white people in the region to bolster the frontier defence. In 1831, the Colonial Secretary, Goderich approved the settlement of Whites in the neutral zone, on the condition that no Boers were allowed.[76]

Cattle theft in the Zuurveld remained prevalent, and the Boers whose livestock was stolen were prohibited from crossing the border themselves to retrieve their cattle.[77]

---

[74] Bezuidenhout, J. P. (1985). Forte en Verdedigingswerke op die Kaapse Oosgrens 1806-1836. *Scientia Militaria, South African Journal of Military Studies*, 15(4), 23-45., p.33
[75] Giliomee, Hermann. Die Afrikaners (Afrikaans Edition). Tafelberg. Kindle Edition., p.124
[76] Kotze C.R., Edited by Muller, C. F. (1984). *500 Years, A History of South Africa* (4th ed.). Academica., P144
[77] Giliomee, Hermann. Die Afrikaners (Afrikaans Edition). Tafelberg. Kindle Edition., p.125

Instead, a Boer who encountered cattle theft had to file a complaint at the nearest military post.[78] A patrol of British troops, led by a British commander, would then accompany the Boer to track down and recover the stolen cattle. Meanwhile, Landdrost Andries Stockenström expressed serious concerns about the military operations carried out by patrols that crossed the border to track and recover stolen cattle. These patrols often involved violence, including the burning of kraals and loss of life. Giliomee refers to an incident where a patrol, led by Governor Somerset's son, Colonel Henry Somerset, mistakenly burned down the wrong kraals twice, resulting in loss of life.[79] According to Stockenström, he was aware of fifty cases where patrols crossed the border and plundered innocent Xhosa kraals.[80] In response to the violence perpetrated by the British authorities against the Xhosas, the Xhosas launched regular counterattacks.

The Mfecane, a period of heightened military conflict, large-scale devastation, and migration in the inland and eastern coastal regions of southern Africa during the 1820s, had profound implications for the Boers residing in the northeastern districts of the Cape. Because of the Mfecane, numerous refugees, known as Fetcanie (isiXhosa for "starving intruders"), migrated from the north, and settled between the Thembu and the San communities, resulting in

---

[78] Giliomee, Hermann. Die Afrikaners (Afrikaans Edition). Tafelberg. Kindle Edition,, p.126
[79] Giliomee, Hermann. Die Afrikaners (Afrikaans Edition). Tafelberg. Kindle Edition., p.127
[80] Giliomee, Hermann. Die Afrikaners (Afrikaans Edition). Tafelberg. Kindle Edition., p.127

considerable devastation among these groups. Many San people fled to the Cape area for protection among the Boers.[81] Andries Stockenström approached the Griqua leader, Adam Kok, in Philippolis and asked him to stop his campaign of extermination against the San because it was driving them into the Cape, where they committed acts of theft in the Tarka and Brak River districts due to hunger. Due to the Boers' lack of gunpowder, according to Field Cornet Pretorius in August 1830, they were unable to recover their stolen livestock.[82] Significant numbers of Mfecane survivors fled southward only to be also attacked by the Griquas, Baster and Koranna tribes, and robbed of their remaining livestock.[83] When they reached the Cape, they were desperate and in a state of starvation and, in turn, attacked many Boer farms and stole their cattle.[84] In February 1826, rumours circulated that the Ngwane, after being driven from their land by Zulu King Shaka, were planning an attack on the Colony. At that time, the ammunition supplies of the Boers were critically low due to restrictions imposed by the British

---

[81] Markram, W. J. (1992). *Stephanus Petrus Erasmus: Grensboerpionier en Voortrekker, 1788-1847* [Master's thesis, University of Stellenbosch]., p.87
[82] Markram, W. J. (1992). *Stephanus Petrus Erasmus: Grensboerpionier en Voortrekker, 1788-1847* [Master's thesis, University of Stellenbosch]., p.89
[83] Markram, W. J. (1992). *Stephanus Petrus Erasmus: Grensboerpionier en Voortrekker, 1788-1847* [Master's thesis, University of Stellenbosch]., p.99
[84] Markram, W. J. (1992). *Stephanus Petrus Erasmus: Grensboerpionier en Voortrekker, 1788-1847* [Master's thesis, University of Stellenbosch]., p.101

colonial government, which forced some to abandon their farms.[85]

Various tribes, including the Ngwane, were attacked by Shaka and robbed of their cattle. In turn, in the second half of 1827, the Ngwane attacked the Thembu and drove them out of their land. Veldkornet Steenkamp from Tarka, together with Colonel Somerset, came across an area where thousands of Thembu bodies, killed by the Ngwane, were found.[86] Under Captain Bawana, approximately 3,000 Thembu with 10,000-12,000 cattle fled into the Cape. The Thembu were peaceful, and the first contact between Boer and Thembu was friendly. After they crossed the border into the Cape, Thembu captain, Bawana, confirmed to Colonel Somerset that they had been treated well by the Boers.[87] In 1828, British landdrost, William Dundas led a force that crossed the border and attacked the Ngwane, seizing 25,000 cattle from them, which were likely originally stolen from the Thembu. A few months later, on 27 August 1828, Colonel Somerset, with a mixed army of British soldiers, Boers, British Settlers, hired Khoi-Khoi soldiers, supported by thousands of Thembu, Gcaleka, and Mpondo auxiliary troops, attacked the Ngwane near present-day Umtata.[88]

---

[85] Markram, W. J. (1992). *Stephanus Petrus Erasmus: Grensboerpionier en Voortrekker, 1788-1847* [Master's thesis, University of Stellenbosch]., p.101
[86] Markram, W. J. (1992). *Stephanus Petrus Erasmus: Grensboerpionier en Voortrekker, 1788-1847* [Master's thesis, University of Stellenbosch]., p.108
[87] Markram, W. J. (1992). *Stephanus Petrus Erasmus: Grensboerpionier en Voortrekker, 1788-1847* [Master's thesis, University of Stellenbosch]., p.108
[88] Markram, W. J. (2001). *Die lewe en werk van Petrus Lafras Uys, 1797-1838* [Doctoral dissertation, Universiteit van Stellenbosch]., p. 78

During this battle, Somerset used light and heavy cannons, and his Xhosa auxiliary troops killed thousands of Ngwane and looted all their cattle.[89]

In the second half of the 1820s, the British government completely abused Boer commandos because they did not have the ability to establish an effective police or military force on the eastern border. Boers from the districts of Brak River and Agter-Sneeuberg complained in a petition to Governor Lowry Cole that they were more on commandos across the border than they were at home, making it impossible for them to attend to their farms and livestock.[90] They were involved in so many commandos that they became despondent. They said that due to the drought, their horses were no longer capable of going on so many commandos. They informed the governor that, when the commandos were out, the Basters attacked their farms in the northeastern districts. The Boers also complained that many commandos were unnecessary because the tribes across the border were mostly peaceful. They also did not want to get involved in disputes between different tribes across the border.[91] Boers from the Albany and Somerset districts handed their own petition to Governor Cole in 1829, requesting him to place more British troops on the border to

---

[89] Giliomee, Hermann. Die Afrikaners (Afrikaans Edition). Tafelberg. Kindle Edition., p.121
[90] Markram, W. J. (1992). *Stephanus Petrus Erasmus: Grensboerpionier en Voortrekker, 1788-1847* [Master's thesis, University of Stellenbosch]., p.51
[91] Markram, W. J. (1992). *Stephanus Petrus Erasmus: Grensboerpionier en Voortrekker, 1788-1847* [Master's thesis, University of Stellenbosch]., p.52

reduce the frequency of commandos. They could not accept that they had been called upon in 1827 and 1828 to fight against tribes that had never caused them any harm.[92] They mentioned to the governor that they were suffering significant losses due to thefts while being away from their farms for extended periods.

Since Colonel Graham placed permanent British troops on the eastern frontier in 1810, they brought an end to the Boers' "habitual freedom," as historians Du Toit and Giliomee described the Boers' self-rule.[93] Complete authority shifted into the hands of the British colonial government. The Boers no longer had control or influence over policy decisions on the eastern frontier or the execution of any military operations. The commandos could still be called up according to the law, but they would serve as a supporting force to the British military and be under the full control of the British colonial government. The stability of the Boers' living conditions and even their right and ability to protect their lives and property were now in the hands of the British government. Alongside this, evangelical Christians, the primary group of propagandists influencing British colonial policy in southern Africa, worked to further weaken the Boers' situation. The leader of the missionaries in southern Africa, Dr. Philip, regarded the Boers as enemies who hindered the missionaries' efforts to Christianise and civilise

---

[92] Markram, W. J. (1992). *Stephanus Petrus Erasmus: Grensboerpionier en Voortrekker, 1788-1847* [Master's thesis, University of Stellenbosch]., p.52
[93] Du Toit, A., & Giliomee, H. (1983). Afrikaner Political Thought. Volume 1: 1780-1850. University of California Press, p16

the indigenous people. Dr. Philip, who had no formal education himself and who previously worked as an apprentice for a linen trader and as a clerk in Dundee, Scotland before getting involved in Wesleyan missionary work, considered the Boers inferior to the English. He criticised the Boers for their "want of intelligence and ... indifference to those comforts that are indispensable to Englishmen"[94] and believed they were filled with "insatiable avarice and rapacity".[95] Although the Boers were in no position of power, had no influence over Xhosa policies, and had no control over military actions, Philip still accused them of stealing land and livestock from the Xhosas. According to Philip, this left the Xhosas with no choice but to steal and plunder.[96] Due to Philip's agitation, the British Colonial Secretary for the Colonies prohibited the "brutal" commandos on 1 August 1834. With the British colonial government's troops on the border being insufficient, the Boers were now defenceless against attacks from the Xhosas or any other invaders.[97]

The conservative newspaper and mouthpiece of British traders in the eastern districts of the Cape, The Grahamstown Journal, advocated for the annexation of more

---

[94] Giliomee, Hermann. Die Afrikaners (Afrikaans Edition). Tafelberg. Kindle Edition., p.88
[95] Giliomee, Hermann. Die Afrikaners (Afrikaans Edition). Tafelberg. Kindle Edition., p.127
[96] Giliomee, Hermann. Die Afrikaners (Afrikaans Edition). Tafelberg. Kindle Edition., p.127-129
[97] Kotze C.R., Edited by Muller, C. F. (1984). *500 Years, A History of South Africa* (4th ed.). Academica., P144

Xhosa land.[98] Meanwhile, Maqoma was allowed once again in 1822 to settle in the Neutral Territory. Over time, other Xhosa captains also entered the Neutral Territory. By 1826, Chungwa, Nqeno, and Botomane and their people had also settled there.[99] The colonial government decided again in 1833 to expel the Xhosa captains Maqoma and Tyhali from the Neutral Territory. There were two problems with this. The Xhosa regarded this land as their birthright, and the British government did not give Maqoma time to harvest his lands. In 1834, on the orders of the colonial government, Colonel Somerset sent out several patrols to burn down the kraals and huts of the Rharhabe Xhosas.[100] The Xhosa had now lost all their grazing lands west of the Kei River and, on top of that, had to make provisions to accommodate the Mfengu and other refugees from the Mfecane. In the 1830s, the reduced land available to the Xhosa was no longer sufficient to sustain their population.[101] In defiance, Maqoma's half-brother, Xhoxho, took his cattle to graze in the Neutral Territory. On 12 December 1834, a British patrol attempted to expel him from the area and wounded him. This was the final provocation that led to the Sixth Xhosa War.[102] At that time, the colonial government had only 775 soldiers

---

[98] Giliomee, Hermann. *Die Afrikaners* (Afrikaans Edition). Tafelberg. Kindle Edition., p.129
[99] Markram, W. J. (2001). *Die lewe en werk van Petrus Lafras Uys, 1797-1838* [Doctoral dissertation, Universiteit van Stellenbosch]., p.88
[100] Markram, W. J. (2001). *Die lewe en werk van Petrus Lafras Uys, 1797-1838* [Doctoral dissertation, Universiteit van Stellenbosch]., p.89
[101] Markram, W. J. (2001). *Die lewe en werk van Petrus Lafras Uys, 1797-1838* [Doctoral dissertation, Universiteit van Stellenbosch]., p.89
[102] Markram, W. J. (2001). *Die lewe en werk van Petrus Lafras Uys, 1797-1838* [Doctoral dissertation, Universiteit van Stellenbosch]., p.90

THE CREATION OF THE BOER IDENTITY

present on the eastern border,[103] including the 21st Light Dragoons, the Cape Corps, and the Royal African Corps. However, these soldiers were poorly trained, with the Royal African Corps consisting mainly of undisciplined criminals.[104] With the abolition of the Boers' commando system, the desperate struggle for survival in which they placed the Xhosas and the restriction of the Boers' ammunition and gunpowder, the British created the perfect storm for the annihilation of the Boers.

On 22 December 1834, Maqoma and Tyhali attacked the eastern border districts of the Cape with a force of 12,000 to 15,000 Xhosa warriors.[105] The Xhosa invasion was so successful that during the first few weeks, hardly any effective defence could be launched. Thousands of Xhosa warriors launched attacks in small units, causing widespread destruction along the border.[106] Stephanus Bernardus Buys was the first Boer to be killed in the war. He was murdered on his farm south of Fort Beaufort by a group of Xhosa attackers. His wife, Cecilia, managed to find shelter with their six young children and later escaped. The Xhosa attackers looted 202 cattle and 16 horses from Buys'

---

[103] Bezuidenhout, P. J. (1985). Forte en Verdedigingswerke op die Kaapse Oosgrens 1806-1836. *Scientia Militaria, South African Journal of Military Studies.*, p.36
[104] Bezuidenhout, P. J. (1985). Forts and Defensive Works on the Cape Eastern Frontier 1806-1836. Scientia Militaria, South African Journal of Military Studies., p.43
[105] Giliomee, Hermann. Die Afrikaners (Afrikaans Edition). Tafelberg. Kindle Edition., p.134
[106] Kotze C.R., Edited by Muller, C. F. (1984). 500 Years, A History of South Africa (4th ed.). Academica., P144

property.[107] Due to the disbandment of the commandos, the Boers were in their weakest situation. Field Commandant G. van Rooyen reported on 29 December 1834 that the Olifantshoek region was in turmoil and being destroyed by the Xhosa invaders. Two days later, Civil Commissioner Duncan Campbell declared that the entire Uitenhage district was overwhelmed by the Xhosa invaders. The Boers formed small groups of 30 to 70 men to protect their properties, but they couldn't stop the ruthless attacks of the Xhosa warriors. Within the first few days of the invasion, thousands of cattle were looted in the Lower Boesmans River district, and most farms along the Boesmans River were burned down. Civil Commissioner Van der Riet reported on 3 January 1835 that a staggering 8,000 cattle had already been stolen in the Olifantshoek area.[108]

The inhabitants of the area were forced to abandon their farms and seek refuge in the Port Elizabeth area. Within a week, about 7,000 border residents were plunged into great distress.[109] By early January 1835, the Xhosas had gained control over the entire eastern border.[110] Piet Retief saved hundreds of people in the Winterberg District when he gathered a large group, including more than two hundred

---

[107] Visagie, J. C. (1980). Louis Jacobus Nel: 'n voortrekkerleier uit die tweede linie. *Journal of Cape History*, 3(1), 52-89., p.76
[108] Markram, W. J. (2001). The life and work of Petrus Lafras Uys, 1797-1838 [Doctoral dissertation, Stellenbosch University]., p.90
[109] Giliomee, Hermann. Die Afrikaners (Afrikaans Edition). Tafelberg. Kindle Edition., p.134
[110] Bezuidenhout, P. J. (1985). Forts and Defensive Works on the Cape Eastern Frontier 1806-1836. Scientia Militaria, South African Journal of Military Studies., p.36

THE CREATION OF THE BOER IDENTITY

women and children, in a laager from where they could effectively resist the Xhosa invaders. Retief and his family suffered significant losses in the war. Their farmhouse was burned down, and all their cattle were stolen.[111] Field Commandant G.R. van Rooyen's commando gathered at Quagga Vlakte, while the Boer families sought refuge mainly at the churches along the Boesmans River and the farms of Rietvalley and Quagga Vlakte.[112] Civil Commissioner Ziervogel reported that fights between Boers from the Brak River district and the Xhosa invaders, who crossed the northeastern border from various directions on 4 January 1834, had begun.[113] Field Corporal Pretorius expressed concern about the scarcity of gunpowder and lead in the northeastern districts while his men had to withstand relentless attacks from the Xhosas without any rest, day and night.[114] In response to the disastrous situation, Governor D'Urban declared martial law in the eastern districts on 3 January 1835.[115] Although commandos had been abolished by the British government on 1 August 1834, D'Urban urgently had to reinstate them out of necessity.

---

[111] Giliomee, Hermann. Die Afrikaners (Afrikaans Edition). Tafelberg. Kindle Edition., p.136
[112] Markram, W. J. (1992). Stephanus Petrus Erasmus: Border Boer Pioneer and Voortrekker, 1788-1847 [Master's thesis, Stellenbosch University]., p.121
[113] Markram, W. J. (1992). Stephanus Petrus Erasmus: Border Boer Pioneer and Voortrekker, 1788-1847 [Master's thesis, Stellenbosch University]., p.121
[114] Markram, W. J. (1992). Stephanus Petrus Erasmus: Border Boer Pioneer and Voortrekker, 1788-1847 [Master's thesis, Stellenbosch University]., p.121
[115] Markram, W. J. (1992). Stephanus Petrus Erasmus: Border Boer Pioneer and Voortrekker, 1788-1847 [Master's thesis, Stellenbosch University]., p.121

The entire civilian population between 18 and 45 years old was called to arms. One able-bodied man had to stay behind on each farm to protect it while all the other Boers joined their commandos.[116] Supplies were requisitioned from the public with the issuance of receipts. During this time, Colonel Harry Smith assumed overall military command of the colony, including the Boer commandos. On 1 January 1835, he hurried from Cape Town to Grahamstown with a force of British troops, covering the 600-mile distance in six days.[117] Colonel Smith divided his troops as well as the Boer commandos into four divisions. The commanders of these four divisions were respectively Colonel John Peddie, Colonel Henry Somerset, Major William Cox, and Field Commandant Stephanus van Wyk, who led commandos from Tarka.[118] Van Wyk had 500 Boers in his commando, while the other Boers were divided among the British officers.[119] During the war, there was tension between members of the Boer commandos and the British regular troops, and several incidents occurred between them. The Boers had a strong aversion to the life of a permanent soldier, which essentially represented the opposite way of life compared to the Boers as individualists and free citizens.

---

[116] Le Roux, P. E. (1946). p.297 By 8 March 1835, at least 1,848 Boers were on commando. Visagie, J. C. (1993). p.79
[117] Bezuidenhout, P. J. (1985). Forts and Defensive Works on the Cape Eastern Frontier 1806-1836. Scientia Militaria, South African Journal of Military Studies., p.36
[118] Visagie, J. C. (1993). Verset teen die burgermilisieplan van 1835. *Historical Association of South Africa (HASA)*, 38(2)., p.78
[119] Le Roux, P. E. (1946). p.297 By 8 March 1835, at least 1,848 Boers were on commando. Visagie, J. C. (1993). p.294

Tempers between the Boers and the British soldiers frequently flared up.[120]

7,000 people fled to Grahamstown and sought shelter there. The English settlers were exempted from commando duty, and they formed self-defence units in towns as volunteers. In Grahamstown, volunteers created the "Committee of Safety" with five leaders from five sections comprising approximately 500 members. Therefore, they were not used in the forefront of battles like the Boers.[121] To counter the Xhosa threat, Colonel Harry Smith ordered on 12 January 1835 that Colonel Somerset drive the Xhosas from the mouth of the Sundays River to Olifantshoek, while Major Gregory was given the task of defending the left bank of the Boesmans River.[122] In early February 1835, Colonel Somerset succeeded in driving the Xhosas out of the Suurberg and Olifantshoek areas. Field Commandant Van Wyk and his men were very active in clearing the area of Xhosas.[123] Field Commandant Rademeyer and his commando were engaged in such intense fighting with the Xhosas that when it seemed they were losing the battle, instead of fleeing, he allowed the Xhosas to surround him. His men formed a circle around him, and after a desperate fight, during which all the Boers' clothes were stained with

---

[120] Visagie, J. C. (1993). Verset teen die burgermilisieplan van 1835. *Historical Association of South Africa (HASA)*, *38*(2)., p.81
[121] Le Roux, P. E. (1946). p.297 By 8 March 1835, at least 1,848 Boers were on commando. Visagie, J. C. (1993). p.294
[122] Markram, W. J. (2001). The Life and Work of Petrus Lafras Uys, 1797-1838 [Doctoral dissertation, Stellenbosch University]., p.91
[123] Le Roux, P. E. (1946). p.297 By 8 March 1835, at least 1,848 Boers were on commando. Visagie, J. C. (1993). p.296

blood, between 60 and 70 Xhosas were killed, and five Boers were killed in the battle, with seven wounded.[124] In January 1835, Colonel Harry Smith ordered Civil Commissioner Harry Rivers to send the Swellendam Commando to Uitenhage. By 12 February 1835, the first division of the commando had arrived in Uitenhage, with the highly respected Field Commandant Jacobus Linde, who was then 75 years old, leading the way.[125]

With the outbreak of the Sixth Frontier War, Piet Uys and his Great Trek reconnaissance commission were in Natal. In January 1835, after receiving news of the Xhosa invasion, Uys's group decided to immediately return home to be with their families.[126] While they were on their way back to the Cape under the guidance of the experienced tracker and hunter Johan Hendrik (Hans Dons) De Lange, they travelled through the Xhosa Chief Hintsa's Gcalekaland by mid-March 1835.[127] Hintsa sent men to warn Uys's group not to follow the usual route to the Colony, and he personally met with Uys to invite them to spend a few days at his kraal near the Tsomo River. According to a report in The Grahams Town Journal of 20 March 1835, Hintsa informed Uys about the current state of the war. Hintsa made it clear to Uys that he desired friendly relations with the British government and

---

[124] Le Roux, P. E. (1946). p.297 By 8 March 1835, at least 1,848 Boers were on commando. Visagie, J. C. (1993). p.297-298
[125] Markram, W. J. (2001). The Life and Work of Petrus Lafras Uys, 1797-1838 [Doctoral dissertation, Stellenbosch University]., p.92
[126] Markram, W. J. (2001). *Die lewe en werk van Petrus Lafras Uys, 1797-1838* [Doctoral dissertation, Universiteit van Stellenbosch]., p.92
[127] Markram, W. J. (2001). *Die lewe en werk van Petrus Lafras Uys, 1797-1838* [Doctoral dissertation, Universiteit van Stellenbosch]., p.93

expressed strong disapproval of approximately 500 of his soldiers who had joined the Xhosa forces in the war. The Xhosa chief categorically denied involvement in the murder of British traders, of which he was accused.

The newspaper reported that Uys and Moolman testified to Hintsa's friendly and open demeanour and that they strongly believed in his innocence.[128] They also confirmed that they had not seen any colonial livestock in Hintsa's territory. Although Hintsa acknowledged owning a few colonial horses, he acquired them through trade. As a goodwill gesture, Hintsa presented Uys's group with oxen and a few horses. He also provided guides to ensure their safe passage to the Cape. Uys, a well-known horse breeder in the eastern Cape, gave Hintsa a thoroughbred horse as a gift. By the end of March 1835, Uys met with Governor D'Urban in Grahamstown and informed him about their journey to Natal and their meeting and discussions with Hintsa.[129] After this, Uys joined the war as a commander under Colonel Somerset. When Uys finally returned home on 23 October 1835, he learned that his wife had been arrested by an English policeman and was en route to Port Elizabeth.[130]

At the end of March 1835, Governor D'Urban, who had meanwhile taken personal command, launched a follow-up operation into Xhosaland with British troops and Boer

---

[128] Markram, W. J. (2001). *Die lewe en werk van Petrus Lafras Uys, 1797-1838* [Doctoral dissertation, Universiteit van Stellenbosch]., p.93

[129] Markram, W. J. (2001). *Die lewe en werk van Petrus Lafras Uys, 1797-1838* [Doctoral dissertation, Universiteit van Stellenbosch]., p.94

[130] Markram, W. J. (2001). *Die lewe en werk van Petrus Lafras Uys, 1797-1838* [Doctoral dissertation, Universiteit van Stellenbosch]., p.98

commandos. The Xhosas were completely defeated and driven across the Kei River, while large quantities of livestock were confiscated.[131] Hintsa surrendered on 30 April 1835.[132] D'Urban annexed the area between the Keiskamma and Kei Rivers on 10 May 1835. He named the newly conquered land the Province of Queen Adelaide and declared that the Rharhabe Xhosas would be expelled from the newly established Province. On 12 May 1835, Hintsa and nine of his bodyguards were shot dead by colonial soldiers, and 2300 of his cattle were looted when he was forced to accompany a patrol, led by Colonel Harry Smith, to gather the Gcaleka's cattle. When attempted to escape, Hintsa was shot while riding a dark reddish-brown horse, which, according to a member of Colonel Smith's bodyguard, was given to him by Piet Uys.[133] Later, Hintsa's body was also mutilated.[134] Afterwards, the troops launched a campaign to destroy the Xhosas' means of subsistence by burning their crops and confiscating their livestock.[135] Peace negotiations took place in September 1835, which led to the signing of peace treaties with the various tribes residing along the eastern border.

---

[131] Le Roux, P. E. (1946). *Die geskiedenis van die burgerkommando's in die Kaapkolonie (1652-1878)* [Doctoral dissertation, University of Stellenbosch]., p.298

[132] Bezuidenhout, P. J. (1985). Forte en Verdedigingswerke op die Kaapse Oosgrens 1806-1836. *Scientia Militaria, South African Journal of Military Studies.*, p.36

[133] Markram, W. J. (2001). *Die lewe en werk van Petrus Lafras Uys, 1797-1838* [Doctoral dissertation, Universiteit van Stellenbosch]., p.96

[134] Giliomee, Hermann. Die Afrikaners (Afrikaans Edition). Tafelberg. Kindle Edition., p.135

[135] Giliomee, Hermann. Die Afrikaners (Afrikaans Edition). Tafelberg. Kindle Edition., p.135

The Christian evangelists were very upset that Governor D'Urban disbanded the Boer commandos and annexed more land from the Xhosas. Dr J. Philip, the Superintendent of the London Missionary Society, with the help of Read, smuggled a Khoi-Khoi man named Andries Stoffels, and a lesser Xhosa captain named Jan Tzatzoe out of the Cape to England to seek support against D'Urban's recent campaign against the Xhosas.[136] Philip paraded the two Africans throughout England and delivered speeches where he maligned the Boers, accused D'Urban of being an oppressor, and absolved the Xhosas of all guilt. On 15 September 1835, Philip delivered a speech at a gay public missionary breakfast in Sheffield where he discussed D'Urban's expulsion of the Xhosas from the Neutral Area, but he used the term "extermination" instead of "expulsion".[137] Dr Philip and Andries Stockenström testified against D'Urban in England before an "Aborigines Committee". The British Secretary of State for the Colonies, Lord Glenelg, reversed D'Urban's border arrangement. In a letter dated 26 December 1835, Glenelg blamed the Boers primarily for all the wars.[138] The annexed territory, the Province of Queen Adelaide, would be returned to the Xhosas by Stockenström, who was promoted to lieutenant governor of the eastern districts, and he was to negotiate

---

[136] Godlonton, R. (1879), Case of the colonists, 2nd ed., Richards, Slater & Co., p.24
[137] Godlonton, R. (1879), Case of the colonists, 2nd ed., Richards, Slater & Co., p.24
[138] Giliomee, Hermann. Die Afrikaners (Afrikaans Edition). Tafelberg. Kindle Edition., p.144

THE BOERS UNDER BRITISH RULE

treaties with the chiefs with the help of missionaries.[139] Stockenström would later be dismissed by Governor Napier because the British settlers could not support his liberal views.

In addition to their services in the Sixth Frontier War, the Boers also contributed 2,330 horses, ninety-two wagons and mostly their own food, for the six months in the field for the war. The government was supposed to bear all these costs. After months in the field, the Boers' clothes, hats, and shoes were completely worn out. The government did not contribute any clothing. Some commando members made clothes from raw cowhide.[140] When the war was over, D'Urban wanted to carry out further operations in the newly acquired territory with his permanent British troops. The Boers had to line up their horses in formation so that the British officers could commandeer the horses for further service. Receipts for £5 per horse were issued to the Boers, but they never received payment for the horses. The Boers had no choice but to give away the saddles along with the horses and walk home from Xhosaland with only their rifles. Weeks later, they arrived home emaciated, with worn-out clothes, sunburned, and without hats or shoes. In many cases, they found their farms burned down and all their herds

---

[139] Kotze C.R., Edited by Muller, C. F. (1984), 500 Years, A History of South Africa, 4th ed., Academica, p.145

[140] Le Roux, P. E. (1946). *Die geskiedenis van die burgerkommando's in die Kaapkolonie (1652-1878)* [Doctoral dissertation, University of Stellenbosch]., p.319

stolen.¹⁴¹ All the livestock that the Boers or British soldiers recovered or confiscated from the Xhosas remained in government possession. It was later sold at auction. Many situations arose where Boers recognised their own herds but did not have the money to buy them back. In many cases, Boers witnessed their beloved horses, with which they always had a strong bond, being sold at auctions. Much of the Boers' livestock was still in the hands of the Xhosas, and there was no chance of getting it back.¹⁴² The Boers lost all their trust in the British government because of these events.

The Sixth Border War of 1834-1835 was a devastating blow to the Boers, plunging them into a state of desperation and distress. The Xhosas burned down 456 farmhouses and looted 5,700 horses, 115,000 cattle, and 161,000 sheep, financially ruining the Boers and leaving them emotionally exhausted.¹⁴³ On 3 March 1836, Thomas Robson, an Englishman, wrote to Governor D'Urban: "I have been again among the Boers residing along the frontier, ie. those plundered by the Kaffirs, and assure you that they are in a most deplorable condition, having nothing to subsist upon, and in many cases are actually starving for the want of common necessaries of nature which she requires for support, and if some means are not shortly made use of to relieve them I certainly am afraid there will be very bad

---

[141] Le Roux, P. E. (1946). *Die geskiedenis van die burgerkommando's in die Kaapkolonie (1652-1878)* [Doctoral dissertation, University of Stellenbosch]., p.320

[142] Le Roux, P. E. (1946). *Die geskiedenis van die burgerkommando's in die Kaapkolonie (1652-1878)* [Doctoral dissertation, University of Stellenbosch]., p.321

[143] Botha, J. P. (2008). Ons Geskiedenis (1st ed.). J.P. Botha., p.93

work".[144] According to the magistrate of Bathurst, Walter Currie, in 1836, the Boers saw no hope for the future in the Cape under British control. He recounted: "One person (a Boer) said that during his father's lifetime and his own, they had been 'cleaned out' five times by the Xhosas... that the future would be like the past in terms of protection; indeed, he believed they were worse off than fifty years ago; in those old days, they would retrieve their livestock if it was stolen, but now their hands were tied while the Xhosas were free (to plunder the Boers)."[145] Furthermore, the British government once again banned the commandos.[146] The confidence in the British government was so low that, on the highest military level, Veldkommandant (Field Commandant) van Wyk demanded a signed document from Colonel Harry Smith affirming their right to defend themselves and their property against attackers.[147] The safety and survival of the Boers were now in the hands of the British, who lacked the will and the ability to ensure it.[148]

Most Boer leaders were wealthy individuals who expected the government to create conditions for trade and

---

[144] Muller, C. F. J. (1946). *Die Britse Owerheid en die Groot Trek* [Doctoral dissertation, University of Stellenbosch]., p.105-p.106
[145] Visagie, J. C. (1993). Verset teen die burgermilisieplan van 1835. Historical Association of South Africa (HASA), 38(2)., p.82
[146] Le Roux, P. E. (1946). Die geskiedenis van die burgerkommando's in die Kaapkolonie (1652-1878) [Doctoral dissertation, University of Stellenbosch]., p.325
[147] Le Roux, P. E. (1946). Die geskiedenis van die burgerkommando's in die Kaapkolonie (1652-1878) [Doctoral dissertation, University of Stellenbosch]., p.329
[148] Le Roux, P. E. (1946). Die geskiedenis van die burgerkommando's in die Kaapkolonie (1652-1878) [Doctoral dissertation, University of Stellenbosch]., p.326

progress by maintaining law and order in the interior and forging a lasting peace with the Xhosa. The British colonial government was unable to protect the lives and property of the Boers, but nevertheless restricted the Boers' rights and means to protect themselves.[149] The mismanagement of land registration highlighted the incompetence of the colonial government in effective administration. The government's inability to meet these expectations further undermined the Boers' trust in British rule. If the British government had met the Boers' needs, they might have stayed in the Cape and, like the Cape Afrikaners, became loyal British citizens. The Boers had no representation or participation in government on any level and there were no effective channels for them to voice their grievances, which reinforced their conviction that only a government established by themselves would promote their interests. Despite their circumstances, the Boers did not simply flee; they purposefully pursued a better future, understanding that peace and prosperity could only be achieved through self-determination.

---

[149] Du Toit, A., & Giliomee, H. (1983). Afrikaner Political Thought. Volume 1: 1780-1850. University of California Press, p.16

Chapter 4:
The Boers Trek

The Boers were compelled to act due to the "unbearable lack of security" along the Cape's eastern border, which posed a significant threat to their survival.[1] They decided to leave the Cape colony. The Great Trek, as the Boers' migration movement would later become known, was a peaceful revolution that allowed the Boers to liberate themselves from British rule without taking up arms against a much larger and stronger power. The Great Trek did, however, not occur out of the blue. The idea of leaving the Cape and settling elsewhere began with a small group of Boers, and it required significant time and sacrifice to gain enough support among the Boers to turn it into a reality. The concept originated with a group of experienced explorers and hunters, such as Johan (Hans Dons) de Lange, Cornelis and Piet Meyer, Abraham and Piet Greyling, and Philip Rudolph Botha – the great-grandfather of Louis Botha, the future Commanding General of the Boer

---

[1] Giliomee, Hermann. Die Afrikaners (Afrikaans Edition). Tafelberg. Kindle Edition., p.139

forces during the Anglo-Boer War.[2] Through the accounts of their journeys into the interior, these explorers and hunters implanted the migration idea among fellow Boers. Initially, the exploration missions sowed the seeds of the migration idea, and as the concept spread and gained traction, it led to further explorations. Later, exploration became purposeful and more official to gather more information about specific regions.[3] The organisers of these exploration missions would then use this information to promote the benefits of certain regions among their fellow Boers.

Formidable forces in the Cape, like the British Government, the media, and the Dutch Reformed Church, actively opposed the idea of migration to stem the tide of the Great Trek. Boer leader Piet Retief published his Manifesto in a Cape newspaper precisely to counter the propaganda against the migration movement. In the opening of his Manifesto, he referred to rumours being spread in the Colony to create prejudice against the Voortrekkers.[4] (Voortrekker is an Afrikaans word meaning Front Trekker – referring to those Boers who left the Cape in the first phase between 1836 to 1839.) For the migration movement to succeed, it was imperative to recruit ample participants. The strategy to achieve this involved persuading the Boer leaders, who already held leadership roles in the community like Field Commandants and Field Cornets in the eastern Cape, to

---

[2] Visagie, J. C. (1992). 'n Besoek aan Mzilikazi in 1830. *Historia, 37*(1), 9-23., p.15
[3] Muller, C. F. J. (1987). *Die oorsprong van die Groot Trek* (2nd ed.). Tafelberg Uitgewers., p.258
[4] Du Toit, A., & Giliomee, H. (1983). *Afrikaner Political Thought. Volume 1: 1780-1850*. University of California Press., p.213-214

embrace the migration idea.⁵ These leaders held a strong sense of responsibility towards their communities and would not be persuaded through negative motivations, such as suppression by the British government, the never-ending border wars, and the "almost continuous series of thefts by the Khoi-Khoi and Xhosa."⁶ to leave everything behind and trek. It would require positive motivation, such as the vision of a homeland with self-governance, to recruit enough people for the migration idea to make the Great Trek a success.⁷ "The Great Trek was the Boer Frontiersman's Declaration of Independence." ~ L. H. Gann and P. Duignan.⁸

The British, however, would not allow a small nation like the Boers to leave the Empire and establish their own independent state. At the time, the British Empire was the largest empire in history and the dominant global power. Arthur Wellesley, a former British military leader and Prime Minister, characterised the British colonies as "significant sources of influence, power, and prosperity for the country".⁹ Later, British Prime Minister John Russel commented to State Secretary Henry Grey: "The loss of any great portion of our Colonies would diminish our importance in the world, and the vultures would soon gather together to despoil us of

---

[5] Muller, C. F. J. (1987). *Die oorsprong van die Groot Trek* (2nd ed.). Tafelberg Uitgewers., p.307
[6] Du Toit, A., & Giliomee, H. (1983). *Afrikaner Political Thought. Volume 1: 1780-1850*. University of California Press., p.16-17
[7] Muller, C. F. J. (1987). *Die oorsprong van die Groot Trek* (2nd ed.). Tafelberg Uitgewers., p.308
[8] Muller, C. F. J. (1987). *Die oorsprong van die Groot Trek* (2nd ed.). Tafelberg Uitgewers., p.10
[9] Muller, C. F. J. (1946). *Die Britse Owerheid en die Groot Trek* [Doctoral dissertation, University of Stellenbosch]., p.307

other parts or our Empire."[10] Grey articulated the mission of the British Empire: "The authority of the British Crown is at this moment the most powerful instrument, under Providence, of maintaining peace and order in many extensive regions of the earth, and thereby assists in diffusing, amongst millions of the human race, the blessings of Christianity and civilisation."[11] On 8 May 1845, Hutt, a member of the British House of Commons, emphasised that it was the duty of the Secretary of State for War and the Colonies "to raise up new Anglo-Saxon nations in southern Africa, Australia, and New Zealand."[12] The Boers leaving the Cape and declaring themselves a free and independent people was an embarrassment for the British authorities. On 11 December 1839, the South African Commercial Advertiser reported: "And can it be supposed for an instant, that she will... permit a handful of Boers... to defy her power...?"[13] The British authorities insisted on the Boers' submission.

During the first half of the 19th century, philanthropists, particularly the evangelical Christians, held considerable influence over British colonial policies. The "organised, semi-educated, evangelically minded and entirely vocal British middle class" primarily relied on Barrow and

---

[10] Muller, C. F. J. (1946). *Die Britse Owerheid en die Groot Trek* [Doctoral dissertation, University of Stellenbosch]., p.306
[11] Muller, C. F. J. (1946). *Die Britse Owerheid en die Groot Trek* [Doctoral dissertation, University of Stellenbosch]., p.307
[12] Muller, C. F. J. (1946). *Die Britse Owerheid en die Groot Trek* [Doctoral dissertation, University of Stellenbosch]., p.307
[13] Muller, C. F. J. (1946). *Die Britse Owerheid en die Groot Trek* [Doctoral dissertation, University of Stellenbosch]., p.326

his followers to understand southern Africa.[14] Especially during the crucial initial phase of the Boers' Great Trek, this group of propagandists dominated the British government. Lord Glenelg, who served as the British Secretary for the Colonies from 1835 to 1839, was a humanitarian and a member of the evangelical Church Missionary Society. His permanent under-secretary, James Stephen, shared many of his liberal ideals. Glenelg replaced Sir Benjamin D'Urban with Sir George Napier because he was convinced of Napier's complete commitment to his philanthropic policies. Glenelg also appointed the philanthropist Andries Stockenström as lieutenant governor of the eastern districts of the Cape colony. The evangelicals, in particular, exerted pressure on the British authorities to pursue Boer migration and annex the areas where they settled. Their propaganda argued that the Boers made the native population less receptive to Christianization by disturbing and preventing them from taking "their rightful place as potential equals of Europeans." Dr Philip who propagated "Annexation up to the Tropics",[15] even claimed that "a progression in skull formation was observed over three consecutive generations among the Khoi-Khoi protected in missionary stations".[16] This spiritual leader of the missionaries in southern Africa advocated for British colonisation of Africa because, as he

---

[14] Muller, C. F. J. (1946). *Die Britse Owerheid en die Groot Trek* [Doctoral dissertation, University of Stellenbosch]., p.63
[15] Muller, C. F. J. (1946). *Die Britse Owerheid en die Groot Trek* [Doctoral dissertation, University of Stellenbosch]., p.396
[16] Muller, C. F. J. (1946). *Die Britse Owerheid en die Groot Trek* [Doctoral dissertation, University of Stellenbosch]., p.62

put it in a letter to Read (the younger) on 19 October 1835: "The Caffres cannot otherwise be saved from annihilation".[17]

Despite numerous appeals from various quarters, including the evangelists, British traders in the Cape, British imperialists, and even in the British Parliament, for immediate and strong action by the British government to halt the Boers' migration movement, the British government initially did little to impede the Great Trek. The financial resources of the British Imperial government couldn't keep pace with the scale of British colonisation. The dire financial situation of the British government since the Napoleonic Wars, along with budget deficits and associated cutbacks until 1842, significantly restrained the implementation of the ideas of these pressure groups. Even in 1842, James Stephen, the permanent under-secretary of the Colonial Office, expressed concern about the financial position of the British Imperial government, stating: "We are recklessly increasing and dispersing our Colonial Empire in all directions creating a demand for naval and military forces which there are no means of meeting, except by weakening that force where its presence is mostly needed."[18] The lieutenant governor for the eastern districts, Andries Stockenström, wrote to Governor D'Urban on 27 September 1836, stating that he had no means to prevent the migration — a statement he also made personally to Piet Retief.[19] Cape Governor D'Urban believed

---

[17] Muller, C. F. J. (1946). *Die Britse Owerheid en die Groot Trek* [Doctoral dissertation, University of Stellenbosch]., p.80

[18] Muller, C. F. J. (1946). *Die Britse Owerheid en die Groot Trek* [Doctoral dissertation, University of Stellenbosch]., p.148

[19] Muller, C. F. J. (1946). *Die Britse Owerheid en die Groot Trek* [Doctoral dissertation, University of Stellenbosch]., p.158

that if the British colonial government were to enact legislation to prevent the Boers from crossing the borders to settle elsewhere, it would incur significant financial expenses. He wrote to Secretary Glenelg on 29 July 1837: "To have endeavoured to prevent, their carrying their designs into effect, by any other means than those of persuasion and argument, would have been altogether useless and worse, ...; and, indeed, as they moved in large bodies of armed and determined men, and crossed a distant border, the arresting their progress by force, would have been probably beyond the means of the military power of the frontiers, and would have had no other effect than that or converting peaceable emigrants into dangerous rebels.[20] Even as the Boers' Great Trek gained momentum, the British Imperial government continued to pressure the Cape colonial government to cut expenditures, as evidenced by Secretary Glenelg's letter to Governor Napier on 6 October 1838: "...that you will adopt such measures as may be within your power for reducing the Expenditure of the Military Establishment of the Colony to the utmost possible extent."[21] Ultimately, the British Treasury had the greatest influence on British policy regarding their actions against the Boers' migration.

When the British Imperial government in London realised that the Boer migration was a large-scale popular movement, they took steps that did not require significant financial expenditure to halt the migration movement. On 13

---

[20] Muller, C. F. J. (1946). *Die Britse Owerheid en die Groot Trek* [Doctoral dissertation, University of Stellenbosch]., p.158
[21] Muller, C. F. J. (1946). *Die Britse Owerheid en die Groot Trek* [Doctoral dissertation, University of Stellenbosch]., p.151

THE CREATION OF THE BOER IDENTITY

August 1836, the British Parliament in Britain passed the "Cape of Good Hope Punishment Act".[22] This legislation stipulated that Boer emigrants could be tried in Cape courts for any crimes committed south of the 25th-degree latitude. The 25th-degree latitude lies just below the present-day Bela-Bela (Warmbaths) in the far northern Limpopo Province of South Africa. This law aimed to put an end to the Boers' migration, but no Boer was ever prosecuted for offences committed beyond the borders of British territory.[23] Nevertheless, the law set a critical precedent by keeping the Boers, even north of the Orange River, outside of British colonial territory, under British jurisdiction. It effectively deprived them of the ability to distance themselves from British subjugation. The "Cape of Good Hope Punishment Act" extended British authority over the Boers wherever they trekked. It stripped the Boers of their right to choose not to be British subjects, thus eroding any prospects of freedom. This policy of persecuting the Boers persisted long after it became clear that the Boers had no intentions of returning to the Cape under British rule or accepting British citizenship.

The British colonial government recognised the considerable influence of the Dutch Reformed Church in the lives of the Boers. They therefore strategically involved the Church to dissuade and counter the Boers' migration plans.[24]

---

[22] Muller, C. F. J. (1987). *Die oorsprong van die Groot Trek* (2nd ed.). Tafelberg Uitgewers., p.391

[23] Muller, C. F. J. (1981). 500 Years - A History of South Africa (3rd ed.). Academica., p.160

[24] J. W. Claasen, (1994) Skotse predikante en die geestelike bearbeiding van die Voortrekkers. HTS Teologiese Studies/Theological Studies, 50.3., p.493

In that era, the Dutch Reformed Church's ministers were appointed and paid by the colonial government and the British governor was also the head of the Church. The Church was therefore prepared to use the Boers' religious convictions as a political lever against the Great Trek. The Dutch Reformed was a central institution in the Boers' cultural heritage, and together with the Dutch language, it formed the foundation of the Boers' culture.[25] The Church employed every resource at its disposal to exploit the "sacred" bond with the Boers to halt the migration. Individual ministers not only attempted to persuade members who wanted to trek to stay, but they also used their considerable social influence within their congregations to shape public opinion against the Trek.[26] They created a negative climate towards the Great Trek in the Cape by fostering negative perceptions of the Great Trek and of the Voortrekkers among those who remained.[27] The Dutch Reformed Church preached that the Boers should patiently wait until the government addressed the circumstances on the eastern frontier.[28] Passivity, however, posed a significant risk to the success of the migration movement in the early stages of the Trek because it could have caused the Trek to come to a standstill. The Boers were conservative, and the prospect of not having their own Dutch Reformed Church minister with

---

[25] Giliomee, Hermann. Die Afrikaners (Afrikaans Edition). Tafelberg. Kindle Edition., p.197
[26] Strauss, P. (2015). Die Kaapse NG Kerk en die Groot Trek: 'n evaluering. *Stellenbosch Theological Journal*, *1*(1), 273-289., p.277
[27] Strauss, P. (2015). Die Kaapse NG Kerk en die Groot Trek: 'n evaluering. *Stellenbosch Theological Journal*, *1*(1), 273-289., p.277
[28] Muller, C. F. J. (1987). *Die oorsprong van die Groot Trek* (2nd ed.). Tafelberg Uitgewers., p.375

them on the Trek would have made the decision to trek exceedingly difficult.

On 20 November 1837, the Synod of the Dutch Reformed Church approved a critical Pastoral Letter,[29] which outlined the Church's stance and strategy against the Great Trek. The Boers' congregations were mostly served by Scottish ministers during this time. These ministers included Reverend Thomas Reid in Colesberg, Reverend Andrew Murray in Graaff-Reinet, Reverend John Taylor in Cradock, Reverend Colin Fraser in Beaufort West, Reverend Alexander Smith in Uitenhage, Reverend Alexander Welsh in Glen Lynden, and Reverend George Morgan in Somerset East.[30] Despite their presence, the Scottish ministers constituted only a quarter of the eligible voters in the 1837 Synod.[31] The pastoral letter was, therefore, largely approved by Cape Afrikaner ministers from the western districts. This pastoral letter was significant as it was binding on the members, congregations, office bearers, and meetings of the Dutch Reformed Church, and everyone had to obey it.[32] The Synod determined that the Great Trek was a "rebellion against lawful authority" because the Boers had withdrawn from British Imperial rule. Consequently, the Voortrekkers

---

[29] Strauss, P. (2015). Die Kaapse NG Kerk en die Groot Trek: 'n evaluering. *Stellenbosch Theological Journal*, 1(1), 273-289., p.277
[30] J. W. Claasen, (1994) Skotse predikante en die geestelike bearbeiding van die Voortrekkers. HTS Teologiese Studies/Theological Studies, 50.3., p.493
[31] J. W. Claasen, (1994) Skotse predikante en die geestelike bearbeiding van die Voortrekkers. HTS Teologiese Studies/Theological Studies, 50.3., p.495
[32] Pont, A. D., (1978). Die herderlijken brief van die Sinode van 1837. HTS Teologiese Studies/Theological Studies. (34)(4), 91-105., p.96

were branded as rebels, and it was decided that everyone must be discouraged from participating in the migration movement.[33] The pastoral letter encouraged the Boers to submit to the British Government as a "divinely appointed authority".[34] The Synod criticised the Boers for expecting the colonial government to "exclusively" cater to their needs, deeming this attitude as "blameworthy".[35] The Synod decided that everyone should patiently wait until "God uses the authority to rectify the temporary problems on the eastern frontier".[36] The Synod advised the Boers to be "faithful and obedient subjects," as this would surely earn them the protection and favour of those who govern them.[37] In its concluding portion, the Synod's pastoral letter has shown to be a political tool against the Boers by elevating Queen Victoria and framing her 1837 ascension to the throne as a divine occurrence.

For the Boers' migration movement to achieve its aims; it now became necessary for enough Boers to also resist against the Church. The Voortrekkers found themselves subject to censorship, being denied the sacrament, their children denied baptism and their marriages excluded from the Church's religious services. The Voortrekkers would trek

---

[33] Pont, A. D., (1978). Die herderlijken brief van die Sinode van 1837. HTS Teologiese Studies/Theological Studies. (34)(4), 91-105., p.97
[34] Pont, A. D., (1978). Die herderlijken brief van die Sinode van 1837. HTS Teologiese Studies/Theological Studies. (34)(4), 91-105., p.91-92
[35] Pont, A. D., (1978). Die herderlijken brief van die Sinode van 1837. HTS Teologiese Studies/Theological Studies. (34)(4), 91-105., p.91-92
[36] Pont, A. D., (1978). Die herderlijken brief van die Sinode van 1837. HTS Teologiese Studies/Theological Studies. (34)(4), 91-105., p.97
[37] Pont, A. D., (1978). Die herderlijken brief van die Sinode van 1837. HTS Teologiese Studies/Theological Studies. (34)(4), 91-105., p.91-92

without the guidance of an ordained minister. The secretary of the synod, Dr William Robertson, later referred to the Bloukrans massacres in Natal, during which more almost three hundred Boers, including 41 men, 56 women, and 185 children were murdered, as well as the murders of Piet Retief and his men by Dingane, as the "punishing hand of God" in a letter.[38] However, for many generations, due to their isolated way of life, there has been a tradition of home worship in Boer culture.[39] The Boers practised a simple, practical religion, devoid of complicated ideologies. In the mornings and evenings, they would read a few verses from their Bible and say a prayer. They refrained from proselytizing or attempting to sway others to their beliefs. The Church, while especially important in their lives, was primarily significant as an institution because they received the sacraments there, baptized their children, and got married. Resistance against the Church emerged. When Reverend Andrew Murray tried to convince Voortrekker leader, Gerrit Maritz and his wife not to trek, Maritz barred him from his house.[40] While the Dutch Reformed Church managed to dissuade some Boers from participating in the Great Trek, it couldn't entirely divert the course of the movement. In 1843, when Dr. A. Faure, the secretary of the Cape Synod, visited the Boers in

---

[38] J. W. Claasen, (1994) Skotse predikante en die geestelike bearbeiding van die Voortrekkers. HTS Teologiese Studies/Theological Studies, 50.3., p.496 and Pont, A. D., (1978). Die herderlijken brief van die Sinode van 1837. HTS Teologiese Studies/Theological Studies. (34)(4), 91-105., p.97
[39] Muller, C. F. J. (1987). *Die oorsprong van die Groot Trek* (2nd ed.). Tafelberg Uitgewers., p.310
[40] J. W. Claasen, (1994) Skotse predikante en die geestelike bearbeiding van die Voortrekkers. HTS Teologiese Studies/Theological Studies, 50.3., p.493

Natal, he no longer referred to them as "wandering rebels," but as "immigrants," indicating a change in the church's attitude towards the Voortrekkers.[41] However, the Cape Church never revoked the decisions made during the Synod of 1837.

A most challenging hurdle to a successful migration was the Boers' deeply ingrained connection to the Cape, which they regarded as their homeland. Boer leaders expressed their affection for the Cape on many occasions and declared that they were compelled to leave the country of their birth, an experience they described as painful. In his manifesto of 1837, when he left the Cape, Piet Retief referred to it as: "the fruitful land of our birth."[42] Andries Pretorius wrote in his letter from the Sand River on 24 February 1839, to Governor D'Urban: "We left our motherland behind with concern and sorrow."[43] The Natalia Volksraad (elected Citizen Council) stated in its "Declaration of Protest" on 11 November 1839: "Compelled to leave their beloved country..."[44] The Volksraad of Origstad, in the later South Africa Republic (ZAR), noted in a Memorial on 7 October 1845: "Having torn ourselves loose from the British Government and departed from our motherland."[45] In 1836,

---

[41] Strauss, P. (2015). Die Kaapse NG Kerk en die Groot Trek: 'n evaluering. *Stellenbosch Theological Journal*, 1(1), 273-289., p.286
[42] Du Toit, A., & Giliomee, H. (1983). *Afrikaner Political Thought. Volume 1: 1780-1850*. University of California Press., p.200
[43] Du Toit, A., & Giliomee, H. (1983). *Afrikaner Political Thought. Volume 1: 1780-1850*. University of California Press., p.200
[44] Du Toit, A., & Giliomee, H. (1983). *Afrikaner Political Thought. Volume 1: 1780-1850*. University of California Press., p.200
[45] Du Toit, A., & Giliomee, H. (1983). *Afrikaner Political Thought. Volume 1: 1780-1850*. University of California Press., p.200

THE CREATION OF THE BOER IDENTITY

after Hendrik Potgieter, one of the first Voortrekker pioneers, had already crossed the Vaal River, Piet Retief wrote in a private letter to his family: "I will postpone the venture (migration) for a while... (I) still live in hope of improvement (of the situation in the Cape)."[46] The Boers' love for their homeland made the decision to migrate personal, and each Boer had to decide for himself what he was willing to sacrifice for freedom.

The complex decision to migrate fundamentally shaped the structure of the Great Trek itself. The Great Trek was not a single massive movement encompassing the entire Boer population. Rather, the history of the Trek can be divided into two primary phases. The initial phase was characterised by the coordinated and structured movement of several significant groups of Trekkers.[47] During this phase, particularly in 1837, the larger trek parties embarked on their trek. The Boers migrated in family units or groups of family units, involving families, women, children, and the elderly. Their large herds of cattle and sheep required the Boers to disperse widely and proceed at a slow pace, rendering them susceptible to potential attacks and impeding their capacity for offensive military actions, which is why they moved in larger groups during the first phase. However, the larger trek groups comprised only around 100 men. A Trek leader Jacob de Klerk left the Cape with eleven families and twenty-seven wagons in late July 1837; his daughter was born on the 7th of

---

[46] Muller, C. F. J. (1987). *Die oorsprong van die Groot Trek* (2nd ed.). Tafelberg Uitgewers., p.261

[47] Du Toit, A., & Giliomee, H. (1983). *Afrikaner Political Thought. Volume 1: 1780-1850*. University of California Press., p.19

the same month, and his 80-year-old father, Jacob de Klerk Sr., also participated in the trek.[48] Following 1839, the safety and security of Boer settlements in Natal and the Highveld had been largely ensured, allowing them to establish essential social and political structures.[49] In the early 1840s, many more people migrated, albeit in smaller groups, primarily as individual families.[50]

The resolute aspiration of the Boers - to achieve independence from British rule - overshadowed the inherent risks of the Trek, including the significant emotional and material losses they suffered, as well as the dangers it posed to them. The direction and distance that the Trek would take them were less important.[51] Already in his manifesto, when Piet Retief joined the migration movement and left the Cape, he declared: "We leave the Colony with the full assurance that the English government has nothing more to demand from us and will allow us to govern ourselves in the future without further interference."[52] After Retief was elected as governor of the Boers when he joined the migration movement, he wrote to Governor D'Urban on 21 July 1837: "That this abandonment of our native country has occasioned us enormous and incalculable losses, but that,

---

[48] Visagie, J. C. (1990). Minder bekende Voortrekkerleiers. *Historia*, 35(1), 39-57., p.42
[49] Du Toit, A., & Giliomee, H. (1983). *Afrikaner Political Thought. Volume 1: 1780-1850*. University of California Press., p.19
[50] Visagie, J. C. (1990). Minder bekende Voortrekkerleiers. *Historia*, 35(1), 39-57., p.57
[51] Muller, C. F. J. (1987). *Die oorsprong van die Groot Trek* (2nd ed.). Tafelberg Uitgewers., p.316
[52] Gie, S. F. (1932). *Geskiedenis vir Suid-Afrika, II* (2nd ed.). Pro Ecclesia-Drukkery, p.296

notwithstanding this, we, on our side, will not show any enmity towards the British nation." "That, consequently, all trade and commerce between us and the British Merchants will, on our part, be free and uninterrupted, as with all other nations, with this understanding, that we desire to be considered as a free and independent people."[53]

Of all the leaders, Hendrik Potgieter likely articulated the Boers' freedom ideal most unequivocally in his letter to Commandant-General Andries Pretorius from Potchefstroom on 28 August 1841: "I do not want to subject myself to any Briton, nor to any other power in the world; and I am no Briton, nor do I hope and trust, will I ever become one, and I pray to the Almighty for this, not only for me, but for our whole united society of burghers (united Boers of Natalia and the highveld region), and I would rather go ten steps forward than one backward."[54] On 24 February 1839, Andries Pretorius conveyed the Boers' determination to govern themselves in freedom, in his letter from the Sand River to Governor D'Urban as follows: "We also notice that the (British) government threatens us much, yet in the first place we know that all proclaim that every man should be free . . . and we know very well that we are a freeborn people,..." "It is vain to nurse the hope that we shall return again, all would rather die than that. . . "[55] The idea of leaving the Cape with the purpose of establishing a country for the Boers where

---

[53] Du Toit, A., & Giliomee, H. (1983). *Afrikaner Political Thought. Volume 1: 1780-1850*. University of California Press., p.214-215
[54] Du Toit, A., & Giliomee, H. (1983). *Afrikaner Political Thought. Volume 1: 1780-1850*. University of California Press., p.217
[55] Du Toit, A., & Giliomee, H. (1983). *Afrikaner Political Thought. Volume 1: 1780-1850*. University of California Press., p.216-217

they can govern themselves, in response to the survival crisis in the eastern Cape ignited a spark in the Boer identity. It motivated hesitant conservatives and captivated the idealists, and it transformed the Trek from a rebellion against British domination into a focused African mission.[56]

The Boers left the Cape precisely to lead a peaceful and tranquil life. Their leaders repeatedly expressed their intentions to live in peace and friendship with the African nations. Piet Retief articulated these intentions in his manifesto: "We declare solemnly that we leave this Colony with the desire to lead a quieter life than we have had up to now. We shall not harm any people, nor take the slightest property from anyone. But if attacked, we will consider ourselves fully justified in defending our persons and property to the utmost against any enemy. We announce that when we have laid down proper laws for our future guidance, copies thereof will be sent to the Colony for general information." "We intend, in the course of our journey and upon our arrival in the land where we are to live, to make our intentions known to the native tribes, as well as our desire to live in peace and friendship with them."[57] When the Great Trek was in a crisis following the attacks on the Potgieter-trek by Mzilikazi, Governor Retief suspected British involvement, possibly through missionaries like Captain Gardener, in sowing mistrust among certain African leaders regarding the intentions of the Boers. He wrote the following

---

[56] Muller, C.F. J., Edited by Muller, C. F. J. (1984). *500 Years, A History of South Africa* (4th ed.). Academica., p. 158
[57] Gie, S. F. (1932). *Geskiedenis vir Suid-Afrika, II* (2nd ed.). Pro Ecclesia-Drukkery, p.296

in his letter to Governor D'Urban on 21 July 1837: "That we have learnt with grief that almost all the native tribes, by whom we are now surrounded, have been instigated to attack us; but although we feel ourselves fully able to resist all our enemies, we would however beg of your Excellency to prevent, as far as lies in your power, such hostilities, so that we may not be compelled to spill human blood, which has already been the case with Matsilikatzi." "That we will prove to the world, by our conduct, that it never has been our intention unlawfully to molest any nation or people; but that, on the contrary, we have no greater satisfaction than in the general peace and amity of all mankind."[58]

The Boers' objective was to acquire uninhabited land and coexist peacefully with other nations. Hendrik Potgieter expressed this goal in a letter to Governor D'Urban on 3 December 1838: "-... we decided to leave the Colony to safeguard our families" "- we regard ourselves as free citizens who can go wherever we choose without harming anyone." "- our aim was a land where there were no (other) nations." "- we want to harm none of the nations present here."[59] Andries Pretorius, in his letter from the Sand River on 24 February 1839 to Governor D'Urban, stated: "we did not go out . . . with aggressive purposes."[60] When they left the Cape, the Boers had concluded peace and friendship

---

[58] Du Toit, A., & Giliomee, H. (1983). *Afrikaner Political Thought. Volume 1: 1780-1850*. University of California Press., p.214-215
[59] Oberholzer, J.. (1989). Die Voortrekkerideaal - Natal of Transvaal?. HTS Teologiese Studies / Theological Studies. 45. 10.4102/hts.v45i3.2316., p.672
[60] Du Toit, A., & Giliomee, H. (1983). *Afrikaner Political Thought. Volume 1: 1780-1850*. University of California Press., p.216-217

agreements with leaders such as Chief Moroka of the Barolong, Sekonyella, Chief of the Batlokwa, Korana Chief David Danser, Pieter Davids, Chief of the Griekwas, and Moshoeshoe, the founder and first paramount chief of the Basotho nation. From the outset, the Boers aimed to acquire land through formal cession or purchase from African tribes. Governor Retief's intentions were most explicit in his comment to the missionary Francis Owen. When they chose Natal as their destination, they decided to negotiate with the Zulu king Dingane. During Retief's first visit to Dingane's kraal, he was asked by Owen if he would use force to acquire land. Retief replied that if no agreement was reached, the Boers would move further north.[61]

Some Boer leaders saw the Great Trek not only as a political-constitutional process but also as a means to expand trade and increase the Boers' access to markets beyond what they had in the eastern Cape. As early as 1825, Petrus Johannes Moolman and 161 other Boers petitioned the British colonial government to develop Port Elizabeth into a free trade zone.[62] This initiative sought to facilitate international trade, given the challenges posed by the long distance to the Cape Town port. Early Boer pioneers like Louis Trichardt and Hendrik Potgieter initially explored the prospect of settling near the Portuguese port in Delagoa Bay (Maputo) to leverage international trade's economic benefits. Governor Piet Retief envisioned free trade with both British

---

[61] Hugo, M. (1988). Piet Retief in die Suid-Afrikaanse geskiedskrywing. *South African Journal of Cultural History*, 2(2), 108-126., p.113
[62] Markram, W. J. (2001). *Die lewe en werk van Petrus Lafras Uys, 1797-1838* [Doctoral dissertation, University of Stellenbosch]., p.70

and other international traders for the future Boer Republic. He articulated this vision in his letter to Governor D'Urban on 21 July 1837: "Consequently, all trade and commerce between us and British traders on our side will be free and uninterrupted, as with all other nations..."[63] Prominent Boer figures such as Piet Uys and Gert Rudolph, who were also farmers and entrepreneurs, had been showing interest in the east coast of Africa for some time because they saw greater economic opportunities there than in the Cape Colony. They regarded the East Coast as a gateway to global markets. This was the primary reason Piet Uys led his exploration commission to Port Natal (Durban) in 1834.[64] Uys's primary objective in the fourteen resolutions he issued on 14 August 1837 along the Caledon River for a future Boer state, was to use Port Natal as a harbour.[65] In these fourteen resolutions, Uys also declared that they aimed to establish their Republic on the same principles of liberty as those adopted by the USA.[66]

The media undertook an extensive propaganda campaign to discredit the legitimacy of the Great Trek. Through Cape newspapers, this propaganda portrayed the Boers as naïve and foolish for relinquishing their temporarily

---

[63] Du Toit, A., & Giliomee, H. (1983). *Afrikaner Political Thought. Volume 1: 1780-1850*. University of California Press., p.214-215
[64] Markram, W. J. (2001). *Die lewe en werk van Petrus Lafras Uys, 1797-1838* [Doctoral dissertation, University of Stellenbosch]., p.70
[65] Markram, W. J. (2001). *Die lewe en werk van Petrus Lafras Uys, 1797-1838* [Doctoral dissertation, University of Stellenbosch]., p.69
[66] Oberholzer, J.. (1989). Die Voortrekkerideaal - Natal of Transvaal?. HTS Teologiese Studies / Theological Studies. 45. 10.4102/hts.v45i3.2316., p.672

unsettled eastern border in exchange for a region ravaged by the Mfecane, where they would be cut off from the Cape's political and religious support systems.[67] De Zuid-Afrikaan, the mouthpiece of the Cape Afrikaner and the only Dutch newspaper in the Cape at the time, condemned the Boers for withdrawing from British authority.[68] In 1837, John Fairbairn, the editor of the Commercial Advertiser and son-in-law of Dr Phillip, an evangelist linked to the London Missionary Society, even suggested that Boers departing from the Cape should be shot on sight unless they immediately returned.[69] Governor D'Urban believed that the Trek could potentially destabilise the Cape Colony, and he made efforts to persuade the Boers to stay. In his correspondence to the British State Secretary, Lord Glenelg, he depicted the departing Boers as "a brave, patient, industrious, orderly and religious people, the cultivators, the defenders and the tax contributors of the country." However, Glenelg's response to D'Urban presented a contrasting perspective. He described the Great Trek as follows: "The motives of this migration were the same as had in all the ages impelled the strong to encroach on the weak, and the powerful and unprincipled to wrest by force or fraud from the comparatively feeble and defenceless, wealth, or property, or dominion."[70] According to the Rev. J. Ayliff, a Wesleyan

---

[67] Muller, C. F. J. (1987). *Die oorsprong van die Groot Trek* (2nd ed.). Tafelberg Uitgewers., p.376
[68] Giliomee, Hermann. Die Afrikaners (Afrikaans Edition). Tafelberg. Kindle Edition., p.154
[69] Giliomee, Hermann. Die Afrikaners (Afrikaans Edition). Tafelberg. Kindle Edition., p.199
[70] Gie, S. F. (1932). *Geskiedenis vir Suid-Afrika, II* (2nd ed.). Pro Ecclesia-Drukkery, p.295

THE CREATION OF THE BOER IDENTITY

Methodist Missionary, the Great Trek's origins were attributed to a sinister influence. He wrote about the Trek: "This mania could never have spread as it did, seeing it involved such fearful sacrifice of property, of ease of life, unless it had been fed by some secret evil influence - that was Satan."[71]

Although Cape Afrikaners made up 66% of the Cape's population, only a small fraction of them participated in the Great Trek. According to Dr Jan C. Visagie, in his book "Voortrekkerstamouers (Voortrekker ancestors) 1835—1845" (2nd edition), only 70 families from Clanwilliam (32), Worcester (24), Cape Town (8), Stellenbosch (4), and Franschhoek (2) embarked on the Great Trek alongside the Boers. This translates to approximately 2.6% of the Voortrekkers, which was about 450 individuals out of the total of 17000. There are several reasons why Cape Afrikaners did not partake in the Great Trek. A significant reason is likely because they did not experience the continuous Xhosa wars, the uncertainty of life, and the material losses faced by the Boers on the eastern border.[72] Another key factor was that Cape Afrikaners had not developed mobility in their culture, as the Boers had done over the preceding century. Cape Afrikaners would develop economically and socially in a more diverse and mature British colonial society, in contrast to the challenges that the

---

[71] Muller, C. F. J. (1987). *Die oorsprong van die Groot Trek* (2nd ed.). Tafelberg Uitgewers., p.256

[72] Van Jaarsveld, F. A. (1963). Anthropo-geographical aspects of the Great Trek: 1836-1863. *Historia, 8*(2), 93-99. P.93

THE BOERS TREK

Boers, founding new independent settlements, would face.[73] The lieutenant governor of the eastern districts, Sir Andries Stockenström, initially thought that the Voortrekkers were just more trekboers (nomadic farmers) who wanted to graze their cattle across the Orange River, and therefore did nothing to prevent the Trek. In his final communication to Piet Retief, Stockenström accused Retief of having abandoned the protection of the British government for the Boers.[74] When Stockenström later realised the gravity of the situation, he insisted that Sir George Napier, D'Urban's successor, pursue the Boers participating in the Great Trek.[75] Cape Afrikaners criticised the Great Trek, but at times, also showed sympathy and solidarity.[76]

In the early 1820s, farmers along the northern border of the Cape dealt with droughts and locust infestations, which harmed the nutritional quality of their soil. To sustain and feed their animals, they sought better pastures in Transorangia (the area north of the Orange River which would later become known as the Free State). In 1825, the colonial government approved this migration as a temporary permit, but the farmers had to return within a specified time limit.[77] When the government later denied permission, these trekboers simply

---

[73] Du Toit, A., & Giliomee, H. (1983). *Afrikaner Political Thought. Volume 1: 1780-1850.* University of California Press., p.20
[74] Giliomee, Hermann. Die Afrikaners (Afrikaans Edition). Tafelberg. Kindle Edition., p.148
[75] Strauss, P. (2015). Die Kaapse NG Kerk en die Groot Trek: 'n evaluering. *Stellenbosch Theological Journal, 1*(1), 273-289. P.276
[76] Giliomee, Hermann. Die Afrikaners (Afrikaans Edition). Tafelberg. Kindle Edition., p.199
[77] Muller, C. F. J. (1987). *Die oorsprong van die Groot Trek* (2nd ed.). Tafelberg Uitgewers., p.229

continued to take their cattle to graze across the border without formal consent. By 1828, the conditions of the land in the Cape were so poor that a sizable number of trekboers remained across the river.[78] The Cape government could no longer contain these movements of the trekboers, and during the drought of 1833 in the Cape, some trekboers ventured as far as the Vaal River for grazing land.[79] The motivations of the trekboers to cross the Cape's border were solely material, and they had developed an allegiance to the British crown. Their leader, M. A. Oberholzer, wrote to the colonial government in 1834, confirming that they had not crossed the border out of malicious intent towards the government. The concept of migration had not taken root among most of the trekboers in Transorangia at this time. On 5 December 1834, 221 trekboers sent a request to Governor D'Urban for permission to take possession of land in the Transorangia area.[80] D'Urban rejected this request. Among the signatories of this request were Sarel Cilliers, who would later become an important Voortrekker leader, and Johannes Jacobus (Lang Hans) Janse van Rensburg, who would later lead one of the first small trek parties to the north. Soon, at least 40% of the trekboers in Transorangia would embrace the idea of migration and join the Voortrekkers.[81] Many of them, such as Cilliers and Casper Kruger, along with his ten-year-old son, Paul, would later join

---

[78] Muller, C. F. J. (1987). *Die oorsprong van die Groot Trek* (2nd ed.). Tafelberg Uitgewers., p.229
[79] Muller, C. F. J. (1987). *Die oorsprong van die Groot Trek* (2nd ed.). Tafelberg Uitgewers., p.232
[80] Visagie, J. C. (1996). Die fyn onderskeid tussen die Voortrekkers en die trekboere. *Historia, 41*(2)., p.2
[81] Visagie, J. C. (1996). Die fyn onderskeid tussen die Voortrekkers en die trekboere. *Historia, 41*(2)., p.3

the trek party led by Andries Hendrik (Hendrik) Potgieter. The crucial distinction between the trekboers of the 19th century and the Boers lay in the fact that the trekboers did not further develop within the Boer cultural identity. They were loyal British subjects who did not participate in the Great Trek and later advocated for the British annexation of the Transorangia region.

The Great Trek coincided with the conclusion of the Mfecane. The Mfecane was a period of widespread warfare and migrations among the Nguni and Sotho-Tswana societies in southern Africa during the 1820s and early 1830s.[82] Socio-economic factors, such as rapid population growth in certain areas resulting in land scarcity, were the underlying causes of the Mfecane. The rise of the Zulu kingdom and the formidable military campaigns led by King Shaka played a pivotal role in initiating and expanding the Mfecane.[83] From north of the Tugela River in Natal, Shaka attacked smaller tribes to the north and south of him. Some of these tribes then fled and, in turn, clashed with other tribes in different regions. Various warlords emerged, leading to intense warfare and conflict that had a devastating impact on the tribes in the interior of southern Africa. Widespread forced migrations occurred, displacing tribes from their original territories. This led to the disintegration of communities and the obliteration of their social structures and traditional ways of life. Numerous communities and settlements were destroyed, and women and children were assimilated into larger tribes as stronger leaders

---

[82] Du Toit, A., & Giliomee, H. (1983). *Afrikaner Political Thought. Volume 1: 1780-1850.* University of California Press., p.19
[83] Van Aswegen, H. J. (1994). Die Mfecane. Werklikheid of mite? *Historia, 39*(1), 19-32., p.31

absorbed weaker groups. Losses of livestock and destruction of crops disrupted agricultural activities and devastated the tribes' economies, causing widespread famine. Large swatches of land, especially surrounding the militarised nations such as the Zulus under Dingane and the Ndebele under Mzilikazi, were left unpopulated.

Boer leaders had undertaken exploratory journeys to central-southern Africa and Natal years before the Great Trek. They knew about the Mfecane and that opportunities existed to settle in extensive depopulated areas.[84] They knew that smaller nations, who had suffered under larger warring nations, would welcome them as allies, and they also established agreements of peace and friendship with many tribes.[85] They knew who the major leaders were and with whom they had to negotiate for land. In many cases, they had already established contact with these leaders, including Dingane and Mzilikazi, before the Trek began. The Boers, however, lacked a comprehensive understanding of the situation. They had no idea of the massive scale and impact of the Mfecane, including the widespread losses and hardships it caused. The most significant consequence of the Mfecane, which the Boers did not comprehend, was the adverse social effects it had on the tribes. The fact that the social systems, tribal structures, and traditions of many tribes were destroyed and replaced with a culture of violence and military control in some, would have a long-lasting impact on the nations in

---

[84] Muller, C. F. J. (1981). 500 Years - A History of South Africa (3rd ed.). Academica., p.157
[85] Muller, C. F. J. (1981). 500 Years - A History of South Africa (3rd ed.). Academica., p.157

southern Africa. It would also have significant consequences for the Boers.

During 1834, the Boer leaders dispatched three exploration expeditions, known as commission treks, to various regions.[86] One of these commission treks was undertaken by Johannes Andries Pretorius and his son Willem Jurgen. Towards the end of 1834, the father and son explored Damaraland, the southern part of present-day Namibia, and returned early in 1835.[87] Another commission trek was the Overvaal (trans-Vaal) exploration commission, which, under the leadership of a Boer named Scholtz, ventured through the highveld up to the Soutpansberg. The third and final exploration commission set out to explore Natal and was led by the widely respected Boer, Piet Uys, with the assistance of the renowned scout, Hans de Lange.[88] Uys's exploration commission departed from the Cape on 8 September 1834, and returned in April 1835, amid the Sixth Border War. Unfortunately, the reports of these three commissions have not been preserved. Nevertheless, it is reasonable to assume that the positive feedback from the Overvaal Commission played a role in influencing figures like Louis Trichardt, Johannes (Lang Hans) van Rensburg, and Hendrik Potgieter to establish themselves in that

---

[86] Giliomee, Hermann. *Die Afrikaners* (Afrikaans Edition). Tafelberg. Kindle Edition., p.147
[87] Markram, W. J. (2001). *Die lewe en werk van Petrus Lafras Uys, 1797-1838* [Doctoral dissertation, University of Stellenbosch]., p.187
[88] Muller, C. F. J. (1987). *Die oorsprong van die Groot Trek* (2nd ed.). Tafelberg Uitgewers., p.272

THE CREATION OF THE BOER IDENTITY

region.[89] Piet Uys's favourable report on his exploration commission in Natal motivated many Boers to join the migration movement and consider settling in the largely depopulated southern part of Natal.[90] In addition to these three exploration commissions, numerous other expeditions were undertaken to explore the interior and Natal.

Between early March and the end of September 1830, a group of twelve Boers embarked on a hunting expedition to what is now Botswana and the Northwest Province of South Africa. While they did indeed go hunting, the purpose of the Meyer-De Lange expedition was to explore the area and to meet the feared Ndebele king, Mzilikazi.[91] Members of the expedition were Cornelis Meyer, his brother Willem Petrus (Piet) Meyer, his son-in-law Abraham Carel Greyling, and the latter's brother, Pieter (Piet) Jacobus Greyling (the Greyling brothers were stepsons of Piet Retief). Also on this expedition were Hans de Lange and his two brothers-in-law, the brothers Paul Dirk Bester and Willem Abraham Bester, Philip Rudolph Botha, J.C. Steyn, and the thirteen-year-old Hans Steyn.[92] This visit to Mzilikazi unfolded in a friendly manner, and after the visit, Mzilikazi displayed goodwill by gifting the Boers with ivory and "a few oxen and cows for

---

[89] Oberholzer, J.. (1989). Die Voortrekkerideaal - Natal of Transvaal? HTS Teologiese Studies / Theological Studies. 45. 10.4102/hts.v45i3.2316. , p.674

[90] Muller, C. F. J. (1987). *Die oorsprong van die Groot Trek* (2nd ed.). Tafelberg Uitgewers., p.282

[91] Visagie, J. C. (1992). 'n Besoek aan Mzilikazi in 1830. *Historia, 37*(1), 9-23., p.p

[92] Visagie, J. C. (1992). 'n Besoek aan Mzilikazi in 1830. *Historia, 37*(1), 9-23., p.14-15

the journey".[93] The discussion between the Boers and Mzilikazi was later revealed in a letter written by Piet Retief in 1836.[94] Retief wrote that the land toward which Hendrik Potgieter's trek was headed was "known to his stepsons" and that it was "healthy, fertile, and blessed with water, fruits, and game." Retief also revealed that "the only people the Boers had to fear (the Ndebele) had offered them land for settlement in the friendliest manner." When the expedition members returned, they reported their positive impressions of the region's "open spaces for farming opportunities". This generated a great deal of enthusiasm amongst the Boers, especially in the Uitenhage district.[95] The enthusiasm was so high that a signature list for those interested in settling in the north was circulated in the area. According to the civil commissioner of Albany and Somerset, Captain Campbell, the excitement was such that the list "quickly gathered over a hundred signatures".[96] Campbell later remarked that the 1830 Meyer-De Lange expedition played a significant role in sparking the idea of migration among the Boers.

During the 1830's, people who wanted to cross the borders of the colony had to obtain prior permission from the government. The most common reasons stated in applications to cross the border were planned hunting expeditions in the

---

[93] Visagie, J. C. (1992). 'n Besoek aan Mzilikazi in 1830. *Historia, 37*(1), 9-23., p.22
[94] Visagie, J. C. (1992). 'n Besoek aan Mzilikazi in 1830. *Historia, 37*(1), 9-23., p.22
[95] Visagie, J. C. (1992). 'n Besoek aan Mzilikazi in 1830. *Historia, 37*(1), 9-23., p.9
[96] Visagie, J. C. (1992). 'n Besoek aan Mzilikazi in 1830. *Historia, 37*(1), 9-23., p.23

interior and the intention to engage in trade with African tribes. On 30 January 1829, Piet Uys, along with Gert Rudolph and Cobus Moolman, obtained permission to hunt elephants in the interior.[97] There is a suspicion that the purpose of this hunting expedition by Uys and his friends was more than hunting and that they likely explored the interior with the intention of potential settlement. A year later, the Meyer-De Lange expedition to Mzilikazi took place. However, this group of explorers and hunters had ventured into the interior before. The Meyer brothers, Piet Meyer, and Cornelis Meyer, along with the Greyling brothers, Abraham, and Piet, had already explored the interior with a trading license in 1828. On their expedition, they encountered Hans de Lange and his party - Philip Botha, Paul Bester, and Willem Abraham Bester at approximately a two-week ox wagon journey away from the border.[98] The fact that there were ties between the 1829 Uys expedition and the Meyer-De Lange expedition to Mzilikazi's territory suggests that the Boers were already contemplating the concept of migration at that time.

The preliminary reconnaissance work preceding the Great Trek appears to have been significantly more organised and methodical than previously assumed. The enthusiasm displayed by the residents of Uitenhage for the Meyer-De Lange expedition to the northwest, even though these explorers were not from that area themselves, holds

---

[97] Markram, W. J. (2001). *Die lewe en werk van Petrus Lafras Uys, 1797-1838* [Doctoral dissertation, University of Stellenbosch]., p.178
[98] Muller, C. F. J. (1987). *Die oorsprong van die Groot Trek* (2nd ed.). Tafelberg Uitgewers., p.249

considerable significance.[99] Piet Uys, along with Gert Rudolph and Cobus Moolman, hailed from Uitenhage, which suggests that communication among Boers from various regions existed regarding exploration ventures and the broader concept of migration. In November 1832, Hans de Lange and Piet Meyer explored Natal without government permission.[100] This expedition by De Lange aptly prepared him to aid Piet Uys in his exploration commission to Natal in 1834. Piet Uys attached great personal significance to his reconnaissance commission, as he saw no future in the Cape. If he hadn't moved to Natal, he would have gone to America. He said to Jacobus, his son: "I don't know what will become of the country's affairs; I will ride to see if I can find any land that will be good for me, my descendants, and compatriots, and if I don't find it, I will go to America, because the oppression is becoming too heavy".[101] This exploration committee of Uys marked the conclusion of the reconnaissance phase of the Great Trek.[102]

Initially, the Boers had to conduct their reconnaissance and groundwork for the Great Trek in secret, due to fears of persecution by the British colonial government.[103] The Boers remembered Slagtersnek and knew

---

[99] Markram, W. J. (2001). *Die lewe en werk van Petrus Lafras Uys, 1797-1838* [Doctoral dissertation, University of Stellenbosch]., p.178-p.179
[100] Muller, C. F. J. (1987). *Die oorsprong van die Groot Trek* (2nd ed.). Tafelberg Uitgewers., p.249
[101] Muller, C. F. J. (1987). *Die oorsprong van die Groot Trek* (2nd ed.). Tafelberg Uitgewers., p.276
[102] Markram, W. J. (2001). *Die lewe en werk van Petrus Lafras Uys, 1797-1838* [Doctoral dissertation, University of Stellenbosch]., p.187
[103] Muller, C. F. J. (1987). *Die oorsprong van die Groot Trek* (2nd ed.). Tafelberg Uitgewers., p.259

how the British government treated "rebels". If prominent Boer leaders were to be prosecuted, it would have delayed the start of the Trek. Not being able to discuss their ideas and plans freely in the open, however, complicated matters significantly. They had to promote the idea of immigration, which was crucial for the success of the migration movement, covertly. They also couldn't openly appoint leaders to actively manage the migration movement, which hindered the organisation of the Trek.[104] The consequence was that many Boers were uninformed about the reconnaissance expeditions and the planning of the migration, which led to them not starting their preparations for the Trek. Governor D'Urban consulted the Attorney General of the Cape, A. Oliphant, to obtain clarity on the legal status of people who had crossed the Colony's borders.[105] According to Oliphant, in his statement on 13 August 1836, existing laws applied only to those who temporarily crossed the borders and considered themselves British subjects during their absence. Individuals who had settled in foreign lands and did not consider themselves British subjects would not be subject to colonial laws.[106] D'Urban and Attorney General Oliphant then concluded that legislation could not prevent migration, and the only way to

---

[104] Muller, C. F. J. (1987). *Die oorsprong van die Groot Trek* (2nd ed.). Tafelberg Uitgewers., p.259

[105] Markram, W. J. (1992). *Stephanus Petrus Erasmus: Grensboerpionier en Voortrekker, 1788-1847* [Master's thesis, University of Stellenbosch]., p.40

[106] Markram, W. J. (1992). *Stephanus Petrus Erasmus: Grensboerpionier en Voortrekker, 1788-1847* [Master's thesis, University of Stellenbosch]., p.40

prevent mass migration was to persuade the Boers to stay.[107] Lieutenant Governor Stockenström then, on 27 August 1836, publicly expressed his opinion that he was not aware of any law preventing British subjects from leaving the Colony and settling in another country, and that "it would be inhumane and oppressive if such a law did exist".[108] While the British colonial government opposed the Boers' migration plans, the statements of D'Urban, Oliphant, and Stockenström opened the door for the migration.[109] Boers could now openly organise, prepare, and leave the Cape, and on 2 February 1837, Piet Retief even published his migration manifesto in the Grahamstown Journal.

The 1834-1835 Border War had a significant impact on the Great Trek, both complicating and expediting the migration. During the war, martial law was enforced, and many Boers were on commando or obligated to defend their farms and those of their neighbours, delaying serious preparations for the Trek until 1836.[110] The war resulted in the largest capital losses on the Boers to date,[111] resulting in a general scarcity of capital among them to fund the Trek.

---

[107] Markram, W. J. (1992). *Stephanus Petrus Erasmus: Grensboerpionier en Voortrekker, 1788-1847* [Master's thesis, University of Stellenbosch]., p.40

[108] Markram, W. J. (1992). *Stephanus Petrus Erasmus: Grensboerpionier en Voortrekker, 1788-1847* [Master's thesis, University of Stellenbosch]., p.41

[109] Markram, W. J. (1992). *Stephanus Petrus Erasmus: Grensboerpionier en Voortrekker, 1788-1847* [Master's thesis, University of Stellenbosch]., p.41

[110] Muller, C. F. J. (1987). *Die oorsprong van die Groot Trek* (2nd ed.). Tafelberg Uitgewers,.p.304

[111] Giliomee, Hermann. Die Afrikaners (Afrikaans Edition). Tafelberg. Kindle Edition, p.88

Xhosa attacks, including cattle theft, the destruction of farms, and pillaging, caused substantial losses for the Boers. Due to the shortage of capital, many Boers had to wait for compensation promised by the colonial government for requisitioned supplies, horses, and wagons used during the conflict.[112] On 6 July 1835, the Boers petitioned the British authorities for war-related compensation, but little to no compensation was received. Farms had to be sold, and due to the influx of properties in the market, English speculators could purchase them at incredibly low prices. Boers traded livestock below its value for necessary supplies like wagons, clothing materials, and tents. They also had to settle all outstanding taxes owed to the government.[113] The transportation of arms and ammunition from Cape Town had to be done clandestinely because Boers were limited to possessing 4.5 kilograms of gunpowder and ammunition.[114] Consequently, they concealed gunpowder in false bottoms of wagons and transported it across the border and buried it on the other side. The destruction of farms, on the other hand, contributed to the Boers' readiness to embrace migration, as burned-down farmhouses already rendered them mobile.[115] When the British colonial secretary, Glenelg, attributed the blame for the Sixth Border War to the Boers and appointed the philanthropic Andries Stockenström as lieutenant

---

[112] Muller, C. F. J. (1987). *Die oorsprong van die Groot Trek* (2nd ed.). Tafelberg Uitgewers,.p.372
[113] Botha, J. P. (2008). Ons Geskiedenis (1st ed.). J.P. Botha., p.98
[114] Botha, J. P. (2008). Ons Geskiedenis (1st ed.). J.P. Botha., p.99
[115] Muller, C. F. J. (1987). *Die oorsprong van die Groot Trek* (2nd ed.). Tafelberg Uitgewers,.p.303

THE BOERS TREK

governor over the eastern districts, it prompted the Boers to commence their Trek.[116]

After Piet Uys returned from his exploratory commission in Natal, the Boers, despite challenges like the Sixth Frontier War, could now begin earnestly preparing for their migration. Someone needed to set the migration in motion. If everyone had waited for each other, the Trek would not have started. The British would not have granted permission to the Boers to emigrate. The Trek now needed a rebel - someone willing to defy the government's will and become the first pioneer. One of the first Boers to receive feedback about Piet Uys' exploration commission was Louis Tregardt. At that time, Tregardt lived in Xhosaland (Gcalekaland – the land of the Xhosa tribe led by Chief Hintsa) through which Uys and his company travelled on their way back to the colony. Tregardt and his eldest son, Carolus, leased 12,000 morgen of land near the White Kei River and Tsomo Mountain, under a 99-year lease agreement with Chief Hintsa.[117] Hans de Lange, who accompanied Uys on the exploration mission to Natal, also lived near Tregardt in Xhosaland at that time.[118] Before Uys returned to the colony, he stayed a few days with Chief Hintsa, who informed him about the situation with the war.[119] Trichardt

---

[116] Muller, C. F. J. (1981). 500 Years - A History of South Africa (3rd ed.). Academica., p.160
[117] Duvenhage, G. D. J. (1963). Wanneer het die Trichardt-trek begin? *Historia, 8*(2), 100-103., p.100
[118] Muller, C. F. J. (1987). *Die oorsprong van die Groot Trek* (2nd ed.). Tafelberg Uitgewers., p. 279
[119] Markram, W. J. (2001). *Die lewe en werk van Petrus Lafras Uys, 1797-1838* [Doctoral dissertation, University of Stellenbosch]., p.203

expected Uys and De Lange back, and he likely received a report about the Natal Exploration Commission from Uys by the end of March 1835.[120]

Louis Trichardt grew up in a revolutionary family. His father, Carolus, played a leading role in the uprising against the VOC government in 1795 when the Boers declared a Republic in Graaff-Reinet. Within the British government at the Cape, Louis Tregardt was known as an outspoken opponent of the British Imperial government. On 30 August 1835, Colonel Harry Smith wrote to D'Urban from King William's Town: "...That villain of a Boer, as well as his family, I understand, is notorious for their hereditary animosity towards the British." They suspected that Tregardt might assist the Xhosa in the war, and Colonel Harry Smith offered a reward of 500 cattle for his capture.[121] By mid-1835, Louis Tregardt was thus seen in the highest Cape government circles as the leader of a potentially dangerous movement.[122] When Hintsa became involved in the war in March 1835 following D'Urban's incursion into Xhosaland, Trichardt decided to trek. After leaving Gcalekaland by the end of March 1835, Tregardt, unaware of any planned British actions against him, lived for six months on the eastern border of Tarka and the Bamboes mountain in the Brak River

---

[120] Markram, W. J. (2001). *Die lewe en werk van Petrus Lafras Uys, 1797-1838* [Doctoral dissertation, University of Stellenbosch]., p.204
[121] Duvenhage, G. D. J. (1963). Wanneer het die Trichardt-trek begin? *Historia*, *8*(2), 100-103., p.101
[122] Muller, C. F. J. (1987). *Die oorsprong van die Groot Trek* (2nd ed.). Tafelberg Uitgewers., p.363

district,[123] where he made all necessary preparations for his Trek. It's possible that Tregardt and his son Carolus joined the Tarka commando for the remainder of the war.[124] On 18 September 1835, Field Cornet J.C. Greyling of Brak River reported that Louis Tregardt had crossed the colony's border.[125] With Louis Tregardt, the entire Great Trek phenomenon began.[126]

During the six months that Tregardt resided on the eastern border of the Tarka area, he most likely engaged in conversations about the migration and shared plans with Hendrik Potgieter and possibly also with Potgieter's cousin Lang Hans van Rensburg.[127] Their movements during the trek indicate that they had already decided on the area where they intended to settle.[128] As predominantly sheep farmers, they preferred the grassy regions of the highveld in the central interior over the mountainous regions of Natal, with the intention of using Delagoa Bay as a port.[129] Furthermore, Potgieter did not trust the English not to annex Natal, despite

---

[123] Visagie, J. C. (1988). Jan en Breggie Pretorius van die Tregardt-trek. *Journal of Cape History*, *13*(1), 14-22., p.19
[124] Visagie, J. C. (1988). Jan en Breggie Pretorius van die Tregardt-trek. *Journal of Cape History*, *13*(1), 14-22., p.20
[125] Visagie, J. C. (1988). Jan en Breggie Pretorius van die Tregardt-trek. *Journal of Cape History*, *13*(1), 14-22., p.20
[126] Muller, C. F. J. (1987). *Die oorsprong van die Groot Trek* (2nd ed.). Tafelberg Uitgewers., p.365
[127] Visagie, J. C. (1988). Jan en Breggie Pretorius van die Tregardt-trek. *Journal of Cape History*, *13*(1), 14-22., p.21
[128] Oberholzer, J.. (1989). Die Voortrekkerideaal - Natal of Transvaal?. HTS Teologiese Studies / Theological Studies. 45. 10.4102/hts.v45i3.2316., p.673
[129] Van Jaarsveld, F. A. (1963). Anthropo-geographical aspects of the Great Trek: 1836-1863. *Historia*, *8*(2), 93-99., p.94

the British Imperial government officially stating that they would not annex Natal.[130] On 12 March 1835, the Cape government informed traders and other residents, who requested the British government to annex Natal, that the Imperial government in London had decided not to annex Natal as a British colony. The Graham's Town Journal published the letter confirming this decision by the British government on 27 March 1835.[131] British State Secretary, Glenelg, once again confirmed the British government's decision not to annex Port Natal on 28 March 1836, despite Captain Gardiner's requests and Governor D'Urban's recommendation of it on 5 December 1835.[132] By September 1835, the first two small trek groups, the Tregardt trek and the Janse van Rensburg trek, had moved northward.[133] The Tregardt trek consisted of seven Boers with their wives (including Tregardt and his wife Martha Elisabeth Susanna, born Bouwer) and thirty-four children, along with about 8,000 sheep, 1,300 cattle, and 80 horses.[134] Van Rensburg had already been living north of the Orange River near the Beersheba mission station since 1830, where he regularly hunted for ivory, horns, and hides.[135] This made it relatively

---

[130] Muller, C. F. J. (1981). 500 Years - A History of South Africa (3rd ed.). Academica., p.162
[131] Muller, C. F. J. (1987). *Die oorsprong van die Groot Trek* (2nd ed.). Tafelberg Uitgewers., p.388
[132] Muller, C. F. J. (1987). *Die oorsprong van die Groot Trek* (2nd ed.). Tafelberg Uitgewers., p.390
[133] Giliomee, Hermann. Die Afrikaners (Afrikaans Edition). Tafelberg. Kindle Edition, p.155
[134] Muller, C. F. J. (1987). *Die oorsprong van die Groot Trek* (2nd ed.). Tafelberg Uitgewers., p.324
[135] Muller, C. F. J. (1987). *Die oorsprong van die Groot Trek* (2nd ed.). Tafelberg Uitgewers., p.317

THE BOERS TREK

easy for him to undertake the journey. Lang Hans Van Rensburg's trek group consisted of forty-nine individuals, ten men, nine women, and thirty children, with 450 cattle, around 3,000 sheep and goats, and thirty horses.

During the early days of the migration movement in the Cape, Hendrik Potgieter, along with Gerrit Maritz, played a significant role in promoting it.[136] After martial law was lifted in the Cape, Potgieter concluded his preparations for the journey and crossed the Orange River in February 1836.[137] Initially, Potgieter's party consisted of only thirty-three able-bodied men, accompanied by their women and children, primarily extended family members, but their numbers grew to around 200 when Sarel Cilliers and Casper Kruger joined them after they crossed the Orange River border.[138] After an election, the larger group again appointed Potgieter as their leader and commandant. Potgieter later acquired the land between the Vet and Vaal rivers, the later Winburg region, by trading it from Chief Makwana of the Batuanga for cattle, and the undertaking to protect Chief Makwana and his people against Mzilikazi.[139] The Winburg region was the first piece of land the Boers acquired from African nations. Hendrik Potgieter later established contact

---

[136] Muller, C. F. J. (1987). *Die oorsprong van die Groot Trek* (2nd ed.). Tafelberg Uitgewers., p.372
[137] Van Zyl, M. C. (1986). Die Slag van Vegkop. *Historia, 31*(2)., p.63
[138] Giliomee, Hermann. Die Afrikaners (Afrikaans Edition). Tafelberg. Kindle Edition, p.156
[139] Botha, J. P. (2008). Ons Geskiedenis (1st ed.). J.P. Botha., p.102

with Tregardt and embarked on an exploratory expedition northward, as far as the other side of the Limpopo River.[140]

Meanwhile, at Strydpoort, Tregardt and Van Rensburg went separate ways, apparently due to Tregardt advising Van Rensburg against excessive ammunition usage while hunting and Van Rensburg's intention to reach Delagoa Bay to sell his ivory. Van Rensburg moved along the right bank of the Limpopo River to its confluence with the Olifants River, where, on approximately 4 August 1836, they were attacked, presumably for their cattle. After a desperate battle that raged through the night, all were slain except for two children. The deceased, eight men, seven women, and fifteen children included Lang Hans Janse van Rensburg with his wife and four children, Sybrand Bronkhorst with his wife and six children, Gysbert Bronkhorst with his wife and one child, Gysbert Bronkhorst Jr. and his spouse, Jacobus de Wet and his spouse, Frederik van Wyk with his wife and two children, Petrus Viljoen with his wife and six children, Hendrik Croucamp with his wife and three children, Nicolaas Prinsloo with his wife and eight children, and Marthinus Prinsloo, a bachelor.[141] A five-year-old boy and a four-year-old girl were apparently spared by the intervention of a Zulu warrior, but they succumbed to malaria shortly thereafter.[142] It's suspected that Van Rensburg, perhaps due to the initial friendliness of

---

[140] Muller, C. F. J. (1981). 500 Years - A History of South Africa (3rd ed.). Academica., p.161
[141] WikiTree. (2023, March 18). Project: Voortrekkers. Retrieved September 13, 2023, from
https://www.wikitree.com/wiki/Project:Voortrekkers
[142] Steyn, J. C. 2016. Afrikanerjoernaal – 'n Vervolgverhaal in 365 episodes. Pretoria: FAK, p.101

the attackers, didn't perceive the need to form a defensive laager or there wasn't enough time to do so. According to Shangana oral traditions, cattle were driven among the wagons to breach the defence before the defenders ran out of ammunition. Tregardt later discovered belongings of the Van Rensburg Trek at the settlement of Soshangane, the founder of the amaShangana tribe in present-day Mozambique.[143] The Tregardt party waited in vain for the Potgieter trek from September 1836 to May 1837 in the vicinity of the later Schoemansdal and Louis Trichardt before proceeding to Delagoa Bay.[144]

The Potgieter trek reached Thaba Nchu (Blesberg), where it stayed for a few months. After that, they travelled north until they reached the Sand River. In May 1836, Potgieter, along with Sarel Cilliers and ten other Boers, left their laager (trek party) and departed on an exploratory journey to explore the areas north of the Vaal River and to contact Louis Tregardt.[145] The remaining trek members dispersed to obtain sufficient grazing for their large herds of cattle. Some moved to the Vaal River, and a few even crossed it, setting up camps in various places. The Liebenberg group camped on the other side of the current Parys area, while Johannes Botha, Hermanus Steyn, and others camped in the bend of the Vaal River southwest of

---

[143] South African Military History Society (2013, April). *Great Trek Anniversary: Military encounters of the Voortrekkers 1*. The South African Military History Society. Retrieved August 7, 2022, from http://samilitaryhistory.org/13/p13aprne.html
[144] Steyn, J. C. 2016. Afrikanerjoernaal – 'n Vervolgverhaal in 365 episodes. Pretoria: FAK, p.101
[145] Van Zyl, M. C. (1986). Die Slag van Vegkop. *Historia, 31*(2)., p.64

Parys.[146] The Potgieter trek did not encounter any problems with the Griquas when they passed by Philippolis, and during their northward journey, they established friendly relations with tribal leaders such as Moroka II of the Barolong, Sikonyella, and Makwana, all of whom had previously suffered greatly under Mzilikazi and saw the Boers as allies.[147]

Mzilikazi's brutal campaigns of destruction in the highveld of southern Africa during the Mfecane, impacted every tribe, from the Bapedi in the northeast to the Bathlaping in the Northern Cape. Nations such as the Bapedi, Bakgatla, and Bahurutse were subjected to violence that left them in desperate poverty and without their land. Many lost their cultural identity when they were assimilated into the Ndebele. Others were massacred and displaced. They couldn't cultivate their land to sustain themselves, and some were even driven to cannibalism to survive. Many had to resettle to survive - the Barolong moved themselves from the western highlands to Thaba Nchu. The central interior was depopulated, and only small groups could find refuge. Larger peoples, like the Venda and Bapedi, managed to sustain themselves in areas on the borders of the later ZAR. All the established tribes in the entire region that later became

---

[146] Van Zyl, M. C. (1986). Die Slag van Vegkop. *Historia, 31*(2)., p.64
[147] Retief, J. (2015)., The Voortrekker and the Ndebele, Part One: Attacks at the Vaal River and Liebenbergskoppie, 21 and 23 August 1836, Military History Journal, 16(6).,
https://www.samilitaryhistory.org/vol166jr.html

known as the Free State, except along the banks of the Caledon and at Thaba Nchu, were displaced.[148]

While Potgieter was still on his reconnaissance expedition in the north, Mzilikazi's Ndebele launched an attack at the Vaal River. However, they did not attack the Voortrekkers but rather the hunting party of Veldkornet Stephanus Erasmus, who happened to be in the area.[149] Erasmus was not a Voortrekker at that time. He left the Cape on 28 June 1836, with his small hunting party after informing the Cape authorities.[150] Stephanus Erasmus' hunting party consisted of eight Boers and a few servants with oxen, horses, and five wagons. The members of the party were Erasmus himself, along with his three sons - Pieter Ernst, Daniel Elardus, and Stephanus Petrus - as well as Pieter Bekker and his son, Carel Kruger, and Johannes Claassen. Several servants also formed part of the expedition.[151] Erasmus and his party reached as far north as the Magaliesberg mountains. However, their hunting attempts were not very successful, and they gradually returned home. The hunting expedition undertaken by Erasmus had motives beyond hunting. There is a possibility that Erasmus wanted to

---

[148] Grönum, W. (1987). *Die Mfecane: Oorsprong, Ontplooiing an Invloed op die Tswana* [Master's thesis, North-West University]., p.120

[149] Markram, W. J. (1992). *Stephanus Petrus Erasmus: Grensboerpionier en Voortrekker, 1788-1847* [Master's thesis, University of Stellenbosch]., p.198

[150] Markram, W. J. (1992). *Stephanus Petrus Erasmus: Grensboerpionier en Voortrekker, 1788-1847* [Master's thesis, University of Stellenbosch]., p.198

[151] Markram, W. J. (1992). *Stephanus Petrus Erasmus: Grensboerpionier en Voortrekker, 1788-1847* [Master's thesis, University of Stellenbosch]., p.201

investigate the conditions in the interior to address his concerns about the violent crime they experienced in his Cape district. Veldkornet J.C. Greyling of Grootrivier and Veldkornet G.H.J. Kruger of Suurberg considered Erasmus' journey as a reconnaissance mission.[152] Before the departure of his hunting expedition, Erasmus became aware of a friendship agreement signed between Governor D'Urban and Mzilikazi earlier that year on 3 March 1836. He was also aware of a wagon and two boxes of gifts that D'Urban had sent to Mzilikazi from Cape Town, through the Ndebele delegation led by Mncumbathe.[153] Therefore, Erasmus had no reason to expect an attack from the Ndebele during his expedition.

The initial attack of the Ndebele on the Boers appears to be the result of a misunderstanding, where the Ndebele mistakenly identified the Boers as Griquas.[154] In August 1836, the Ndebele, led by Marap, undertook a punitive expedition against the Bataung, accusing them, along with a group of Griquas, of stealing cattle from the Ndebele. It was during this expedition that the Ndebele encountered the wagons of the Boer hunters.[155] Erasmus' camp was positioned on the northern bank of the Vaal River,

---

[152] Markram, W. J. (1992). *Stephanus Petrus Erasmus: Grensboerpionier en Voortrekker, 1788-1847* [Master's thesis, University of Stellenbosch]., p.198

[153] Markram, W. J. (1992). *Stephanus Petrus Erasmus: Grensboerpionier en Voortrekker, 1788-1847* [Master's thesis, University of Stellenbosch]., p.200-201

[154] Grönum, W. (1987). *Die Mfecane: Oorsprong, Ontplooiing an Invloed op die Tswana* [Master's thesis, North-West University]., p.115

[155] Grönum, W. (1987). *Die Mfecane: Oorsprong, Ontplooiing an Invloed op die Tswana* [Master's thesis, North-West University]., p.115

approximately fifty kilometres south of Potchefstroom, during the attack. On the morning of Sunday, 21 August 1836, Erasmus, and his son Pieter left their camp to go hunting. Meanwhile, Erasmus' other two sons and Johannes Claassen went out to collect the bucks that had been hunted the previous day. Carel Kruger remained at the camp, while the movements of Pieter Bekker and his son were unknown.[156] While Erasmus and his son were hunting, Khaliphi, Mzilikazi's supreme commander, attacked the camp with 500 to 600 warriors.[157] When Erasmus and his son returned to their camp in the evening, they found their wagons surrounded by the Ndebele force. Erasmus made two unsuccessful attempts to reach the wagons.[158] The Ndebele tried to capture Erasmus and his son, but they successfully evaded the ambush. In a state of shock and mourning after the loss of their family and friends, they undertook a journey of fifty kilometres to reach the Voortrekker families of the Potgieter trek.[159]

---

[156] Retief, J. (2015)., The Voortrekker and the Ndebele, Part One: Attacks at the Vaal River and Liebenbergskoppie, 21 and 23 August 1836, Military History Journal, 16(6).,
https://www.samilitaryhistory.org/vol166jr.html

[157] Retief, J. (2015)., The Voortrekker and the Ndebele, Part One: Attacks at the Vaal River and Liebenbergskoppie, 21 and 23 August 1836, Military History Journal, 16(6).,
https://www.samilitaryhistory.org/vol166jr.html

[158] Markram, W. J. (1992). *Stephanus Petrus Erasmus: Grensboerpionier en Voortrekker, 1788-1847* [Master's thesis, University of Stellenbosch]., p.202

[159] Retief, J. (2015)., The Voortrekker and the Ndebele, Part One: Attacks at the Vaal River and Liebenbergskoppie, 21 and 23 August 1836, Military History Journal, 16(6).,
https://www.samilitaryhistory.org/vol166jr.html

Bekker and his son, like Erasmus and his son, were able to evade the Ndebele and joined the Erasmuses on their way to the Voortrekkers along the Vaal River. On Monday, 22 August 1836, they reached the Voortrekker camp after travelling through the night. Erasmus informed the Voortrekkers of the attack on his camp and urged them to prepare for a possible attack.[160] The Potgieter-Voortrekkers were divided into two camps. The main camp, which Erasmus and his group joined, was located a few kilometres southwest of Parys, while the Liebenberg camp was a few kilometres to the north.[161] Before Erasmus arrived, the Potgieter trekkers did not expect an attack from the Ndebele because they were unaware that Mzilikazi's territorial claims extended so far south. They were unprepared and did not form a defensive laager. The news of the attack on Erasmus' camp came as a shock to them. They immediately formed a laager with their wagons and closed the gaps between the wheels with thorn tree branches. Rudolph Bronkhorst's mother sent him to warn the Liebenbergs.[162] According to news from the missionary Reverend Venable sometime later, Erasmus' sons, Stephanus Junior, and Daniel, along with Carel Kruger, were initially spared by the Ndebele. They

---

[160] Markram, W. J. (1992). *Stephanus Petrus Erasmus: Grensboerpionier en Voortrekker, 1788-1847* [Master's thesis, University of Stellenbosch]., p.203

[161] Retief, J. (2015)., The Voortrekker and the Ndebele, Part One: Attacks at the Vaal River and Liebenbergskoppie, 21 and 23 August 1836, Military History Journal, 16(6).,
https://www.samilitaryhistory.org/vol166jr.html

[162] Retief, J. (2015)., The Voortrekker and the Ndebele, Part One: Attacks at the Vaal River and Liebenbergskoppie, 21 and 23 August 1836, Military History Journal, 16(6).,
https://www.samilitaryhistory.org/vol166jr.html

were kept alive to demonstrate the process of yoking the oxen to the king. Zetini, Khaliphi's second-in-command, had them executed when they attempted to escape during their journey to Mosega. Erasmus would continue to search, but he never saw his two sons or Carel Kruger again. Johannes Claassen was presumed dead as there was no news of him.[163] Erasmus could only return to his campsite six days later. At the camp, he found the bodies of five servants. His five wagons were later seen by the American missionaries at Mosega.[164]

After the impi (army/regiment) launched their attack on Erasmus' camp, they divided into two groups. The larger contingent marched towards the Potgieter laager, while a smaller group set their sights on a hill, now known as Liebenbergskoppie.[165] The Boers were unaware of the Ndebele's approach. Desperate to find his missing sons and recover his wagons, Erasmus gathered a group of eleven volunteers to assist him in the search. When they rode to his camp the next morning, they encountered a force of approximately 500 Ndebele warriors. The Ndebele attacked

---

[163] Retief, J. (2015)., The Voortrekker and the Ndebele, Part One: Attacks at the Vaal River and Liebenbergskoppie, 21 and 23 August 1836, Military History Journal, 16(6).,
https://www.samilitaryhistory.org/vol166jr.html
[164] Retief, J. (2015)., The Voortrekker and the Ndebele, Part One: Attacks at the Vaal River and Liebenbergskoppie, 21 and 23 August 1836, Military History Journal, 16(6).,
https://www.samilitaryhistory.org/vol166jr.html
[165] Retief, J. (2015)., The Voortrekker and the Ndebele, Part One: Attacks at the Vaal River and Liebenbergskoppie, 21 and 23 August 1836, Military History Journal, 16(6).,
https://www.samilitaryhistory.org/vol166jr.html

them and forced them into a fighting retreat.[166] Around 10:00, the young Diederik Frans Kruger, who was tending to cattle in the field, was pulled onto the back of his horse by his father, who was one of the retreating riders, and taken to the Boer laager. Shortly after their arrival, the first shot was fired, claiming the life of a Ndebele warrior within 100 meters of the camp.[167]

Within the laager, where the eleven-year-old Paul Kruger also sought shelter, only thirty-five able-bodied men had to defend the camp. In the absence of Potgieter, Johannes Lodewikus Petrus Botha took command, supported by leaders such as Stephanus Erasmus, Daniel Kruger, Stephanus Fourie, Lucas Badenhorst, and Christiaan Harmse.[168] The Ndebele, unfamiliar with the Boer laager-defence tactics, repeatedly attacked the camp, but the fortifications and firepower of the Boers successfully repelled each attack. By 3:00 pm, the Ndebele had ceased their attack. The Boers had lost Adolf Bronkhorst during the battle, while Christiaan Harmse's son, Christiaan Junior, had died earlier outside the camp when he was murdered while tending to their livestock in the field. The American

---
[166] Retief, J. (2015)., The Voortrekker and the Ndebele, Part One: Attacks at the Vaal River and Liebenbergskoppie, 21 and 23 August 1836, Military History Journal, 16(6).,
https://www.samilitaryhistory.org/vol166jr.html
[167] Markram, W. J. (1992). *Stephanus Petrus Erasmus: Grensboerpionier en Voortrekker, 1788-1847* [Master's thesis, University of Stellenbosch]., p.205
[168] Retief, J. (2015)., The Voortrekker and the Ndebele, Part One: Attacks at the Vaal River and Liebenbergskoppie, 21 and 23 August 1836, Military History Journal, 16(6).,
https://www.samilitaryhistory.org/vol166jr.html

missionaries at Mosega estimated the Ndebele's losses at around fifty.[169] The Battle of Vaal River was the first skirmish between the Boers and the Ndebele, as well as the first battle fought by Boers in the region that would later become the South African Republic (ZAR), also known as the Transvaal.[170]

The Liebenberg family was led by the patriarch, Barend Liebenberg, and consisted of his wife, four married sons, a married daughter, and their children. An unmarried schoolteacher named MacDonald was also part of the group.[171] The Liebenberg family was overwhelmed and plundered by the Ndebele warriors while they were trying to flee to the Potgieter camp before dawn on Tuesday, 23 August 1836.[172] When they were attacked by the Ndebele, Christiaan Liebenberg, one of Barend's sons, was away with the Potgieter reconnaissance commission. All six men of the Liebenberg family were killed, including Barend Liebenberg Senior, his sons Hendrik, Stephanus, and Barend Junior, his

---

[169] Retief, J. (2015)., The Voortrekker and the Ndebele, Part One: Attacks at the Vaal River and Liebenbergskoppie, 21 and 23 August 1836, Military History Journal, 16(6).,
https://www.samilitaryhistory.org/vol166jr.html
[170] Markram, W. J. (1992). *Stephanus Petrus Erasmus: Grensboerpionier en Voortrekker, 1788-1847* [Master's thesis, University of Stellenbosch]., p.208
[171] Retief, J. (2015)., The Voortrekker and the Ndebele, Part One: Attacks at the Vaal River and Liebenbergskoppie, 21 and 23 August 1836, Military History Journal, 16(6).,
https://www.samilitaryhistory.org/vol166jr.html
[172] Retief, J. (2015)., The Voortrekker and the Ndebele, Part One: Attacks at the Vaal River and Liebenbergskoppie, 21 and 23 August 1836, Military History Journal, 16(6).,
https://www.samilitaryhistory.org/vol166jr.html

son-in-law Johannes du Toit, and the schoolmaster MacDonald. Hendrik Liebenberg's wife and Johannes du Toit's wife were also murdered. The latter succumbed to her injuries the following day. The Ndebele also killed six children and twelve servants, bringing the total death toll in the Liebenberg camp to twenty-six. However, some of the women and children managed to escape.[173] Stephanus Liebenberg's wife, Hester Pienaar, and her four children were preparing their wagon to flee when the attackers intercepted them. They managed to escape when Hermanus Jacobus Potgieter and five men arrived and attacked the Ndebele warriors. Barend Johannes Liebenberg was tending to sheep when the attack occurred, but he was never found.[174]

Among the survivors, Christiaan Liebenberg's eldest daughter recovered from twenty-one stab wounds. The wives of Barend Liebenberg Senior and Christiaan Liebenberg were seriously injured but ultimately survived. Christiaan Liebenberg's three children and all four of Hendrik Liebenberg's children also managed to escape with their lives. Four of Johannes du Toit's children were later found safe in a wagon where they had hidden.[175] Rudolph

---

[173] Retief, J. (2015)., The Voortrekker and the Ndebele, Part One: Attacks at the Vaal River and Liebenbergskoppie, 21 and 23 August 1836, Military History Journal, 16(6).,
https://www.samilitaryhistory.org/vol166jr.html
[174] Retief, J. (2015)., The Voortrekker and the Ndebele, Part One: Attacks at the Vaal River and Liebenbergskoppie, 21 and 23 August 1836, Military History Journal, 16(6).,
https://www.samilitaryhistory.org/vol166jr.html
[175] Retief, J. (2015)., The Voortrekker and the Ndebele, Part One: Attacks at the Vaal River and Liebenbergskoppie, 21 and 23 August 1836,

Bronkhorst, who was sent by his mother to warn the Liebenberg family of the potential danger, never returned. Later, his horse returned to the camp, wounded by an assagai.[176]

These unprovoked attacks by Mzilikazi plunged the Boers into mourning and exposed them to further attacks. They also lost a significant number of livestock. At this time, Stephanus Erasmus was deeply concerned about the fate of his two missing sons. He and another person returned to his hunting camp six days after the attack, where they discovered the bodies of five servants. There were no signs of his sons.[177] The Boers stayed in the protection of their laager at Kopjeskraal for about a week to ensure that the Ndebele had left the area. During this time, they buried the victims of both attacks at Kopjeskraal.[178] On 31 August 1836, the Potgieter trek divided into two groups. One group moved southwards towards the Vals River and eventually to Thaba Nchu, while the other group moved eastwards towards the origin of the Rhenoster River and camped at a hill called Doornkop. This

---

Military History Journal, 16(6).,
https://www.samilitaryhistory.org/vol166jr.html
[176] Retief, J. (2015)., The Voortrekker and the Ndebele, Part One: Attacks at the Vaal River and Liebenbergskoppie, 21 and 23 August 1836, Military History Journal, 16(6).,
https://www.samilitaryhistory.org/vol166jr.html
[177] Markram, W. J. (1992). *Stephanus Petrus Erasmus: Grensboerpionier en Voortrekker, 1788-1847* [Master's thesis, University of Stellenbosch]., p.213
[178] Retief, J. (2016). The Voortrekker and the Ndebele, Part Two: The Battle of Vegkop, 20 October 1836. *Military History Journal, 17*(1).,
https://www.samilitaryhistory.org/vol171jr.html

hill later became known as Vegkop.[179] Potgieter and his reconnaissance committee, whose prolonged absence had raised serious concerns about their safety, returned on 2 September 1836.[180] In their journey, lasting more than three months, they covered about 1,500 miles. They arrived at the Liebenberg massacre site and followed the wagon tracks from there. The Potgieter trek spread out again, searching for grazing and water for their herds of sheep and cattle. On 17 October 1836, their peace was disrupted when two Mantatee (baThlokoa) came to warn them of a large Ndebele impi approaching.[181]

The Boers realised that fleeing was not an option because they would be vulnerable in their scattered individual wagons and their herds of cattle and sheep would slow them down.[182] This left them with only two alternatives: victory or annihilation. They created a defensive laager with their wagons and prepared to repel the coming attack. The laager was established south of Doornkop. Potgieter sent out a three-man reconnaissance patrol, consisting of Nicolaas Potgieter, Jan Celliers, and Joachim Botha. The patrol

---

[179] Retief, J. (2016). The Voortrekker and the Ndebele, Part Two: The Battle of Vegkop, 20 October 1836. *Military History Journal, 17*(1)., https://www.samilitaryhistory.org/vol171jr.html

[180] Retief, J. (2016). The Voortrekker and the Ndebele, Part Two: The Battle of Vegkop, 20 October 1836. *Military History Journal, 17*(1)., https://www.samilitaryhistory.org/vol171jr.html

[181] Retief, J. (2016). The Voortrekker and the Ndebele, Part Two: The Battle of Vegkop, 20 October 1836. *Military History Journal, 17*(1)., https://www.samilitaryhistory.org/vol171jr.html

[182] Retief, J. (2016). The Voortrekker and the Ndebele, Part Two: The Battle of Vegkop, 20 October 1836. *Military History Journal, 17*(1)., https://www.samilitaryhistory.org/vol171jr.html

reported that 3,000 to 5,000 Ndebele warriors, the bulk of King Mzilikazi's army, were a few hours' ride away.[183] That night, few of them could sleep. They remained vigilant, listening for any suspicious sounds, and praying. The memories of the previous attacks at Liebenbergskoppie and Kopjeskraal were still fresh in their minds. They had no illusions about the challenges that the next day would bring.[184]

At dawn, the following morning the thirty-six able-bodied men of the laager, including Hendrik Potgieter, Sarel Celliers, J.L. Botha, Jacobus Potgieter, Hermanus Potgieter, Joachim Botha, and Piet Botha, formed a commando and set off on horseback to track down the Ndebele. Their mission was twofold: to try to negotiate with the Ndebele to avoid bloodshed, and to protect the laager by keeping the enemy at bay.[185] After about an hour's ride, approximately ten kilometres from the laager, they encountered the Ndebele who were eating. Using a Khoi-Khoi translator, the Boers asked the Ndebele why they wanted to harm the Boers. In response, the Ndebele warriors stood up and shouted

---

[183] Retief, J. (2016). The Voortrekker and the Ndebele, Part Two: The Battle of Vegkop, 20 October 1836. *Military History Journal*, *17*(1)., https://www.samilitaryhistory.org/vol171jr.html
[184] Retief, J. (2016). The Voortrekker and the Ndebele, Part Two: The Battle of Vegkop, 20 October 1836. *Military History Journal*, *17*(1)., https://www.samilitaryhistory.org/vol171jr.html
[185] Retief, J. (2016). The Voortrekker and the Ndebele, Part Two: The Battle of Vegkop, 20 October 1836. *Military History Journal*, *17*(1)., https://www.samilitaryhistory.org/vol171jr.html

"Mzilikazi!" and launched an attack.[186] The mobility of the Boers, who were skilled horsemen and marksmen, gave them a significant advantage. The Ndebele continued to attack relentlessly, but the Boers managed to stay out of their reach. The Boers' tactic during this phase of the battle was to fall back out of range of the Ndebele, reload, fire a volley, and then fall back again to reload their muskets. Sarel Celliers noted that he had fired about forty-six shots during the Ndebele attack, and if that was the average, there would have been about 1,600 shots fired at the Ndebele, causing significant losses among the Ndebele warriors. This phase of the battle, during which no Boer was injured, lasted about three hours. According to a reporter from the Graham's Town Journal who visited the Boer laagers there shortly after the event, it was believed that about 200 Ndebele warriors were killed during this phase of the battle. The loss of several Ndebele leaders during this early confrontation would later have an impact on their subsequent attack on the Boer laager.[187]

The Boers were running out of ammunition when they arrived at the laager and quickly closed the gate in preparation for the impending attack. However, a few members of the commando, including Louw du Plessis, Floris Visser, and Marthinus van der Merwe, rode past the laager. They returned a few days later and were thereafter

---

[186] Retief, J. (2016). The Voortrekker and the Ndebele, Part Two: The Battle of Vegkop, 20 October 1836. *Military History Journal, 17*(1).,
https://www.samilitaryhistory.org/vol171jr.html
[187] Retief, J. (2016). The Voortrekker and the Ndebele, Part Two: The Battle of Vegkop, 20 October 1836. *Military History Journal, 17*(1).,
https://www.samilitaryhistory.org/vol171jr.html

criticised as cowards.[188] Less than forty able-bodied men in the laager were possibly assisted by boys, including the eleven-year-old Paul Kruger, and servants who could handle firearms. The women, who grew up on the eastern frontier, were skilled with muskets and assisted by either shooting or loading ammunition for their husbands.[189] The Ndebele impi surrounded the laager and divided into three groups, taking positions about 500 meters away from the laager, well beyond the effective range of a musket. Another group of warriors began gathering the cattle. After the running battle, the Ndebele warriors were hungry and slaughtered and ate about eighty cattle. Tension was palpable inside the laager, and some individuals tried to challenge the Ndebele to start the fight by waving either a white or red flag. Potgieter ordered his men not to start shooting until the enemy was about twenty to thirty meters away from the laager.[190]

Without warning, the Ndebele impi launched a fierce attack on the laager from all directions. Their synchronised beating on their shields with their spears, along with their terrifying battle cries, was unnerving for the Boer

---

[188] Retief, J. (2016). The Voortrekker and the Ndebele, Part Two: The Battle of Vegkop, 20 October 1836. *Military History Journal, 17*(1)., https://www.samilitaryhistory.org/vol171jr.html
[189] Retief, J. (2016). The Voortrekker and the Ndebele, Part Two: The Battle of Vegkop, 20 October 1836. *Military History Journal, 17*(1)., https://www.samilitaryhistory.org/vol171jr.html
[190] Retief, J. (2016). The Voortrekker and the Ndebele, Part Two: The Battle of Vegkop, 20 October 1836. *Military History Journal, 17*(1)., https://www.samilitaryhistory.org/vol171jr.html

defenders.[191] As the impi advanced, they came together and ran shoulder to shoulder, making it impossible for the defenders not to hit more than one warrior with each buckshot round. However, the Ndebele warriors continued to attack in large numbers, even over the bodies of their fallen comrades.[192] When they reached the outer perimeter of the laager, the warriors tried to break through the defence. They tried to remove the thorn trees and move or overturn the wagons but without success. They then attempted to enter the laager by placing their shields on the thorn branches and climbing over them and onto the wagons. Others tried to crawl under the branches and penetrate the laager from below. Not a single warrior succeeded in infiltrating the laager.[193] Amid the chaos of the battle, the horses inside the laager became excited and kicked up dust clouds, while the smoke from the gunfire further obscured visibility. When the Ndebele warriors realised that their attempts to break through to the laager were futile and that they were suffering heavy losses, they lost heart and changed tactics. Their stabbing spears were ineffective, and they began to throw their throwing spears over the wagons and into the laager in an attempt to hit their opponents from a distance. This tactic caused losses among the Boer defenders. After the battle,

---

[191] Retief, J. (2016). The Voortrekker and the Ndebele, Part Two: The Battle of Vegkop, 20 October 1836. *Military History Journal*, *17*(1)., https://www.samilitaryhistory.org/vol171jr.html
[192] Retief, J. (2016). The Voortrekker and the Ndebele, Part Two: The Battle of Vegkop, 20 October 1836. *Military History Journal*, *17*(1)., https://www.samilitaryhistory.org/vol171jr.html
[193] Retief, J. (2016). The Voortrekker and the Ndebele, Part Two: The Battle of Vegkop, 20 October 1836. *Military History Journal*, *17*(1)., https://www.samilitaryhistory.org/vol171jr.html

more than 1,100 spears were found inside the laager.[194] The attack on the laager, which began around noon, was short but intense and lasted no longer than half an hour.

Two Boers lost their lives during the Battle of Vegkop, while fourteen others were wounded. Nicolaas Potgieter and Piet Botha, the brother and son-in-law of Hendrik Potgieter, were buried on the battlefield that same evening. It is estimated that about 400 Ndebele warriors were killed in the battle, with 184 bodies found around the laager.[195] The Ndebele plundered about 6,000 cattle and 41,000 sheep and goats from the Boers, leaving them without trek oxen and facing famine due to the loss of their milk cows and sheep. Sarel Celliers recounted how his children cried for food, and he had nothing to give them.[196] In an attempt to recover some of the stolen animals, a commando was sent out three days after the battle, but it was unsuccessful. During the intense fighting, no assegai reached the tents in the inner circle of the laager, but many wagons on the perimeter suffered serious damage, with some wagon tents having up to a hundred assegai holes. With the bodies of dead Ndebele warriors around the laager, the Boers were forced to move their wagons to the Rhenoster Spruit, about

---

[194] Retief, J. (2016). The Voortrekker and the Ndebele, Part Two: The Battle of Vegkop, 20 October 1836. *Military History Journal, 17*(1)., https://www.samilitaryhistory.org/vol171jr.html
[195] Retief, J. (2016). The Voortrekker and the Ndebele, Part Two: The Battle of Vegkop, 20 October 1836. *Military History Journal, 17*(1)., https://www.samilitaryhistory.org/vol171jr.html
[196] Retief, J. (2016). The Voortrekker and the Ndebele, Part Two: The Battle of Vegkop, 20 October 1836. *Military History Journal, 17*(1)., https://www.samilitaryhistory.org/vol171jr.html

four hundred meters away, using horses and manpower because they had no draft animals.[197] The Potgieter trek went in search of help, and after two weeks, Chief Moroka of the Barolong people came to their aid with two hundred trek oxen. The impoverished group of Boers left Doornkop, which was renamed Vegkop after the battle, and reached Thaba Nchu by mid-November 1836. Upon their arrival at Thaba Nchu, they were warmly received by Reverend Achbell and Chief Moroka, who provided them with essential supplies. The Boers were deeply grateful to the Barolong people for generations.[198]

During the period between Potgieter's departure and Gerrit Maritz's trek from the Cape in September 1836, the migration movement reached a critical turning point. Few Boers were ready to follow Potgieter, and a lack of action could have paralyzed the entire migration movement.[199] Throughout 1836, Gerrit Maritz, initially in secret, widely discussed and promoted the migration concept across the Boer districts. During this time, even before Piet Retief and other leaders had decided to trek, Maritz effectively persuaded hundreds of families to join the vanguard trekkers, significantly aiding Potgieter's efforts.[200] Following

---

[197] Retief, J. (2016). The Voortrekker and the Ndebele, Part Two: The Battle of Vegkop, 20 October 1836. *Military History Journal, 17*(1)., https://www.samilitaryhistory.org/vol171jr.html
[198] Retief, J. (2016). The Voortrekker and the Ndebele, Part Two: The Battle of Vegkop, 20 October 1836. *Military History Journal, 17*(1)., https://www.samilitaryhistory.org/vol171jr.html
[199] Muller, C. F. J. (1987). *Die oorsprong van die Groot Trek* (2nd ed.). Tafelberg Uitgewers., p.375
[200] Muller, C. F. J. (1987). *Die oorsprong van die Groot Trek* (2nd ed.). Tafelberg Uitgewers., p.376

Mzilikazi's attacks on the Potgieter trek, Maritz mobilised the Boers and encouraged them to support Potgieter. Despite counterpropaganda by the media and the Dutch Reformed Church, which portrayed these attacks as evidence of a foolish migration idea, families from all over the Cape's eastern frontier and from the northern frontier and Swellendam, began their treks.[201] Gerrit Maritz, a wagon maker and entrepreneur,[202] more known for his intellectual abilities than military prowess, left the Cape in September 1836 with over seven hundred people, including about one hundred men. The Maritz trek initially moved in smaller groups to ensure sufficient grazing for their livestock and to resist potential actions by the colonial administration. They joined the Potgieter trek at Thaba Nchu.

On 2 December 1836, the two Boer treks held a general meeting in the Potgieter camp to elect a Burgerraad (citizens' council). The Burgerraad, consisting of seven members, was democratically elected by secret ballot. Maritz was elected as the "President," while Potgieter was elected as the "Laagerkommandant" (military commander). This election of the Burgerraad was an important milestone in the history of southern Africa because it was the first democratic election on southern African soil.[203] In addition to administrative matters, the Burgerraad also had to address King Mzilikazi's attack on the Boers. The attack at Vegkop

---

[201] Muller, C. F. J. (1987). *Die oorsprong van die Groot Trek* (2nd ed.). Tafelberg Uitgewers., p.376-p.377
[202] Botha, J. P. (2008). Ons Geskiedenis (1st ed.). J.P. Botha., p.103
[203] Retief, J. (2016). The Voortrekker and the Ndebele, Part Two: The Battle of Vegkop, 20 October 1836. *Military History Journal, 17*(1).,
https://www.samilitaryhistory.org/vol171jr.html

left the Potgieter trek in a state of poverty. For these subsistence farmers, livestock, especially cattle, were of utmost importance, and they were eager to recover the animals that had been taken by Mzilikazi. The Burgerraad decided to go and retrieve the stolen cattle to eliminate the threat from Mzilikazi.[204]

The Burgerraad had planned a commando against Mzilikazi, which was supposed to depart on 20 December 1836, but it was postponed due to bad weather. Maritz was also concerned that the commando was not strong enough. To strengthen their numbers, he recruited volunteers from Treks which were still on their way to Thaba Nchu from the south. Maritz returned on 29 December 1836 to handle the preparations.[205] Stephanus Erasmus was still uncertain about the fate of his sons. There were rumours that the Ndebele had abducted them, and Erasmus joined the commando in the hope of finding them alive in Mosega.[206] The commando consisted of 107 Boers, assisted by forty mounted Griquas led by Chief Pieter Dawids and sixty fighters from the Barolong tribe under the leadership of Chief Matlaba

---

[204] Retief, J. (2016). The Voortrekker and the Ndebele, Part Two: The Battle of Vegkop, 20 October 1836. *Military History Journal, 17*(1).,
https://www.samilitaryhistory.org/vol171jr.html
[205] Retief, J. (2016). The Voortrekker and the Ndebele, Part Two: The Battle of Vegkop, 20 October 1836. *Military History Journal, 17*(1).,
https://www.samilitaryhistory.org/vol171jr.html
[206] Markram, W. J. (1992). *Stephanus Petrus Erasmus: Grensboerpionier en Voortrekker, 1788-1847* [Master's thesis, University of Stellenbosch]., p.213

(Matshabe).²⁰⁷ The supporting forces were tasked with controlling the recaptured cattle during the campaign.

The commando against Mzilikazi was divided into two when it departed from Thaba Nchu for Mosega. The Boers under Potgieter departed on 2 January 1837, followed by Maritz's division the next day.²⁰⁸ Their target was Motsenyateng, the military capital of Mzilikazi, which was in the Mosega basin, about 10 km south of the current town of Zeerust. This settlement housed about 2,000 Ndebele warriors, which formed the largest part of the Ndebele army. It was also the residence of the commander-in-chief of Mzilikazi's impis, Khalipi.²⁰⁹ According to witnesses who participated in the battle, Jan Viljoen, Okkert Oosthuizen, and Koert Grobler, the commando set out early in the morning of 17 January 1837.²¹⁰ Boer leaders considered the element of surprise necessary for the success of the commando because they realised the enemy's superiority. They achieved total surprise, thanks to Chief Motlabe and his men who silenced the Ndebele's Batswana herdsmen and prevented them from warning the Ndebele forces.²¹¹

---

[207] Retief, J. (2016). The Voortrekker and the Ndebele, Part Two: The Battle of Vegkop, 20 October 1836. *Military History Journal, 17*(1)., https://www.samilitaryhistory.org/vol171jr.html

[208] Retief, J. (2016). The Voortrekker and the Ndebele, Part Two: The Battle of Vegkop, 20 October 1836. *Military History Journal, 17*(1)., https://www.samilitaryhistory.org/vol171jr.html

[209] Retief, J. (2016). The Voortrekker and the Ndebele, Part Two: The Battle of Vegkop, 20 October 1836. *Military History Journal, 17*(1)., https://www.samilitaryhistory.org/vol171jr.html

[210] Grönum, W. (1987). *Die Mfecane: Oorsprong, Ontplooiing an Invloed op die Tswana* [Master's thesis, North-West University]., p.116

[211] Grönum, W. (1987). *Die Mfecane: Oorsprong, Ontplooiing an Invloed op die Tswana* [Master's thesis, North-West University]., p.117

When the Ndebele were startled by the sound of gunshots, they were shocked and tried to escape through the narrow openings of their huts. In a state of total confusion, they fled, but they were pursued by Potgieter's division. Another group of Ndebele simultaneously tried to flee before an attack by Maritz and his men.[212] Potgieter's division attacked the nearest kraal, which happened to be only a few hundred meters away from the missionaries' homes. Some Ndebele sought refuge in the house and in the marshland behind it, drawing fire from the attackers and placing the mission station in the middle of a fierce firefight. A stray bullet flew through a window where Dr Venable and his wife were lying in bed.[213] After the first kraal was set on fire, Maritz moved towards the mission station and reassured Dr. Wilson, the missionary. He offered the missionaries the option to leave with the commando, as it would not be safe to stay behind with the Ndebele. Initially, the attack progressed quickly, but when more Ndebele became aware of the noise, they started to resist and slow down the attackers.[214]

---

[212] Retief, J. (2016). The Voortrekker and the Ndebele, Part Two: The Battle of Vegkop, 20 October 1836. *Military History Journal*, *17*(1)., https://www.samilitaryhistory.org/vol171jr.html
[213] Retief, J. (2016). The Voortrekker and the Ndebele, Part Two: The Battle of Vegkop, 20 October 1836. *Military History Journal*, *17*(1)., https://www.samilitaryhistory.org/vol171jr.html
[214] Retief, J. (2016). The Voortrekker and the Ndebele, Part Two: The Battle of Vegkop, 20 October 1836. *Military History Journal*, *17*(1)., https://www.samilitaryhistory.org/vol171jr.html

THE BOERS TREK

While the sun was rising, some Boers and auxiliary forces began gathering the cattle from one kraal to another.[215] Meanwhile, three groups of Ndebeles gathered near the modern railway farm, which was just a short distance from the missionary's residence. In the absence of Mzilikazi and Khalipi, some indunas attempted to launch a counterattack using the "horns of the bull" formation. However, the Boers were aware of this tactic and quickly responded by focusing their fire on the emerging horns, which forced the enemy to abandon the counterattack and flee northwards to the present-day village of Zeerust.[216] The commando also advanced northwards and systematically attacked and set fire to several kraals while the auxiliaries gathered the cattle. About fourteen or fifteen kraals were destroyed in the process. Those who could escape did so hastily, but some Ndebele women also became victims of the conflict and were hit by shots or killed by the auxiliaries' assegais. The battle ended between 11:30 and 12:00."[217] After the battle, Field Cornet Stephanus Erasmus learned from the missionary Reverend Venable about the fate of his two sons and left for home. He arrived at his farm in the Cape Colony in September 1836, where he immediately began preparing for his trek to the north.

---

[215] Retief, J. (2016). The Voortrekker and the Ndebele, Part Two: The Battle of Vegkop, 20 October 1836. *Military History Journal, 17*(1)., https://www.samilitaryhistory.org/vol171jr.html

[216] Retief, J. (2016). The Voortrekker and the Ndebele, Part Two: The Battle of Vegkop, 20 October 1836. *Military History Journal, 17*(1)., https://www.samilitaryhistory.org/vol171jr.html

[217] Retief, J. (2016). The Voortrekker and the Ndebele, Part Two: The Battle of Vegkop, 20 October 1836. *Military History Journal, 17*(1)., https://www.samilitaryhistory.org/vol171jr.html

The diverse group of attackers, Boers, Griquas, and Barolong soldiers with shields and spears, along with the five missionaries and their two children and 6,500 cattle, set out back towards Thaba Nchu, following the same path they had come from.[218] The commando travelled through the night on the first evening to put distance between themselves and the Ndebele, reducing the risk of a counterattack. They rested the following morning for about an hour around 11:00 and then continued their journey until late the next night. When they reached Kommando-Drift, the commando stopped for a few days to preliminarily divide the cattle to compensate the Griquas and Barolong for their contributions to the commando.[219] Afterwards, the group split, with some heading to Thaba Nchu and others following with wagons and animals. Maritz and the missionaries travelled at a slower pace and eventually arrived at Thaba Nchu on 31 January 1837, where they were warmly received by Reverend Archbell.[220] During the attack on the Ndebele, an estimated 200 to 400 were killed, while no Boers were killed or injured, but two auxiliaries lost their lives. At Thaba Nchu, a second division of the cattle took place to compensate the members of the Potgieter trek for their losses during the battles at the

---

[218] Retief, J. (2016). The Voortrekker and the Ndebele, Part Two: The Battle of Vegkop, 20 October 1836. *Military History Journal, 17*(1)., https://www.samilitaryhistory.org/vol171jr.html
[219] Retief, J. (2016). The Voortrekker and the Ndebele, Part Two: The Battle of Vegkop, 20 October 1836. *Military History Journal, 17*(1)., https://www.samilitaryhistory.org/vol171jr.html
[220] Retief, J. (2016). The Voortrekker and the Ndebele, Part Two: The Battle of Vegkop, 20 October 1836. *Military History Journal, 17*(1)., https://www.samilitaryhistory.org/vol171jr.html

Vaal River and Vegkop. The remaining cattle were divided among the members of the commando.[221]

The Boers had unresolved issues with Mzilikazi, as many of Potgieter's people fell into poverty after the Ndebele attacks. Furthermore, Mzilikazi's threat posed a danger to the migration movement, as many Boers still in the Cape might choose to stay due to the insecurity of the area between the Vet and Vaal rivers - a region already acquired by the Boers from the Bataung - as well as the unpopulated areas under Mzilikazi's control. Approximately two thousand Boers from all the trek groups that had already left the Cape had now gathered at Thaba Nchu and were now camped between Thaba Nchu and the Vet River.[222] Issues of importance to the migration movement had to be discussed and decided upon. These matters included the election of leadership, constitutional issues, relations with neighbouring nations, future relations with the British Government, the organisation of their Church after their ex-communication by the Dutch Reformed Church, and the determination of their ultimate settlement destination.[223] The Boers awaited Piet Retief's arrival from the Winterberg region of the Cape Colony with great anticipation. It is clear that the Boers requested Retief to join them as their leader. According to his farewell letter to

---

[221] Retief, J. (2016). The Voortrekker and the Ndebele, Part Two: The Battle of Vegkop, 20 October 1836. *Military History Journal*, *17*(1)., https://www.samilitaryhistory.org/vol171jr.html

[222] Muller, C. F. J. (1981). 500 Years - A History of South Africa (3rd ed.). Academica., p.161

[223] Retief, J. (2016). The Voortrekker and the Ndebele, Part Two: The Battle of Vegkop, 20 October 1836. *Military History Journal*, *17*(1)., https://www.samilitaryhistory.org/vol171jr.html

Stockenström, dated 1 February 1837, Retief planned to join the Boers who already were in the Transorangia, not as an ordinary Boer, but as their leader.[224]

Piet Retief initially did not want to emigrate. He first tried to work with the colonial authorities to improve conditions on the eastern frontier.[225] After numerous conversations and correspondence with Stockenström, it became clear to Retief by the end of October 1836 that the situation in the Cape would not improve. He realized that the Boers could only establish a peaceful and secure way of life through migration. When the highly respected Retief made the decision to trek, it had a significant impact on the migration movement. He actively encouraged fellow Boers to exchange the turbulent British-Xhosa border for a peaceful existence within a Boer republic. On 2 February 1837, he published his manifesto in the Grahamstown Journal: "We leave this colony with the full assurance that the English government requires nothing more from us, and that we can govern ourselves without their interference in the future." Along with his manifesto, the newspaper published a list of 366 new Voortrekkers.[226] Subsequently, in February 1837, Piet Retief led a group of one hundred Boers, including men, women, and children, out of the Cape Colony.[227] Among

---

[224] Hugo, M. (1988). Piet Retief in die Suid-Afrikaanse geskiedskrywing. *South African Journal of Cultural History*, 2(2), 108-126., p.113
[225] Hugo, M. (1988). Piet Retief in die Suid-Afrikaanse geskiedskrywing. *South African Journal of Cultural History*, 2(2), 108-126., p.113
[226] Muller, C. F. J. (1981). 500 Years - A History of South Africa (3rd ed.). Academica., p.161
[227] Giliomee, Hermann. Die Afrikaners (Afrikaans Edition). Tafelberg. Kindle Edition, p.155

them were his own family, James Edwards and his family, three Greyling families, seven Rensburg families, two Malan families, three Viljoen families, one Meyer family, one Van Dijk family, two Joubert families, one Dreyer family, three Van Staden families, and a schoolmaster named Alfred Smith.[228]

During an assembly known as volksvergadering (people's meeting) in April 1837 and on 6 June 1837 at Winburg, the Boers elected Retief to serve as both their governor and hoofkommandant (commander-in-chief). Maritz assumed the roles of President of the Council of Policy, the highest legislative and administrative entity that later transformed into the Volksraad of the Republic of Natalia, and landrost (magistrate). The members elected to the Volksraad were J.G.L. Bronkhorst, L.S. van Vuuren, E.F. Liebenberg, P.J. Greyling, and M. Oosthuizen. A provisional constitution known as the First Constitution, consisting of nine articles, was drafted and adopted. The nine articles of this constitution were: All political offices were to be elected by the people; Every Boer was recognised as a citizen of the new State; All citizens or burghers were entitled to equal rights and eligibility for any office; The Dutch Reformed Church was established as the State Church; Slavery was explicitly prohibited; Non-Boers could join the Boers, provided they declared, under oath, no affiliation with the London Missionary Society; The State must aim to maintain friendly relations with other nations; Land and property for the new State were to be acquired through legal treaty,

---

[228] History of the Emigrant Boers in South Africa" (2nd ed., 1888) by G. M. Theal, published by Swan Sonnenschein, Lowrey & Co., p.82

cession, or purchase; In case of legal uncertainties, the old laws of the Batavian Republic were to be referenced. This straightforward Constitution was also known as Retief's Grondwet (Retief's Constitution).[229]

Hendrik Potgieter's absence from any elected position was most likely due to his decision not to stand as a candidate. Potgieter had early on expressed his preference for the highveld as his ultimate destination, in contrast to other Boer leaders who favoured Natal.[230] Until September 1837, the Boers held several meetings and assemblies to deliberate and strategise on important matters. One of Retief's first actions as the Boers' governor was to engage the leaders of the surrounding nations, including Chiefs Moroka, Towane, Sekonyela, and Moshoeshoe, to establish agreements of peace and friendship.[231] Retief would soon be reminded that, due to their strong individualism, the absence of class distinctions in their culture and their inherent inclination towards localism, the Boers could not easily be controlled, and internal disagreements could not easily be resolved. With his first decision, the appointment of Reverend Erasmus Smit as the official Boer preacher, half of the Boers did not agree. Many preferred the Wesleyan missionary, Reverend James Archbell.

---

[229] Voigt, J. C. (1899). *Fifty Years of the History of the Republic in South Africa 1795-1845 I*. E.P. Dutton & Co., p. 335
[230] Hugo, M. (1988). Piet Retief in die Suid-Afrikaanse geskiedskrywing. *South African Journal of Cultural History*, 2(2), 108-126., p.113
[231] Hugo, M. (1988). Piet Retief in die Suid-Afrikaanse geskiedskrywing. *South African Journal of Cultural History*, 2(2), 108-126., p.113

THE BOERS TREK

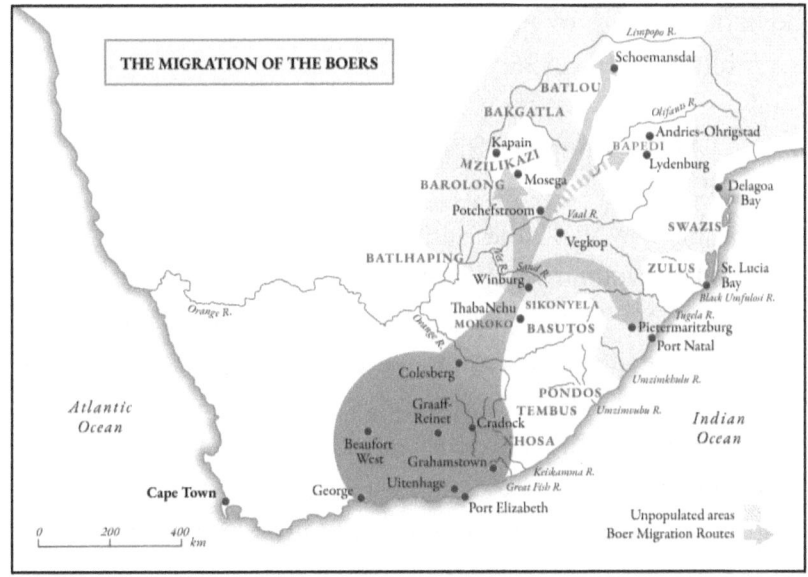

Map 3: The Migration Routes of the Boers

Nevertheless, Retief's elevated status and appointment as their leader were well-founded. Piet Retief commanded respect not only within the Boer community but also among English settlers, British authorities, and Governor D'urban. In the Cape, Retief readily engaged with authorities to better the living conditions of his people, even engaging directly with the governor when necessary.[232] Historian G.E. Cory noted Retief's exceptional military capabilities during the Sixth Frontier War: "In no instance did the military under Colonel Somerset make any stand against the enemy such as that made by the Winterberg Boers under Piet Retief".[233] D'Urban was so impressed by Retief's military prowess that

---

[232] Hugo, M. (1988). Piet Retief in die Suid-Afrikaanse geskiedskrywing. *South African Journal of Cultural History*, 2(2), 108-126., p.113
[233] Cory, G. E. (1919). *The Rise of South Africa, Vol. III*. Longman's, Green & Co., London., p.89

he honoured him by naming a military post in the Winterberg after him in early 1836.[234]

Another popular Boer leader, Piet Uys, was unable to attend the Volksvergadering (People's Assembly) as he was still on his way to Thaba Nchu. Uys, along with his trek group of more than 100 people, crossed the colonial border in April 1837.[235] Consequently, Uys's party was not present for the Boers' leadership elections, nor did they participate in the formation of the nine resolutions on 6 June 1837. The Uys trek, like many other trek parties, consisted of family groups and friends who formed a cohesive bond, that made embracing a leader from another migration group difficult.[236] On 14 August 1837, Piet Uys issued a statement, signed by 170 individuals, confirming that they would not submit to the recently formulated resolutions.[237] Uys believed that elections and a constitution should be deferred until the formal acquisition of their forthcoming territory was finalised and until the entirety of the Boers had concluded their migration, enabling universal participation in the electoral process, not exclusively by the vanguard pioneers. According to Uys, they should be governed by the traditional Boer structures of field cornets and commandants until an official constitution of their new land comes into effect. Uys's address to his compatriots culminated in a notable resolution:

---

[234] Hugo, M. (1988). Piet Retief in die Suid-Afrikaanse geskiedskrywing. *South African Journal of Cultural History*, 2(2), 108-126., p.112
[235] Markram, W. J. (2001). *Die lewe en werk van Petrus Lafras Uys, 1797-1838* [Doctoral dissertation, University of Stellenbosch]., p.225
[236] Markram, W. J. (2001). *Die lewe en werk van Petrus Lafras Uys, 1797-1838* [Doctoral dissertation, University of Stellenbosch]., p.227
[237] Botha, J. P. (2008). Ons Geskiedenis (1st ed.). J.P. Botha., p.106

"We intend to construct our settlement upon the same principles of freedom embraced by the United States of America...".[238]

It is unclear whether Piet Uys met Dingane during his exploration commission to Natal in 1834 to negotiate about land. Uys nevertheless seemed confident in their settlement plans in the largely depopulated southern region of Natal, between the Tugela and Umzimvubu Rivers. Reverend George Champion, an American missionary, documented on 28 June 1835, that information from fellow missionary Dr. Newton Adams indicated a Boer group had met with Dingane and gained approval to establish themselves in Natal. Champion reaffirmed this account in a letter dated 15 July 1835 to Anderson in Boston.[239] Both Uys and Retief were eager to obtain the harbour of Port Natal that would facilitate the import and export of goods. They were also eager to relocate to the coastal plain of Natal.[240]

The Boers were aware of the British government's official decision to not annex Natal,[241] and for that reason, they continued to explore the possibility of settling in Natal. English settlers and traders from the Cape petitioned King William IV to occupy Port Natal. Governor D'Urban referred

---

[238] Theal, G. M. (1913). *Willem Adriaan van der Dtel and other Historical Sketches*. Thomas Maskew Miller, Publisher., p.286
[239] Markram, W. J. (2001). *Die lewe en werk van Petrus Lafras Uys, 1797-1838* [Doctoral dissertation, University of Stellenbosch]., p.199
[240] Giliomee, Hermann. Die Afrikaners (Afrikaans Edition). Tafelberg. Kindle Edition, p.157
[241] Muller, C. F. J. (1981). 500 Years - A History of South Africa (3rd ed.). Academica., p.163

this petition to the British colonial secretary on 17 June 1834. British Minister T Spring Rice informed D'Urban on 10 November 1834 that the government could not comply and in March of the next year, the request to annex Natal was formally denied due to financial concerns.[242] On 12 March 1835, the Cape government secretary informed traders and other inhabitants of the Cape Colony that the Imperial government decided against annexing Natal as a British colony. The colonial secretary's letter confirming the British authorities' decision against annexing Natal was published in The Graham's Town Journal on 27 March 1835. A year later, on 29 March 1836, Glenelg once again wrote to D'Urban, the letter which the governor received in Cape Town on 11 July 1836, that the British government had once again decided not to annex Natal, despite renewed requests.

Following the British government's official refusal to annex Natal, the small group of British settlers, hunters, and traders at Port Natal, including Alexander Biggar, supported the Boers' migration to southern Natal.[243] In contrast, the philanthropist and evangelist, Captain A.F. Gardiner, held a different perspective. Gardiner was stationed at Port Natal as a missionary on 29 January 1835 to convert the Zulus to Christianity. On 3 March 1835 he requested an interview with State Secretary Glenelg and shortly thereafter visited Glenelg.[244] Subsequently, on 6 May 1835, Captain Gardiner

---

[242] Markram, W. J. (2001). *Die lewe en werk van Petrus Lafras Uys, 1797-1838* [Doctoral dissertation, University of Stellenbosch]., p.185
[243] Muller, C. F. J. (1981). 500 Years - A History of South Africa (3rd ed.). Academica., p.163
[244] Muller, C. F. J. (1987). *Die oorsprong van die Groot Trek* (2nd ed.). Tafelberg Uitgewers., p.390

entered a treaty with Dingane which ceded the area around Port Natal to the British crown, on the condition that the British extradite all Zulu refugees who had escaped from Dingane's rule. Gardiner's actions aroused suspicions, and Retief possibly referred to him when, after his election as governor of the Boers, he wrote the following letter to the Cape Governor D'Urban on 21 July 1837: "...That we have learnt with grief that almost all the native tribes, by whom we are now surrounded, have been instigated to attack us; but although we feel ourselves fully able to resist all our enemies, we would however beg of your Excellency to prevent, as far as lies in your power, such hostilities, so that we may not be compelled to spill human blood, which has already been the case with Matsilikatzi..."[245]

Meanwhile, the Boer leaders, during the time they spent together, apparently unsuccessfully tried to persuade Potgieter to also move to Natal. Potgieter wanted to distance himself as much as possible from the British government by establishing a settlement across the Vaal River.[246] Among the leaders of smaller trek parties, independent choices were exercised, regardless of previous affiliations. Christiaan Liebenberg and Sarel Cilliers, both long-term members of the Potgieter trek, chose Natal, while JGS Bronkhorst and Gert Kruger remained under Potgieter's leadership. Other Boers

---

[245] Du Toit, A., & Giliomee, H. (1983). *Afrikaner Political Thought. Volume 1: 1780-1850*. University of California Press., p.215
[246] Giliomee, Hermann. Die Afrikaners (Afrikaans Edition). Tafelberg. Kindle Edition, p.157

like Pieter Daniel Jacobs remained in the Winburg area.[247] However, neither of these two regions had been definitively secured for settlement. Governor Retief, on behalf of the Boers, sent a message to Mzilikazi, the Ndebele king, in which he offered peace in exchange for the cattle that Mzilikazi had confiscated from the Boers but Mzilikazi did not respond to his proposal.[248] It was decided that, while Governor Retief undertook the critical mission to negotiate the territory in southern Natal with Dingane, other Boer leaders such as Potgieter, Uys, and Gert Rudolph went on a mission to neutralise the Ndebele threat in the western highveld region.[249] Removing the Mzilikazi threat from the highveld was crucial for peace and security in the region. Boer leaders considered the impending campaign against Mzilikazi of such importance to the migration movement that even Andries Pretorius, who hadn't started his trek yet joined them for their upcoming battle with Mzilikazi.

The "Nine Days Battle," which took place from 4 to 12 November 1837, broke the Ndebele dominance in the region. A commando of 360 Boers, led by Hendrik Potgieter and Piet Uys, launched an extensive attack on the Ndebele, to destroy all their concentration points. They were assisted by the Tswana leader, Moiloa II of the Bahurutshe, and the

---

[247] Oberholzer, J.. (1989). Die Voortrekkerideaal - Natal of Transvaal?. HTS Teologiese Studies / Theological Studies. 45. 10.4102/hts.v45i3.2316., p.677
[248] Voigt, J. C. (1899). *Fifty Years of the History of the Republic in South Africa 1795-1845 II*. E.P. Dutton & Co., p2
[249] Muller, C. F. J. (1981). 500 Years - A History of South Africa (3rd ed.). Academica., p.163

Barolong under the leadership of Chief Motlabe.[250] The attackers carried out a systematic search and destroy operation, and no Ndebele kraal was left untouched. On 4 November, the Ndebele kraal of Karnpu was attacked, during which the Ndebele offered limited resistance, after which the kraal was set on fire by the Barolong fighters. In the following days, the Boers drove away the Ndebele, who sought shelter in the Enzelsberg area. The "Battle of Koppieskraal" on 6 November included an attack on scattered huts of Kobalonta, which led to the Ndebele retreating northward.[251] In a counterattack, Marap, with reinforcements from Silkaatskop, fiercely fought back, but he suffered significant losses and ultimately withdrew. Meanwhile, Mzilikaze began to evacuate all his settlements, and women and children were escorted out of the area by Gundwane with the Mnyama Makanda regiment. Kalipi, Sebeku, and two cattle-fighting regiments (which attack by releasing cattle on their enemy) defended the main settlement of Kopanyeng. The Boers attacked Silkaatskop, and the Ndebele were forced to retreat in the south-southwest direction.[252]

On 8 November Mzilikazi attempted to personally influence the outcome of the battles by taking a leading

---

[250] Grönum, W. (1987). *Die Mfecane: Oorsprong, Ontplooiing an Invloed op die Tswana* [Master's thesis, North-West University]., p.118-119
[251] Grönum, W. (1987). *Die Mfecane: Oorsprong, Ontplooiing an Invloed op die Tswana* [Master's thesis, North-West University]., p.118-119
[252] Grönum, W. (1987). *Die Mfecane: Oorsprong, Ontplooiing an Invloed op die Tswana* [Master's thesis, North-West University]., p.118-119

position on Maaierskop.²⁵³ Meanwhile, Kalipi and Sebuku set up an ambush parallel to the approaching routed Ndebeles from Silkaatskop. The ambush failed and led to losses among their own forces. In their defensive attempts on 9 November, the Ndebele tried to protect Kopanyeng by deploying the fighting bull regiments in the middle, with Kampu and Marap on the right flank and Kalipi and Sebeku on the left flank. The release of the cattle led to chaos among the Ndebele due to their panic under the Boers' gunfire. Kopanyeng was burned down. Mzilikazi's forces tried to evade the Boers' relentless pursuit by seeking refuge behind the "Dwarsberg" on 10 November. However, the Boers continued the pursuit and attacked the Ndebele's rear guard. The Ndebele's attempts to set up ambushes on 11 November failed, and thereafter, Ndebele groups began surrendering to the Boers.²⁵⁴ After being scattered by the Boers, Mzilikazi and his remaining followers fled from Marico to the eastern parts of modern-day Botswana. In 1840, they settled in an area that later became known as Matabeleland, located in present-day Zimbabwe.²⁵⁵ There was now no significant power posing a threat to the Boers on the highveld.²⁵⁶

---

[253] Grönum, W. (1987). *Die Mfecane: Oorsprong, Ontplooiing an Invloed op die Tswana* [Master's thesis, North-West University]., p.118-119

[254] Grönum, W. (1987). *Die Mfecane: Oorsprong, Ontplooiing an Invloed op die Tswana* [Master's thesis, North-West University]., p.118-119

[255] Retief, J. (2016). The Voortrekker and the Ndebele, Part Two: The Battle of Vegkop, 20 October 1836. *Military History Journal, 17*(1)., https://www.samilitaryhistory.org/vol171jr.html

[256] Giliomee, Hermann. Die Afrikaners (Afrikaans Edition). Tafelberg. Kindle Edition, p.157

THE BOERS TREK

Following the victory over Mzilikazi and the Ndebele's retreat across the Limpopo River, Potgieter asserted Boer ownership of the land north of the Vaal River, previously controlled by Mzilikazi, using the principle of conquest. On 3 December 1838, as the Boers reached their camp at the Sand River, Potgieter, mindful of the Cape of Good Hope Punishment Act, wrote the following letter to Governor D'Urban, notifying him of the events regarding Mzilikazi:
"...And so we emigrants have seen fit, for the security of our families, to leave the Colony, and not only in view of His Excellency's laws, but mainly because we were not able to maintain our wives and children...
Since we have left the Colony in peace and have had no ill intentions of doing anything illegal, we regard ourselves as free citizens who might go where we please without acting to the detriment of any other, as all nations are free and go where they like.
And we cannot understand why we should be accused of such an unforgiveable crime from which, in terms of section 5 of your proclamation, not even time can absolve us.
(Referring to the Cape of Good Hope Punishment Act.)
It is our desire to live in peace with His Excellency and with all nations, as will become evident.
[We concluded peace treaties with the different chiefs that we encountered, Danser, Maroka, Pieter Davids, Sikonjala and Makwana.]
Our objective was to reach a country where there were no other peoples, and while on our journey in the upper reaches of the Vaal River in Makwana's country the bloodthirsty tyrant Musilicaats fell on us, and murdered some of our families in a bloodthirsty way and took away many cattle.

Upon this we retreated to Doorenkop at the Renoster River, where he fell on us a second time with a countless horde, and again killed two people and took away our last cattle so that we were to starve to death.

Maroka, Pieter Davids and Mr Archbell assisted us to get to Maroka, whereupon we went on patrol, with a little help from Maroka, Pieter Davids and Sikonjala, with a view to getting back our cattle. In this way we got back some of our cattle, and later a second patrol we again regained a few.

Many of us are still destitute because of this bloodthirsty tyrant Musilicaats.

From Makwana, who had also been ruined by Musilicaats, we bought a part of the country, since we do not want to do anything to the disadvantage of the nations that are here.

But we are definitely occupying [Musilicaats's] country until he returns our cattle to us, though he has fled so far away that we do not know where he is. We do not believe that this is an unjust cause that we are now representing to you. And so we ask Your Excellency on what grounds we are to be regarded as bloodthirsty enemies (of the British government), to such an extent that even time will not protect us from punishment...

We did not ask for the assistance given us by Maroka and Sikonjala. They did it from their own free will because they had also been cruelly and bloodthirstily devastated by the same Musilicaats. Many of them who had survived would have starved to death, and not only that but great parts of the country were depopulated and devastated by the same tyrant

Musilicaats and are still lying empty. Because of us, the nations that are still here can live in peace..."[257]

Piet Retief left his camp at Kerkenberg on the Drakensberg with fifteen men in October 1837 on his crucial mission to negotiate for land with the Zulu king, Dingane. At that time, the Zulu king and his warriors resided north of the Tugela River, but his influence extended across the entire Natal region encompassing the land from the Drakensberg Mountains in the west to the sea, extending as far south as the Umzimvubu River.[258] The entire region south of the Tugela was part of the vacant land created by his predecessor, Shaka, which he maintained for his kingdom.[259] It was this very land that Retief sought to negotiate for on behalf of his people. Governor Retief first visited Port Natal, where about thirty English traders lived permanently or in intervals between hunting expeditions because from there, he could dispatch a message to Dingane to arrange a meeting with him. Some of these English traders exercised a degree of control akin to that of Zulu chiefs over several thousand local refugees who had sought refuge at the port. Most of these English traders, notably Alexander Biggar who had already formed an amicable relationship with several Boers in the Cape, extended a warm welcome to Retief. The governor suspected that Dingane, likely incited by

---

[257] Du Toit, A., & Giliomee, H. (1983). *Afrikaner Political Thought. Volume 1: 1780-1850*. University of California Press., p.215-216
[258] Theal, G. M. (1886). *Boers and Bantu: A History of the Wanderings and Wars of the Emigrant Farmers from their leaving the Cape Colony to the overthrow of Dingan*. Saul Solomon and Co., p.98
[259] Walker, E. A. (1965). *The Great Trek* (5th ed.). Adam & Charles Black, London., p.149

philanthropic elements among the English settlers in Port Natal, was instigating against the Boers, as evidenced by his letter of 9 September 1837 to Stockenström.[260] Retief also knew that Dingane had previously also launched an attack on Mzilikazi on the highveld, and to increase the chances of success in the upcoming negotiations, he wanted to make sure that Dingane knew they had a common enemy in Mzilikazi. Therefore, in his letter to Dingane from Port Natal on 21 October 1837, to arrange a meeting with him, Retief explained and justified the Boers' actions against Mzilikazi.[261]

On 31 October 1837, while Retief was already on his way to Dingane, he received a letter from Dingane, granting him an audience. Dingane also sent a small herd of sheep and sheepskins to Retief, which his warriors had taken from Mzilikazi and which he suspected might have originally belonged to Retief's people.[262] Retief arrived at Dingane's capital, uMgungundlovu (isiZulu for the secret place of the elephant), or Dingaanstad as it was known to the Boers, on 5 November 1837. However, the governor had to wait for two days before King Dingane ka Senzangakona would see him because the Zulu king was waiting for Captain Allen Gardiner to advise him on his discussions with Retief.[263]

---

[260] Hugo, M. (1988). Piet Retief in die Suid-Afrikaanse geskiedskrywing. *South African Journal of Cultural History*, 2(2), 108-126., p.116
[261] Hugo, M. (1988). Piet Retief in die Suid-Afrikaanse geskiedskrywing. *South African Journal of Cultural History*, 2(2), 108-126., p.113
[262] Hugo, M. (1988). Piet Retief in die Suid-Afrikaanse geskiedskrywing. *South African Journal of Cultural History*, 2(2), 108-126., p.116
[263] Hugo, M. (1988). Piet Retief in die Suid-Afrikaanse geskiedskrywing. *South African Journal of Cultural History*, 2(2), 108-126., p.116

Gardener, however, failed to appear. While Retief was engaged in negotiating a land transaction with Dingane in uMgungundlovu, his kinsmen were locked in a nine-day battle against Mzilikazi to secure the western highveld. During these negotiations, the Zulu king expressed his willingness to cede the land between the Tugela and Umzimvubu rivers to the Boers. However, Dingane's condition was that Retief must first recover cattle recently stolen from his people in Zoeloeland by Sikonyela's Batlokua,[264] Retief was pleased with the outcome of the negotiations because he was confident that he could fulfil the condition of the land transaction by recovering the stolen cattle for the Zulus. Nonetheless, he may have been perplexed by Sikoyela's actions. Despite the existing friendship treaty with the Boers, Sikonyela attempted to implicate them in his cattle theft. He conducted the cattle theft on horseback, wearing clothing resembling that of the Boers, and deliberately followed the trail of the stolen cattle right through the vicinity of the Boers' encampments.[265]

Unbeknownst to Retief during his visit to uMgungundlovu, the negotiations with Dingane were far from successful. In truth, Dingane had secretly resolved to exterminate the amaBhunu (the Boers) - men, women, and children - and was merely biding his time. When Retief informed him of the Boers' struggles with Mzilikazi in his

---

[264] Muller, C.F.J. (1973). The Period of the Great Trek, 1834-1854. C.F.J. Muller (Ed.), Five Hundred Years. A History of South Africa (pp.146-182). (3rd ed.). Academia. ,p.163
[265] Theal, G. M. (1888). *History of the Emigrant Boers in South Africa* (2nd ed.). Swan, Sonnenschein, Lowrey and Co., p.103

letter, it was not news to Dingane, as his own sources had already informed him of Potgieter and Maritz's first punitive expedition against Mzilikazi. What startled Dingane, however, was the realization that the Boers could inflict considerable damage on Mzilikazi without suffering any casualties in battle. Moreover, they managed to seize thousands of cattle from the Ndebele king. Dingane himself, after the Boers' first punitive expedition against Mzilikazi in the winter of 1837, sent a large Zulu army to attack Mzilikazi, but the Zulus could not gain the upper hand over the Ndebele and had to withdraw their forces.[266] Dingane feared that, with a strong neighbour like the Boers, he would not remain on the Zulu throne for long. He could also not fathom that Retief would peacefully depart Natal if he did not cede land to the Boers. Before Retief departed from uMgungundlovu, Dingane had already issued orders to one of his Indunas (captains) to eliminate the Retief party during their journey back to Port Natal. However, the Induna refused to carry out these deadly orders and instead fled to Port Natal with six hundred of his people. Incensed by this defiance, Dingane ruthlessly massacred all the Induna's people, except for the Induna himself and a small group who managed to reach Port Natal safely.[267]

Dingane acquired the Zulu throne through violence, and he was determined to retain his rule through force. On 28

---

[266] Grobler, J. E. H. (2010). Afrikaner- en Zoeloeperspektiewe op die Slag van Bloedrivier, 16 Desember 1838. *Tydskrif vir Geesteswetenskappe, 50*(3). pp.363-382, p.366

[267] Walker, E. A. (1965). *The Great Trek* (5th ed.). Adam & Charles Black, London., p.162

September 1828 Dingane conspired with Mhlangana (his half-brother), Mbopha KaSithayi (Shaka's chief councillor), and Mkabayi KaJama (Shaka's aunt) to assassinate Shaka. After the assassination of Shaka, the Zulu people hoped for a period of peace, but Dingane quickly moved to consolidate his power within the Zulu empire. Several important royal Abantwana (princes) and regional factions and chiefdoms could, however, not readily transfer their loyalty from Shaka to Dingane.[268] To eliminate potential challengers, Dingane embarked on a campaign to eliminate those amakhosi (royals) whom he suspected of disloyalty. While he spared his half-brothers, Gqugqu and Mpande KaSenzangakhona, because he deemed them too weak to pose a threat, he did not hesitate to eliminate the princes Ngwadi, Mhlangana, and Ngqojana.[269] The first opposition to Dingane's rule came from Nqetho, the inkosi (chief) of the Qwabe clan, who was forced to flee southward across the Tugela River along with his entire clan.[270] Dingane's brutality persisted in the years that followed. He massacred nearly the entire Cele clan in 1831 and launched an attack against the Qadi clan in 1837.[271] This cruelty led to widespread desertion from his ranks. In

---

[268] Shamase, M. Z. (1999). *The reign of King Mpande and his relations with the Republic of Natalia and its successor, the British colony of Natal* [Doctoral dissertation, University of Zululand]., p.60-61
[269] Shamase, M. Z. (1999). *The reign of King Mpande and his relations with the Republic of Natalia and its successor, the British colony of Natal* [Doctoral dissertation, University of Zululand]., p.61
[270] Shamase, M. Z. (1999). *The reign of King Mpande and his relations with the Republic of Natalia and its successor, the British colony of Natal* [Doctoral dissertation, University of Zululand]., p.62
[271] Shamase, M. Z. (1999). *The reign of King Mpande and his relations with the Republic of Natalia and its successor, the British colony of Natal* [Doctoral dissertation, University of Zululand]., p.62

response to these desertions and to strengthen his position within the Zulu Empire, Dingane waged wars against external forces he perceived as threats, including the Swazi, Bheje of the Khumalo at Ngome, the San, Mzilikazi, and the Boers.[272]

During Retief's absence, he left his stepson, Abraham Greyling, in charge of his trek party. Retief had given instructions to Greyling that no one should descend the mountain until his return.[273] On his journey back from uMgungundlovu, Retief dispatched two men to the camps with a message that his negotiations with Dingane for land had been successful. The two men reached the encampments on the Drakensberg on 11 November 1837, and within a few days, people began their descent from the mountain with their wagons. When Retief rejoined his trek on 27 November 1837, nearly 1,000 wagons were scattered in the vicinity of Doornkop, south of the Tugela River.[274] During this time, before Retief departed once again towards the end of December 1837 to recover Dingane's stolen cattle from Sikonyella, Andries Pretorius paid a visit to the camps in Natal after he participated in the expedition against Mzilikazi. The following day, Gerrit Maritz and Gert

---

[272] Shamase, M. Z. (1999). *The reign of King Mpande and his relations with the Republic of Natalia and its successor, the British colony of Natal* [Doctoral dissertation, University of Zululand]., p.62
[273] Hugo, M. (1988). Piet Retief in die Suid-Afrikaanse geskiedskrywing. *South African Journal of Cultural History*, *2*(2), 108-126., p.117
[274] Hugo, M. (1988). Piet Retief in die Suid-Afrikaanse geskiedskrywing. *South African Journal of Cultural History*, *2*(2), 108-126., p.117

Rudolph also arrived from the campaign against Mzilikazi.[275] A large gathering took place in Retief's camp on Monday, 18 December 1837, during which Retief and Piet Uys resolved their disputes. B. Liebenberg, on behalf of the Boers, requested Piet Uys to take an oath of allegiance to the governor, as everyone else had done. Uys pledged to do so once his trek had descended from the Drakensberg.[276]

On 26 December 1837, Retief set out with a small commando of fifty men, accompanied by a group of representatives from Dingane, to Sikonyella, who lived near present-day Ficksburg. He returned to his trek on 11 January 1838, with seven hundred cattle, sixty-three horses, and 11 rifles that he had taken from Sikonyela.[277] Retief then started preparations for his second visit to uMgungundlovu, aimed at returning Dingane's cattle and formalising the treaty for their land transaction. On 16 January 1838, the Boers held another public meeting, known as a "volksvergadering", to deliberate further negotiations with Dingane. During this gathering, several Boers expressed concerns about Retief's upcoming visit to uMgungundlovu. Gerrit Maritz, in particular, distrusted Dingane. Maritz offered to go in Retief's place to finalise the contract with Dingane, but Retief was hesitant to take any steps that might undermine Dingane's trust in the Boers, endangering the critical land transaction.

---

[275] Jansen, E. G. (1938). *Die Voortrekkers in Natal.*,
https://archive.org/details/VoortrekkersInNatal
[276] Jansen, E. G. (1938). *Die Voortrekkers in Natal.*,
https://archive.org/details/VoortrekkersInNatal
[277] Jansen, E. G. (1938). *Die Voortrekkers in Natal.*,
https://archive.org/details/VoortrekkersInNatal

THE CREATION OF THE BOER IDENTITY

On 25 January 1838, Governor Retief, along with a company of one hundred people, including four boys (one of which was his own twelve-year-old son, Pieter Retief junior), the English interpreter Thomas Halstead, and thirty auxiliaries departed for uMgungundlovu.[278] By this time Dingane had become aware that the Boers had successfully broken Mzilikazi's power at Kapain and that Retief could take the cattle and guns from Sikonyela without firing a single shot. When he heard that Retief was on his way to finalise the land transaction, he devised a plan to murder Retief and his companions. He concealed 3,000 warriors within the huts surrounding his residence, preparing for an ambush against Retief and his party.[279] Retief and his group arrived at uMgungundlovu on 3 February 1838. Dingane expressed his contentment with Retief's efforts in upholding their agreement to return the cattle. Over the next two days, Dingane entertained the Boers with captivating dance performances, simulated battles, and a regiment of warriors who initiated a rhythmic display by beating their shields. When, on the morning of 6 February 1838, Dingane sealed the land transaction with his mark on the treaty, Retief was assured and convinced of Dingane's good faith.[280] Suddenly, on Dingane's order: "For me, my warriors grab them, grab

---

[278] Muller, C.F.J. (1969). The Period of the Great Trek, 1834-1854. C.F.J. Muller (Ed.), Five Hundred Years. A History of South Africa (pp.122-156). Academia. ,p.139
[279] Walker, E. A. (1965). *The Great Trek* (5th ed.). Adam & Charles Black, London., p.163
[280] Hugo, M. (1988). Piet Retief in die Suid-Afrikaanse geskiedskrywing. *South African Journal of Cultural History*, 2(2), 108-126., p.118

THE BOERS TREK

hold of them, and kill, kill the wizards!",[281] the Boers were attacked and overwhelmed by his amabutho (Zulu military units) which included the dancing warriors, as well as those hidden in the huts. The Boers defended themselves with pocket knives, resulting in twenty Zulu warriors being killed and a large number wounded.[282] The Boers, whose names are listed here,[283] were taken to a nearby hill, the hill of

---

[281] Grobler, J. (2011). The Retief Massacre of 6 February 1838 revisited. *Historia*, *56*(2), pp.113-132., p.119
[282] Grobler, J. (2011). The Retief Massacre of 6 February 1838 revisited. *Historia*, *56*(2), pp.113-132., p.119
[283] Pieter Mauritz Retief, Pieter Retief junior (Piet Retief's son, age 12), Abraham Greyling (Retief's stephson), Lucas Petrus Johannes Meyer (Retief's son-in-law); Johannes Diederik Aucamp; Willem Johannes Basson; Johannes Breed, Petrus Gerhardus Breed (brother of Johannes); Joachim Botha; Gerhardus Cornelis Bothma; Pieter Josuas Hendrik Cilliers; Matthys de Beer, Stephanus Johannes de Beer (Matthys de Beer's son); Izak Jacobus Johannes de Clercq, Matthys Pieter Taute (stephbrother of Izak de Clerq?); Jacobus (Jan) de Wet, Hendrik de Wet; Marthinus Esterhuysen, Samuel Esterhuysen; Reinier Nicolaas Johannes Grobler; Johannes Petrus Paulus Hugo; Johannes Hendrik Claassen; Piet Klopper, Balthasar Marthinus Klopper, Coenraad Christoffel Klopper, Lucas Cornelis Klopper (Coenraad Klopper's son), JC Beukes (Coenraad Kolopper's son-in-law?); Jan Hendrik Labuschagne, Frans Labuschagne (Hendrik Labuschagne's son); Barend Johannes Liebenberg; Hercules Phillippus Malan; Jacobus Johannes Opperman, Jacobus (Kootjie) Opperman (11 years old); Marthinus Jacobus Oosthuizen, Johannes Hendrik Lodewyk Oosthuysen, Jacobus Nicolaas Oosthuisen (12 years old); Frederik Pretorius, Mathys Van As Pretorius; Isaak Jacobus Robertse; Stephanus Johannes Scheepers; Barend Petrus van den Berg; Andries van Dyk (his family would later be murdered by at the Blaauwkrans Massacre on 17 February 1838); Johannes Frederick van der Merwe (father of Johanna van der Merwe); Johannes Christiaan van Schalkwyk; Gerrit Willem Visagie; Johannes Beukes; Johannes Scheepers, Gerrit Scheepers, Marthinus Scheepers; Jan Robberts; Barend Oosthuysen; Pieter Johannes Petrus Jordaan; Johannes de Klerk; Abraham de Klerk; Stephanus Smit; Stephanus Petrus Janse van Vuuren; Matthys Pretorius, Jan Pretorius, Marthinus Gerhardus Petrus Pretorius; Barend Jacobus Petrus van den Berg, Piet van den Berg; Jacobus Joosten; Charl Maré; Pieter Breed, Daniel

execution, Kwa-Matiwane, where everyone was beaten to death with knobkerries. The murder of Retief was the opening act in Dingane's war aimed at exterminating the entire Boer community in Natal.

The next day, Dingane sent two of his indunas (captains) to the missionary, Rev. Francis Owen, who had witnessed the massacre of Retief and his people, to reassure him that the missionaries and all the British in Natal were safe because they were (king) George's people and therefor also his people. Owen recorded the words of the induna in his diary as follows: "Feb. 7th. — In the morning two Indoonas with an attendant called... They had been sent by the king to inform me that it was not his intention to kill either me or the other missionaries, ...he could live in peace with us, for we were his people. All George's people, meaning the British were his, i.e., he liked them, but the Boers were not his people: nor were they George's..."[284] Dingane had previously explained his worldview to the missionary Owens: "I and my people believe that there is only one God - I am that God. We believe that there is only one place to

---

Liebenberg (12 year old), Jacobus Hattingh; Christiaan de Beer, Jan de Beer; Gerrit Bothma; Hermanus Fourie; Christiaan Breytenbach; Thomas Caldecott Halstead, Retief's translator); About 30 "agterryers" (auxiliaries). [Source: WikiTree. (2023, March 18). Project: Voortrekkers. Retrieved September 13, 2023, from: https://www.wikitree.com/wiki/Project:Voortrekkers]

[284] Historical Publications Southern Africa (n.d.). *The Diary of the Rev. F. Owen, Missionary with Dingane, together with the accounts of Zulu affairs by the interpreters, Messrs. Hully and Kirkman*. Retrieved October 4, 2023, from https://hipsa.org.za/publication/the-diary-of-the-rev-f-owen-missionary-with-Dingane-together-with-the-accounts-of-zulu-affairs-by-the-interpreters-messrs-hully-and-kirkman/

which all good people go - that is Zululand. We believe that there is one place where all bad people go: There, (pointing to a rocky hill in the distance - Kwa-Matiwane), there is hell, where all my wicked people go. The Chief who lives there is Umatiwane, the head of the Amangwane. I put him to death and made him the Devil-Chief of all wicked people who die. You see, then, that there are but two Chiefs in this country, Umatiwane and myself. I am the great Chief - the God of the living. Umatiwane is the great Chief of the wicked." In his doctoral thesis, M.Z. Shamase shows that Dingane's "izibongo" (praise poems) refer to these murders:
"Owad!' uPiti kumaBhunu,
[Who devoured Piet among Boers]
Wamud!a wamtshobotshe!a;
[He completely obliterated him from the earth's face]
Od!' uMzibhelibheli kumaBhunu,
[Who devoured Mzibhelibheli among Boers]
Wad!' uPhuzukuh!okoza kumaBhunu,
[You devoured Phuzukuhlokoza among Boers]
Wad!' uHwahwini kumaBhunu,
[You devoured Hwahwini among Boers]
Wad!' uJanomude kumaBhunu,
[You devoured Janomude among Boers]
Wad!' uJanejembu!uki kumaBhunu,
[You devoured Janejembuluki among Boers]
Wad!' uMazinyansakansaka kumaBhunu,
[You devoured Mazinyansakansaka among Boers]
Wad!' oSisini kumaBhunu ... "

[You devoured Sisini among Boers..."] [285]
Dingane's reign would also soon end violently.

On the same day that Retief and his companions were murdered, Dingane dispatched six to seven thousand warriors to massacre the Boer trek groups along the Bloukrans and Boesmans rivers, as well as elsewhere along the banks of the Tugela River.[286] At around 01:00 in the morning of 17 February 1838, the Zulu force launched a surprise attack on the unsuspecting Boers. Most Boers were scattered over an extensive area covering sixty-five kilometres by forty kilometres, in search of grazing for their large herds of cattle, leaving them extremely vulnerable. They were attacked over a front of thirty-two kilometres.[287] There were only eight hundred able-bodied Boer men to defend their laagers against this overwhelming Zulu force.[288] The Liebenbergs, Besters, De Beers, Prinsloos, and most of the Bezuidenhout family members were wiped out. Daniël Bezuidenhout, who was severely wounded, managed to escape the attack on his wagons and went to warn other families, but not before his entire family, including his wife, Elizabeth Cecilia Bezuidenhout (née Smit), and their 11-month-old baby were

---

[285] Shamase, M. Z. (1999). *The reign of King Mpande and his relations with the Republic of Natalia and its successor, the British colony of Natal* [Doctoral dissertation, University of Zululand]., p.62-63
[286] Giliomee, Hermann. Die Afrikaners (Afrikaans Edition). Tafelberg. Kindle Edition., p.158
[287] Walker, E. A. (1965). *The Great Trek* (5th ed.). Adam & Charles Black, London., p.166
[288] Giliomee, Hermann. Die Afrikaners (Afrikaans Edition). Tafelberg. Kindle Edition., p.158

killed.[289] The Bothma family's defences were breached, leading to the murder of the entire family.[290] The Bothas, Breytenbachs, and Smit families also suffered heavy losses, and further south, the Rossouws were similarly attacked. In an attempt to escape the Zulu attack, the Engelbrecht and Greyling families sought refuge with the Robbertse family, located between the Groot and Kleinmoordspruit, but they too were overwhelmed and massacred by the Zulus. Retief's camp at Doornkop was not attacked because the Zulu attackers were stopped before they could reach that far.

The Boers formed several groups to launch counterattacks. Sarel Cilliers, along with five other men, including the eighteen-year-old Marthinus Oosthuizen, were some of the first to launch mounted counterattacks against the Zulus. They came across a hill, which later became Rensburg Hill, where Hans van Rensburg and his people were trapped after being driven from their wagons by the Zulus. When Van Rensburg signalled that they were running low on gunpowder, Oosthuizen loaded himself and his horse with as much gunpowder as they could carry and charged through the Zulu warriors to get it to the Van Rensburgs.[291] They then succeeded in driving the Zulus away from there. Approximately 196 men, women, and children, who had been warned in time, sought refuge at Retief's camp at

---

[289] WikiTree. (2023, March 18). Project: Voortrekkers. Retrieved September 13, 2023, from
https://www.wikitree.com/wiki/Project:Voortrekkers
[290] Walker, E. A. (1965). *The Great Trek* (5th ed.). Adam & Charles Black, London., p.166-167
[291] Walker, E. A. (1965). *The Great Trek* (5th ed.). Adam & Charles Black, London., p.167

Doornkop.²⁹² From there, Piet Greyling, stepson of Piet Retief and brother of Abraham Greyling who was murdered along with Retief at Mgungundhlovu, led a group of Boers to help the people in the Bloukrans River Valley. Hans de Lange left his three-month-old baby at his camp by the Kleinboesmans River and launched an attack on the retreating Zulus. After Gerrit Maritz successfully repelled the Zulu attack on his camp, Saailaer, in the afternoon, he also went to assist the people in the Grootmoordspruit Valley.²⁹³ The Boers suffered heavy losses during the Weenen Massacres, as the event is known today, but they managed to repel the Zulu regiments' attack.²⁹⁴

The Boers faced devastating losses during these events. Forty-one men, fifty-six women, and 185 Boer children lost their lives,²⁹⁵ alongside 252 Khoi-Khoi and

---

²⁹² The South African Military History Society (n.d.). *South African Military History Society Eastern Cape Branch Newsletter / Nuusbrief August/ Augustus 2013: Great Trek Anniversary: Military encounters of the Voortrekkers 4.* http://samilitaryhistory.org/13/p13augne.html
²⁹³ WikiTree. (2023, March 18). Project: Voortrekkers. Retrieved September 13, 2023, from https://www.wikitree.com/wiki/Project:Voortrekkers
²⁹⁴ Grobler, J. E. H. (2010). Afrikaner- en Zoeloeperspektiewe op die Slag van Bloedrivier, 16 Desember 1838. *Tydskrif vir Geesteswetenskappe, 50*(3). pp.363-382, p.367
²⁹⁵ The following names of the Boers who were murdered at the Weenen Massacres were sources from the WikiTree Voortrekker Project: WikiTree. (2023, March 18). Project: Voortrekkers. Retrieved September 13, 2023, from https://www.wikitree.com/wiki/Project:Voortrekkers . This is an ongoing project and the identities of some of the people are still being researched.: Andries Bester and his wife Appolona (Vosloo) Bester.; Wynand Bezuidenhout and his wife Elizabeth (Liebenberg) Bezuidenhout. Six of their 13 children died, including their daughter, Susanna Botha. Daniel Bezuidenhout survived the attack. His wife Elizabeth Cecilia (Smit) Bezuidenhout died. Their 11-month-old baby

THE BOERS TREK

was killed in Daniels's arms.; George Biggar. The 18-year-old son of the English trader Alexander Biggar was sent by his father to warn the Boers. The distraught Alexander Bigger then joined the Boers in their later battle with the Zulus at Blood River.; Johannes Botha the elder, Johannes Botha the younger, Roelof Botha and his wife Susanna (Bezuidenhout) Botha; Abraham Bothma and his wife Getruida Bothma, Catharina Aletta Elizabeth Bothma (12), Johannes Arnoldus Bothma (11), Anna Maria Bothma (9), Lodewyk Christoffel Bothma (8), Louw Bothma the elder, Louw Bothma the younger.; Jacobus Coetzee, Sr; Christian de Beer and his wife Marth Cornelia (Bezuidenhout) de Beer and four children, Arnoldus Stephanus de Beer, Stephanns de Beer, Zacharias de Beer.; Thomas Frederik Dreyer.; Piet de Wet and his wife Marie (Botha) de Wet and their seven children; Louisa Johanna Margaretha (Jacobs} du Preez, wife of Pieter Daniel du Preez and seven children; Gerhardus Engelbrecht and his wife Anna Magrieta (van der Merwe) Engelbrecht and one of their children.; Laurens Erasmus and his wife Geertruyda Christina (Joubert) Erasmus.; Willem Jacobs and three of his children; Jacobus Petrus (Jubert) Joubert amd his wife Rachel Cornelia (van Jaarsveld) Joubert. Anna Francina (Roets) Joubert, wife of Abraham Benjamin Joubert who was not there and one child. Adriaan Josua Jacobus Joubert, his wife Susanna Catharina (Roos) Joubert, their 10-year-old son Josua Adriaan Joubert and their daughter Catherina Roos. Maria Magdalena (Badenhorst) Joubert, wife of Jan Christoffel Joubert and their son Jan Hendrik Joubert. Probate indicates that Maria and Jan died with all their children, who are not named.; Hester Magdelene (van den Berg) Liebenberg, widow of Barend Johannes Liebenberg who died with Retief, and three of her children, probably Phillipus, Paul and Jan. Christina Susanna (van der Merwe) Liebenberg, wife of Johannes Petrus Liebenberg. They had been married one month. He survived. Christian Lochenberg, Hendrik Lochenberg the younger, Hendrik Lochenberg the elder and his wife Maria Martha (Krugel) Loggenberg. Three of Hendrik seniors' children (probably adults) died as well.; Nicolaas Casparus le Roux, his daughters Anna Elisabeth Le Roux. His son Jan Christiaan le Roux and another daughter Clasina Le Roux Nicolaas survived.; Joachimus Prinsloo and seven of his children died. His daughter Catherine Prinsloo, who was severely wounded, survived.; Charl Petrus Roos and his wife Christina Hendrina (Joubert) and their three children were murdered. Johannes Gysbertus Roos (Charl's brother) and his wife Aletta Helena (Vorster) Roos and their son Johannes Gysbertus Roos and his wife Elizabeth Johanna (van der Berg) Roos and two children were murdered. The Roos children who died were: three children of Charl Petrus Roos, two children of Johannes Gysbertus Roos Snr., two children

Basutos, who accompanied the Boers, who were also killed. Entire families were wiped out. In some cases, the victims' bodies were horribly mutilated.[296] Tens of thousands of their sheep, cattle, and horses were stolen, and despite their counterattacks, they couldn't recover many of them.[297] Following these counterattacks, the men faced the grim task of searching for both survivors and the deceased. Retief's encampment at Doornkop became a sanctuary for many seeking refuge and wounded who needed treatment.[298] Many chose to stay there until the fear of another Zulu attack had subsided. Among the wounded was Johanna van der Merwe, a 12-year-old girl, whose father had been killed alongside

---

of Johannes Gysbertus Roos Jnr.; Jan Josua van den Berg and his wife Petronella Christina Elizabeth (Smit) van den Berg and four of their seven children died.; Helena Catharina Van der Merwe, wife of Johannes Frederick van der Merwe who were murdered with Retief. Her children died as well. Their daughter Johanna van der Merwe, who was severely wounded, survived.; Zacharia (Kruger) van Dyk, mother of Andries van Dyk and Frans van Dyk. Frans Johannes van Dyk, Francina Petronella (de Lange) van Dyk, wife of Andries Jacobus van Dyk who died with Retief. The nine of their children who were killed were: Anna Johanna Maria van Dyk (wife of H Fourie), Johannes Hendrik van Dyk, Andries Frans Jacobus Johannes van Dyk, Zacharia Susara van Dyk, Dorothea Hermina van Dyk, Sybrand van Dyk, Hesje Martha Aletta van Dyk, Willem van Dyk, Baba van Dyk. Susara Sophia Elizabeth (Potgieter) van Dyk, wife of Joshep van Dyk and her daughter-in-law Francina (de Lange) van Dyk, wife of Joseph van Dyk (Jnr.).; David Schalk Viljoen and his wife Catherina Aletta (Bothma) Viljoen, Pieter Nicolaas Viljoen (probably a cousin of David)

[296] Theal, G. M. (1886). *Boers and Bantu: A History of the Wanderings and Wars of the Emigrant Farmers from their leaving the Cape Colony to the overthrow of Dingan*. Saul Solomon and Co., p.106

[297] Muller, C.F.J. (1969). The Period of the Great Trek, 1834-1854. C.F.J. Muller (Ed.), Five Hundred Years. A History of South Africa (pp.122-156). Academia. ,p.139-140

[298] Jansen, E. G. (1938). *Die Voortrekkers in Natal.*,
https://archive.org/details/VoortrekkersInNatal

Piet Retief. Johanna survived despite sustaining twenty-five and Catharina Prinsloo also survived with twenty-three assegai wounds.

Dingane's attempt to obliterate the Boer community in Natal was unsuccessful due to the effective, swiftly organised counterattacks by small groups of Boers. The Great Murder, however, left the Boers in a crisis and jeopardised the entire migration movement of the Boers in Natal. They now realise that their governor and his companions have probably been murdered. The decision of whether to remain in Natal or return across the mountains was effectively made for them by Dingane when he plundered their cattle and essential resources. Many trek parties now lost their draught oxen, essential for pulling their wagons, rendering them immobile. In Boer culture, their women were always their wellspring of courage, remaining steadfast in challenging times even when the men wavered. Dingane's act of spilling innocent blood demanded accountability. Susanna Smit articulated their stance eloquently: "God will not leave him unrecompensed, nor will our men acquit him".[299]

After the Weenen Massacres, the Boers found themselves in disarray and fearing further attacks from Dingane. They gathered in three large camps near Maritz's laager, which overlooked the Bushman's River. Patrols, under the leadership of Hans de Lange, continuously scouted

---

[299] Walker, E. A. (1965). *The Great Trek* (5th ed.). Adam & Charles Black, London., p.168

the area for potential Zulu attacks.[300] Fortunately, the swollen Tugela River acted as a natural barrier, protecting them from such assaults.[301] Acting leader Gerrit Maritz dispatched messengers to the Boers in the Winburg area and north of the Vaal River to inform them of the situation and request assistance. Hendrik Potgieter and Piet Uys immediately answered the call. Piet Uys now moved his entire trek party across the Drakensberg mountains, uniting with his people on the banks of the Tugela on 1 March 1838.[302] With the loss of Retief, there was a pressing need for leadership among the Boers.

---

[300] Walker, E. A. (1965). *The Great Trek* (5th ed.). Adam & Charles Black, London., p.169
[301] Walker, E. A. (1965). *The Great Trek* (5th ed.). Adam & Charles Black, London., p.169
[302] Markram, W. J. (2001). *Die lewe en werk van Petrus Lafras Uys, 1797-1838* [Doctoral dissertation, University of Stellenbosch]., p.255

Chapter 5:
The Boers Republics

On 28 March 1838 the Boers elected their Volksraad (People's Council). The Volksraad, which was officially known as "die Raad van Representanten van het Volk" (the Council of Representatives of the People), consisted of twenty-four members. They also drew up a constitution that was called the "Regulatien en Instructien" (Regulations and Instructions).[1] However, they did not appoint a governor to replace Retief.[2] Maritz retained his previous position and took on the additional role of Orphan Master to handle all the estates of those who had perished in the Great Murder.[3] The Boers considered their entire territory, including Natalia, their Winburg territory and the territory of Mzilikazi north of the Vaal River, which they obtained by conquest, as a single unit. This was the reason why the Boers of Natal, including

---

[1] Storm, J.M.G. (1989). Die konvensie van Sandrivier as die afsluiting van die Groot Trek. *HTS Teologiese Studies / Theological Studies, 45*(3), 680-695., p.685
[2] Markram, W. J. (2001). *Die lewe en werk van Petrus Lafras Uys, 1797-1838* [Doctoral dissertation, University of Stellenbosch]., p.255
[3] Walker, E. A. (1965). *The Great Trek* (5th ed.). Adam & Charles Black, London., p.170

Uys, Maritz and others, and even Andries Pretorius who was still in the Cape, partook in the campaign against Mizilikazi. However, the Volksraad of Natalia did not interfere in the area beyond the Drakensberg and north of the Vaal and Potgieter and his Council were left in peace to manage the area there.[4] Driven by a desire for retribution and the need to recover their vital livestock, the Boers decided to mount an expedition against Dingane. Uys was appointed general field commandant to lead the forthcoming expedition against Dingane.[5] Potgieter would command his own men during the expedition.

Meanwhile, the Boers dispatched messengers to Port Natal to gather more information regarding the fate of Governor Retief and his men. In Port Natal, they discovered that the group of English settlers were already aware of the murders of Retief and his companions and that the English settlers attempted to warn the Boers about the recent attacks, but unfortunately, their messengers arrived too late. Tragically, 18-year-old George Bigger lost his life while on a mission to alert the Boers, leaving his father, Alexander Bigger, in grief. The English settlers at Port Natal realised that they would not be untouched by the consequences of the Zulu conflict with the Boers. With Dingane preoccupied with the Boers, the English settlers and their Zulu refugee followers began planning a campaign of "plunder and

---

[4] Storm, J.M.G. (1989). Die konvensie van Sandrivier as die afsluiting van die Groot Trek. *HTS Teologiese Studies / Theological Studies, 45*(3), 680-695., p.685

[5] Uys, I.S. (1979). The Battle of Italeni. *The South African Military History Society, Military History Journal, 4*(5)., The Battle of Italeni - Military History Society - Journal (samilitaryhistory.org)

revenge" against the Zulus.[6] On 13 March 1838, Reverend Owen documented that the English settlers formally declared war against Dingane.[7] Captain Allen Gardiner and his group left Port Natal on 25 March 1838, as he assumed that the Boers would not permit him to continue his missionary work in Hambanathi, a presumption that may have been correct. Two missionaries, the American Daniel Lindley and "Owen of uMgungundlovu",[8] offered their services to the Boers. However, the Boers declined Owen's services.

On 13 March 1838, the Natal English, with their army of Zulu refugees, embarked on their mission against Dingane. Robert Biggar, a son of Alexander Biggar, led the expedition. Although Robert held command, the English "chiefs" effectively oversaw their own people.[9] A dispute arose shortly after their departure, as John Cane's and Henry Ogle's Zulu wards disputed over who would lead the attack, resulting in fifty Zulus sustaining serious injuries. Ogle's faction swore vengeance.[10] Four days after leaving the port, they encountered an unprotected Zulu kraal at Untunjambili,

---

[6] Cubbin, A. E. (1988). The English alliance with the Voortrekkers against the Zulus during March and April 1838. *Historia, 33*(2), 63-73., p.64

[7] Cubbin, A. E. (1988). The English alliance with the Voortrekkers against the Zulus during March and April 1838. *Historia, 33*(2), 63-73., p.64

[8] Walker, E. A. (1965). *The Great Trek* (5th ed.). Adam & Charles Black, London., p.170

[9] Theal, G. M. (1886). *Boers and Bantu: A History of the Wanderings and Wars of the Emigrant Farmers from their leaving the Cape Colony to the overthrow of Dingan.* Saul Solomon and Co., p.108

[10] Cubbin, A. E. (1988). The English alliance with the Voortrekkers against the Zulus during March and April 1838. *Historia, 33*(2), 63-73., p.66

THE CREATION OF THE BOER IDENTITY

where the men were involved in Dingane's campaign against the Boers. They looted 4,000 head of cattle and took five hundred women and children. Both the missionary societies and the British government ignored this act of forced slavery. During the campaign, the army of the Port Natal English suffered two casualties. One was bitten by a snake and the other had been summarily executed by Cane for attempting to steal cattle before the loot was divided. When they returned to Port Natal, according to Rev Daniel Lindley, "cattle mania rages in the land".[11]

On 5 and 6 April 1838 the first commando sent by the Boers to confront Dingane departed from their laagers (encampments) heading towards uMgungundlovu.[12] This commando consisted of 347 men, including fifteen-year-old Dirkie Uys, the son of Piet Uys. On 10 April 1838 they found themselves in a deep gorge. On the other side of the gorge was a narrow passage leading to uMgungundlovu, with hills on both sides. A Zulu regiment was positioned on each of these hills, and at the end of the gorge, a third impi was concealed in the valley, of which the Boers were unaware. This was the ambush set by Zulu commanders Ndlela kaSompisi and Nzobo kaSobadli, and it proved highly effective. The estimated combined strength of the three

---

[11] Cubbin, A. E. (1988). The English alliance with the Voortrekkers against the Zulus during March and April 1838. *Historia, 33*(2), 63-73., p.67

[12] Uys, I.S. (1979). The Battle of Italeni. *The South African Military History Society, Military History Journal*, 4(5)., The Battle of Italeni - Military History Society - Journal (samilitaryhistory.org)

regiments was between 6000 and 7000 warriors.[13] After moving through a few dongas, the Boers stopped to consider their next course of action. Despite the overwhelming odds and challenging terrain, they decided to launch an attack. It was decided that Uys would attack the more experienced White Shield regiment, which was positioned on the hill in front of them, while Potgieter would attack the regiment on the left hill.

Uys's commando moved incredibly close to the Zulu regiment, so close that Gert Viljoen jokingly asked Uys's second in command, Filed Cornet Koos (Grootvoet) Potgieter, if they were about to engage the Zulus in hand-to-hand combat.[14] Uys and his commando moved to within approximately twenty meters of the Zulus, dismounted from their horses, and simultaneously opened fire. The intense attack lasted only a few minutes but inflicted significant losses upon the Zulu forces. When Pieter Nel, a left-handed Boer sharpshooter, shot the leader of the Zulu warriors in that section, the Zulu force scattered in all directions down the hill.[15] Piet Uys noticed that two Malan brothers, who were pursuing the fleeing Zulus, were riding right into an ambush. He, along with a group of about fifteen men, which included Dawid Malan, Gert, Louis, Pieter, and Willem Nel, Jan and Jacobus Moolman, Jan Landman, Jan de Jager, Jan Meyer,

---

[13] Markram, W. J. (2001). *Die lewe en werk van Petrus Lafras Uys, 1797-1838* [Doctoral dissertation, University of Stellenbosch]., p.261

[14] Uys, I.S. (1979). The Battle of Italeni. *The South African Military History Society, Military History Journal,* 4(5)., The Battle of Italeni - Military History Society - Journal (samilitaryhistory.org)

[15] Markram, W. J. (2001). *Die lewe en werk van Petrus Lafras Uys, 1797-1838* [Doctoral dissertation, University of Stellenbosch]., p.262

Jan Steenkamp, and a Boer named Snyman, rushed to rescue the two Malan brothers.[16] However, as they reached them and were making their way back to the commando, they found themselves cut off and partially surrounded by Zulu warriors.

The Zulus attacked them with throwing assegais, and Uys was struck in the lower back with a spear. He pulled out the spear and tried to fend off the attackers, but due to blood loss, he lost consciousness and fell from his horse. His friends, including his son Dirkie, Jacobus Moolman, Jan Moolman, and Jan Meyer, rushed to his aid. He then asked to be laid down on the ground and informed them that he would die, but they should try to save their own lives. However, Dirkie Uys couldn't leave his father, and he was fatally stabbed alongside his father.[17] Most of the other members of the commando managed to shoot their way out and escape. Landman and a few other Boers attempted to recover their packhorses and baggage that had been taken by the Zulus but were unsuccessful. The commando then tried to reach the camps as quickly as possible. They were pursued by a number of Zulus but managed to drive off the pursuers a few hours later. They could finally dismount at midnight.[18]

---

[16] Uys, I.S. (1979). The Battle of Italeni. *The South African Military History Society, Military History Journal*, 4(5)., The Battle of Italeni - Military History Society - Journal (samilitaryhistory.org)

[17] Markram, W. J. (2001). *Die lewe en werk van Petrus Lafras Uys, 1797-1838* [Doctoral dissertation, University of Stellenbosch]., p.264

[18] Markram, W. J. (2001). *Die lewe en werk van Petrus Lafras Uys, 1797-1838* [Doctoral dissertation, University of Stellenbosch]., p.266

Meanwhile, Potgieter didn't attack simultaneously with Uys. He was more cautious and first scouted the area.[19] Potgieter personally led the initial attack, riding with twenty-five men up the hill to within about fifty meters of the Zulus, where they halted and opened fire. The Zulu immediately launched a large counterattack, forcing Potgieter to retreat. During the retreat, Frans Labuschagne was killed after his horse was wounded in the hip, rendering him immobile.[20] Joseph Kruger was killed when he dismounted and fired on the attacking Zulus.[21] Potgieter's retreating commando struggled to navigate the gullies, but they managed to keep their packhorses with their supplies and ammunition. The pursuing Zulu warriors were hot on their heels. Potgieter and his men repeatedly stopped and fired at the Zulus, resulting in a significant number of casualties among the Zulu.[22]

Ten Boers lost their lives in the Battle of Italeni.[23] The news of the defeat of the commando, now renamed Vlugkommando (the Fleeing Commando), sparked panic in the laagers. What made the defeat at Italeni particularly

---

[19] Markram, W. J. (2001). *Die lewe en werk van Petrus Lafras Uys, 1797-1838* [Doctoral dissertation, University of Stellenbosch]., p.266
[20] Uys, I.S. (1979). The Battle of Italeni. *The South African Military History Society, Military History Journal*, 4(5)., The Battle of Italeni - Military History Society - Journal (samilitaryhistory.org)
[21] Markram, W. J. (2001). *Die lewe en werk van Petrus Lafras Uys, 1797-1838* [Doctoral dissertation, University of Stellenbosch]., p.267
[22] Markram, W. J. (2001). *Die lewe en werk van Petrus Lafras Uys, 1797-1838* [Doctoral dissertation, University of Stellenbosch]., p.269
[23] The Boers who lost their lives in the battle of Italeni were Pieter (Piet) Lafras Uys, Dirk Cornelis Uys (Piet Uys' fifteen-year-old son), Joseph Kruger, Francois Labuachagne, Dawid Malan, Jacobus Malan (son of Dawid Malan), Johannes Malan (son of Dawid Malan), Pieter Nel, Louis Nel (Pieter Nel's brother), and Theunis Nel.

concerning was that, unlike the murders of Retief and the attacks on unsuspecting camps of men, women, and children in the middle of the night during the Great Murder, this defeat occurred in broad daylight in a fair battle between the two forces. One of the most talented Boer military leaders, who had achieved significant successes against the Xhosa in the Cape and Mzilikazi's Ndebele on the highveld, was killed on the battlefield. Amidst the emotions, some branded Potgieter as a coward, after which he and his people departed back across the Drakensberg. From there, he went to Mooirivier, where he, in November 1838, established the first Boer settlement of the future South African Republic (ZAR), Potchefstroom.[24] The Boers in Natal, whose distress and anxiety had now intensified, had to discuss among themselves once again whether to stay in Natal or trek with Potgieter over the Drakensberg. From their perspective, they had legally acquired the land south of the Tugela through their treaty with Dingane, and they had sacrificed so much already. For the sake of those who had already paid the highest price, they couldn't turn their backs on Natal. They still had to get their cattle back from Dingane, but they decided to delay the next commando against Dingane until after the winter, as their horses were in poor condition.[25]

On Friday, 13 April 1838, the English at Port Natal, led by John Cane, set out to attack the Zulus. This force

---

[24] Theal, G. M. (1886). *Boers and Bantu: A History of the Wanderings and Wars of the Emigrant Farmers from their leaving the Cape Colony to the overthrow of Dingan*. Saul Solomon and Co., p.111
[25] Jansen, E. G. (1938). *Die Voortrekkers in Natal.*, https://archive.org/details/VoortrekkersInNatal

consisted of eighteen English settlers, thirty Khoi-Khoi, and three thousand Zulu followers, including four hundred armed with guns. Before the break of dawn on 17 April 1838, they encircled and attacked the military umuzi (kraal) of Ndondakusuka. They rained gunfire on the huts with devastating results, setting the kraal ablaze.[26] Several large Zulu impis, under the command of Prince Mpande with assistance from Nkosi Ndlela, Zulu, and Nongalaza, launched attacks from the northern ridges. The powerful weaponry of the Port Natal army fended off their assaults multiple times, but eventually, Mpande's Zulus broke through, and hand-to-hand combat followed. When John Cane and Robert Biggar were killed, the Port Natal regiments dropped their weapons and made a desperate attempt to flee.[27] Only four English settlers, one of whom was Richard (Dick) King survived the battle,[28] and only two or three Khoi-Khoi and very few of the Port Natal Zulus made it back to the port.[29] The remaining English settlers in the port found refuge aboard the Comet, which was anchored in the bay and later sailed to the Cape Colony. The Zulus then besieged the port settlement, looting and killing as they went until they withdrew on 4 May

---

[26] Cubbin, A. E. (1988). The English alliance with the Voortrekkers against the Zulus during March and April 1838. *Historia, 33*(2), 63-73., p.68
[27] Cubbin, A. E. (1988). The English alliance with the Voortrekkers against the Zulus during March and April 1838. *Historia, 33*(2), 63-73., p.68
[28] The English settlers who died in their battle with Mpande's impis were John Cane, Robert Biggar, John Stubbs, Carl Blanckenberg, Thomas Carden, John Russel, Richard and William Wood, Henry Batt, John or Thomas Campbell, and Richard Lovedale.
[29] Cubbin, A. E. (1988). The English alliance with the Voortrekkers against the Zulus during March and April 1838. *Historia, 33*(2), 63-73., p.69

1838.³⁰ The few settlers, including Alexander Biggar, who chose to stay had to rely on the kindness and limited resources of the struggling Boers for support.³¹

At this juncture, several Boer families made their way to Natal from the Cape. The most notable trek, consisting of thirty-nine families, was led by Karel Pieter Landman.³² Shortly after their arrival, Landman was appointed as head commandant of the Boer laagers in Natal. In early May 1838, he, along with Gerrit Maritz, led a commando to visit Port Natal with the intention of deliberating with the remaining English residents there. They reached Port Natal on 12 May 1838. Maritz aimed to replenish supplies and purchased goods, livestock, gunpowder, and even a ten-pounder cannon from English traders. Landman was there to officially take control of Port Natal on behalf of the Boers. The English welcomed this development and, on 16 May 1838, provided Landman with a written statement confirming their inability to defend themselves against the Zulus.³³ At the request of the English settlers, Landman agreed to relocate his people to

---

³⁰Cubbin, A. E. (1988). The English alliance with the Voortrekkers against the Zulus during March and April 1838. *Historia, 33*(2), 63-73., p.70
³¹ Cubbin, A. E. (1988). The English alliance with the Voortrekkers against the Zulus during March and April 1838. *Historia, 33*(2), 63-73., p.70
³² Theal, G. M. (1886). *Boers and Bantu: A History of the Wanderings and Wars of the Emigrant Farmers from their leaving the Cape Colony to the overthrow of Dingan.* Saul Solomon and Co., p.112
³³ Markram, W. J. (2001). *Die lewe en werk van Petrus Lafras Uys, 1797-1838* [Doctoral dissertation, University of Stellenbosch]., p.281

Port Natal and establish his laager there.[34] Several camps were set up in the vicinity of Port Natal, including Lourens Badenhorst's laager, likely located at Congella, and Jacobus Uys's laager at the mouth of the Umlaas River.[35] All of these laagers were under the leadership of Karel Landman, who positioned himself at the mouth of the Umgeni River. Landman appointed Lourens Badenhorst as the magistrate of Port Natal and William Cowie as Field Cornet.[36]

During the winter of 1838, the Boers in Natal faced dire circumstances. There were days when there was barely enough food to go around, a measles outbreak plagued the people, and the weather was cold, wet, and muddy. Adding to their woes, in July, a fire broke out in one of the camps.[37] The laagers were filled with widows and orphans, and many people were sick and wounded, requiring medical care. Gerrit Maritz was now gravely ill due to malaria. After Piet Retief's murder in uMgungundlovu, Piet Uys's death in the Battle of Italeni, and Maritz's illness, the Boers had now, apart from Potgieter in Potchefstroom, lost all their senior leaders. It was during this time and under these circumstances that the British government threatened them to annex Natal by military force, "to protect the natives in Natal against

---

[34] Theal, G. M. (1886). *Boers and Bantu: A History of the Wanderings and Wars of the Emigrant Farmers from their leaving the Cape Colony to the overthrow of Dingan.* Saul Solomon and Co., p.112
[35] Jansen, E. G. (1938). *Die Voortrekkers in Natal.*,
https://archive.org/details/VoortrekkersInNatal
[36] Theal, G. M. (1886). *Boers and Bantu: A History of the Wanderings and Wars of the Emigrant Farmers from their leaving the Cape Colony to the overthrow of Dingan.* Saul Solomon and Co., p.113
[37] Steyn, J. C. (2016). *Afrikanerjoernaal: ń Vervolgverhaal in 365 episodes.* Firefly Publications (PTY) Ltd., p.113

extermination or slavery by the Boers".[38] By the end of July, several laagers relocated upstream to the Boesmans River, a few kilometres above the present-day town of Estcourt. They settled in a large hollow area on both sides of the river, and these camps became known as Gatslaer (Hole laager) due to their location in a hollow.[39] Gatslaer, consisting of approximately 300 wagons, was composed of three separate laagers. Kommandant Jacobus (Grootvoet) Potgieter, Jan Du Plessis, and Joachim Prinsloo stood on the right bank, in a larger camp known as Dubbellaer (Double laager) and on the left bank were the laagers of Gert Rudolf and Hans de Lange.[40]

On the morning of Monday, 13 August 1838, two cattle herders, Botha and Bothma, alerted the laagers that a large Zulu army was on its way. Hans de Lange quickly organised a commando and rode out to try and halt the Zulus, but they had to quickly retreat to the safety of the laagers. All the Boers reached the laagers safely, except for Hans Froneman, a cattle herder, who was killed by the approaching Zulus in the field. Approximately 10,000 Zulus, led by the experienced commander Ndhlela nTuli, launched an attack on the laagers, but this time, the Boers were forewarned and

---

[38] Napier to Glenelg on 18 May 1838, [Muller, C. F. J. (1946), p.420]; Napier's public statement of 21 May 1838, [Muller, C. F. J. (1946), p.309]
[39] Jansen, E. G. (1938). *Die Voortrekkers in Natal.*, https://archive.org/details/VoortrekkersInNatal
[40] Jansen, E. G. (1938). *Die Voortrekkers in Natal.*, https://archive.org/details/VoortrekkersInNatal

had time to prepare their defences.[41] Anna Elizabeth Steenkamp, a niece of Piet Retief, described the attack as follows: "The Zulu hordes, thousands upon thousands, stretched as far as the eye could reach. It was terrible to see. I cannot describe their numbers; for one would think that all Heathendom had assembled to destroy us."[42] With only seventy-five able-bodied men to defend Gatslaer and their gunpowder damper than they wanted, everyone in the laagers, men, women, and children, had to take up arms or support those who were fighting. nTuli's forces attacked throughout the day, but after multiple failed attempts to breach the laagers, they withdrew beyond the range of the Boer muskets for the night. That night was a night of heightened vigilance for the Boers. They increased the number of sentries and lit lanterns around the laagers to guard against surprise attacks. Meanwhile, just beyond reach, the Zulus feasted on the stolen cattle, and the Boers had to listen to the bellowing and bleating of the wounded animals as they were slaughtered by the Zulus.[43]

Early the following morning, De Lange and his commando once again set out to engage the Zulu army, attempting to lure them within firing range. Just like the

---

[41] The South African Military History Society (n.d.). SOUTH AFRICAN MILITARY HISTORY SOCIETY EASTERN CAPE BRANCH Newsletter / Nuusbrief 108 September 2013: Great Trek Anniversary: Military encounters of the Voortrekkers 6. http://samilitaryhistory.org/13/p13augne.html
[42] Voigt, J. C. (1899). *Fifty years of the history of the Republic in South Africa - 1795-1845 - Vol.II*. E.P. Dutton & Co., p.74
[43] Walker, E. A. (1965). *The Great Trek* (5th ed.). Adam & Charles Black, London., p.177

previous day, they were forced to retreat to the laagers. The 14th unfolded much like the 13th, with relentless Zulu attacks on the laagers, which, despite their determination, they couldn't overrun. On the morning of the 15th, after two days of continuous fighting, nTuli withdrew his forces. However, before he left, he seized most of the Boers' cattle.[44] Reinforcements arrived from Maritz's camp. They left the younger Boers to finish off the Zulu wounded while the men pursued the retreating Zulu army to recover their stolen cattle.[45] They managed to retrieve some livestock, but the retreating Zulu force was too large, and they eventually had to abandon the pursuit. Following the intense two-day battle, in which the Boers lost only one man named Vlotman, they renamed Gatslaer to Veglaer (Fighting Laager). It took them five days to clear the approximately two hundred Zulu bodies from the vicinity of the laager. Subsequently, the Boers from Veglaer disbanded and relocated to Maritz's camp on the Little Tugela River.[46]

The loss of their cattle plunged the Boers further into distress. They were already grappling with illness and a scarcity of food. Gerrit Maritz's health had now deteriorated significantly, and on 23 September 1838, he passed away at the age of forty-two. Maritz had been a cornerstone for the

---

[44] The South African Military History Society (n.d.). South African Military History Siciety Eastern Cape Branch, Newsletter / Nuusbrief 108 September 2013: Great Trek Anniversary: Military encounters of the Voortrekkers 6. http://samilitaryhistory.org/13/p13augne.html
[45] Walker, E. A. (1965). *The Great Trek* (5th ed.). Adam & Charles Black, London., p.178
[46] Jansen, E. G. (1938). *Die Voortrekkers in Natal.*, https://archive.org/details/VoortrekkersInNatal

Boers in Natal and a major source of inspiration for them. His death left even the most resilient among them overwhelmed with despair and profound sadness.[47] The Boers now found themselves in a period of intense adversity and suffering, desperately in need of some positive news. In their darkest hour, Boer messengers did deliver the much-needed good news. Andries Pretorius was preparing to join them and provided precise instructions on the necessary preparations for a commando against Dingane, aimed at reclaiming their cattle and securing their lives in Natalia.

In the meantime, however, efforts were underway to urge the British government to halt the Boers' freedom movement. On 6 March 1838, Sir W. Molesworth, a member of the British House of Commons, initiated the Boer debate in the British parliament: "the most extraordinary events are taking place in the (Cape) colony, which prove the inability and feebleness of the colonial government. A formidable body of Cape Boors (Boers)... carrying along with them their wives and children, sheep, cattle, waggons, household stuff, and farming utensils, have left the colony, and set our authority at defiance!" In reference to resolutions adopted by the Boers at the Caledon River on 14 August 1837, Molesworth added: "their intent is to establish a settlement on the same principles of liberty as those adopted by the United States of America.... They are in open rebellion!"[48] Molesworth told the British parliament: "No one can tell

---

[47] Voigt, J. C. (1899). *Fifty Years of the History of the Republic in South Africa (1795-1845), Volume II*. E.P.Dutton &Co., p.81
[48] Muller, C. F. J. (1946). *Die Britse Owerheid en die Groot Trek* [Doctoral dissertation, University of Stellenbosch]., p.321-p.322

THE CREATION OF THE BOER IDENTITY

what disastrous commotions may be produced by this Tartar horde of wandering Boors (Boers)."[49] Shortly after his appointment, the new governor of the Cape colony, Sir George Napier, engaged in a conversation with a Boer trek party at the Orange River as they were departing the Cape. His objective was to determine if the Boers could be persuaded to return to the Cape if he promised "to do for them all and more than D'Urban had tried to do".[50] However, the Boers told him that they didn't trust the British government and declined the proposition and chose not to return. Napier realised that he couldn't prevent the Boers from trekking, but he was also unwilling to tolerate defiance against the British Empire.

In a letter to Secretary Glenelg on 18 May 1838, Napier recommended that Port Natal be militarily occupied to protect the natives of Natal (the Zulus) from extermination or slavery by the Boers.[51] On 21 May 1838, he issued a public proclamation to the Boers: "His Excellency warns all those who have already emigrated or, may still be disposed to emigrate,... as her Majesty's subjects, that their migration into the interior cannot absolve them from their allegiance as British subjects...".[52] Napier also prohibited the migration of Boers from the Cape to support their fellow Boers in their

---

[49] Muller, C. F. J. (1946). *Die Britse Owerheid en die Groot Trek* [Doctoral dissertation, University of Stellenbosch]., p.166
[50] Walker, E. A. (1965). *The Great Trek* (5th ed.). Adam & Charles Black, London., p.183
[51] Muller, C. F. J. (1946). *Die Britse Owerheid en die Groot Trek* [Doctoral dissertation, University of Stellenbosch]., p.420
[52] Muller, C. F. J. (1946). *Die Britse Owerheid en die Groot Trek* [Doctoral dissertation, University of Stellenbosch]., p.309

THE BOER REPUBLICS

struggle against the Zulus.[53] In October 1838, Napier, in a letter to Glenelg, referred to a letter from E. Parker in which he mentioned the Boers' anticipated commando against Dingane, saying: "I fear the destruction and massacre of human life will be unparalleled."[54] In another letter to Glenelg on 16 October 1838, Napier once again requested that the British government annex Port Natal to cut off all ammunition intended for the Boers: "...by which means alone I can prevent aggressions against the native tribes by these emigrant farmers, and thus to stop further bloodshed."[55] Napier tells Glenelg that by annexing Port Natal, the British nation and the British government will clearly demonstrate to the Boers that they will not tolerate any form of aggression against the natives.[56] By mid-November 1838 Napier dispatched Major Samuel Charters to occupy the Boer port of Port Natal.[57] In his instructions from Napier, Charters was directed to exercise caution in his interactions with the Boers and avoid any actions or expressions that could be interpreted as recognition of them as an independent people.[58] On 20 November 1838, Napier explained his motivation for the occupation of Port Natal to Glenelg: "they (the Boers) would

---

[53] Walker, E. A. (1965). *The Great Trek* (5th ed.). Adam & Charles Black, London., p. 183-p.184
[54] Muller, C. F. J. (1946). *Die Britse Owerheid en die Groot Trek* [Doctoral dissertation, University of Stellenbosch]., p.421
[55] Muller, C. F. J. (1946). *Die Britse Owerheid en die Groot Trek* [Doctoral dissertation, University of Stellenbosch]., p.421
[56] Muller, C. F. J. (1946). *Die Britse Owerheid en die Groot Trek* [Doctoral dissertation, University of Stellenbosch]., p.421
[57] Walker, E. A. (1965). *The Great Trek* (5th ed.). Adam & Charles Black, London., p. 184
[58] Muller, C. F. J. (1946). *Die Britse Owerheid en die Groot Trek* [Doctoral dissertation, University of Stellenbosch]., p.309-310

soon form a separate (sic) colony or Republic, and set the British Nation at defiance!"[59]

Andries Wilhelmus Jacobus Pretorius was the last of the prominent Boer leaders to leave the Cape. Pretorius was a respected and affluent Boer from Graaff-Reinet, standing over two meters tall.[60] He also distinguished himself as a brilliant military and political strategist and organiser.[61] After visiting the Boers on the highveld and in Natal from October 1837 to January 1838, he began advertising various farms and properties in the village of Graaff-Reinet as early as January 1838.[62] During 1838, while converting his properties into cash and preparing for his trek, he continued to promote the migration idea among the Boers who had not yet joined the migration movement. He also made unsuccessful attempts to find a "good (Dutch Reformed) preacher" for the Boers. During Pretorius's earlier visits to the Voortrekkers, he gained a thorough understanding of the opportunities and dangers of the Boers' circumstances in the highveld and Natal.[63] He participated in the Boers' campaign against Mzilikazi alongside Potgieter and Uys and spent time with

---

[59] Muller, C. F. J. (1946). *Die Britse Owerheid en die Groot Trek* [Doctoral dissertation, University of Stellenbosch]., p.312-p.313
[60] Steyn, J. C. (2016). *Afrikanerjoernaal: ń Vervolgverhaal in 365 episodes*. Firefly Publications (PTY) Ltd., p.115
[61] Giliomee, Hermann. Die Afrikaners (Afrikaans Edition). Tafelberg. Kindle Edition., p.158
[62] Muller, C. F. J. (1971). Andries Pretorius se grondverkopings in Graaffreinet, 1837 tot 1838: 'n hersiening van dr. G.S. Preller se gevolgtrekkings. *Historia, 16*(1), 2-8., p.2
[63] Muller, C. F. J. (1971). Andries Pretorius se grondverkopings in Graaffreinet, 1837 tot 1838: 'n hersiening van dr. G.S. Preller se gevolgtrekkings. *Historia, 16*(1), 2-8., p.7

Piet Retief and his people before Retief's fateful second visit to Dingane. He also visited Port Natal, where he purchased a beautiful farm at a reasonable price. Upon receiving news of the devastating events in Natal, he could keenly sense the physical and emotional distress of the people. Pretorius also had a comprehensive understanding of the military needs and security issues of the Boers in Natal. After his land sales, when he left the Cape in September 1838, he thoroughly equipped himself at the supply depot in Graaff-Reinet for the anticipated challenges that awaited him and his people in Natal.[64]

Andries Pretorius left his trek at the Sand River and continued to Natal with sixty able-bodied men. The Boers were delighted when he arrived at the banks of the Tugela River on 22 November 1838. On 28 November 1838, during a Volksraad meeting, he was unanimously elected as the commandant-general for the upcoming commando against Dingane.[65] Revenge was certainly high on most Boers' agenda with this commando because many had lost family members, including children, during Dingane's brutal attacks. The leadership's goal for the commando against Dingane was to recover the cattle and possessions that Dingane had plundered during his attacks on the Boers, without which they could not survive. Pretorius would later send a message to Dingane, offering peace if he returned the Boers' possessions, but Dingane ignored his message. The Boers

---

[64] Muller, C. F. J. (1971). Andries Pretorius se grondverkopings in Graaffreinet, 1837 tot 1838: 'n hersiening van dr. G.S. Preller se gevolgtrekkings. *Historia, 16*(1), 2-8., p.8
[65] Voigt, J. C. (1899). *Fifty Years of the History of the Republic in South Africa 1795-1845 II*. E.P. Dutton & Co., p.85

had been preparing for this commando over the past few months, and over the next few days, Pretorius made sure that every preparation for the commando was meticulously made. He assembled the commando and outlined the strategy for the campaign. The commando consisted of 464 mounted Boers, including the commandants, with 230 coming from the highveld on the other side of the Drakensberg to assist their brethren.[66] Three Englishmen from Port Natal, who had joined the Boers after the Zulus ravaged Port Natal, participated in the commando with sixty of their Zulu refugee followers.[67] The leaders of the commando were Andries Pretorius, Carel Pieter Landman (second-in-command), Pieter Daniel Jacobs, Gerrit Jacobus Potgieter, Hans de Lange, Stephanus Erasmus, Piet Moolman, Louis Nel, Bart Pretorius, and Alexander Biggar, who was in charge of his Zulu followers.[68] Stephanus Maritz, the brother of the late Gerrit Maritz, was left in command of the Boer laagers.[69]

Pretorius had no illusions about the danger the emerging commando posed to the Boers in the face of the overwhelming numerical superiority of the Zulus. He knew it was a massive gamble. In the development of his strategy for the upcoming commando, he drew from the lessons they had learned from their experiences facing Mzilikazi at Veglaer on

---

[66] Jansen, E. G. (1938). *Die Voortrekkers in Natal.*, https://archive.org/details/VoortrekkersInNatal
[67] De Jong, R. C. (1979). Die Slag van Bloedrivier - 16 Desember 1838., *Scientia Militaria, South African Journal of Military Studies*, 9(4)., p.34
[68] Voigt, J. C. (1899). *Fifty Years of the History of the Republic in South Africa 1795-1845 II*. E.P. Dutton & Co., p.87-p.88
[69] Walker, E. A. (1965). *The Great Trek* (5th ed.). Adam & Charles Black, London., p.184

16 October 1836, and their defeat by Dingane at Italeni in April 1838. The hilly terrain of Zululand did not suit the Boers' specialised method of warfare, namely a mobile mounted commando. The strategy for the upcoming battle would combine a mounted commando and a wagon laager commando. The plan was to advance against Dingane's forces with enough wagons, and when they reached the battlefield, they would fight from the fortified laager. Mounted commandos would undertake reconnaissance missions and follow-up operations against the enemy. The commando had sixty-four wagons loaded with supplies, several of which were loaded with ammunition. The Boers were armed with single- or double-barreled muzzle-loading rifles with various calibres, ranging from four to ten-pounders, and they also brought three small cannons.[70] Other provisions mainly included boerbeskuit (rusks), biltong (dried meat), coffee, and tobacco.[71] Two days after being appointed as commandant-general of the Boers, Pretorius led the commando, with the ox-wagons, into Zululand.

In the days when the commando advanced deeper into Zululand, Pretorius assigned Hans de Lange the task of continuous reconnaissance to precisely locate the Zulu forces. Each evening, the commando set up their laager where they could safely spend the night, and Pretorius posted

---

[70] Grobler, J. E. H. (2010). Afrikaner- en Zoeloeperspektiewe op die Slag van Bloedrivier, 16 Desember 1838. *Tydskrif vir Geesteswetenskappe*, *50*(3). pp.363-382, p.371

[71] Voigt, J. C. (1899). *Fifty Years of the History of the Republic in South Africa 1795-1845 II*. E.P. Dutton & Co., p.87

sentinels every night to prevent any surprises.[72] At the same time, Zulu spies continually reported the Boers' progress to Dingane. Pretorius realised that Dingane knew they were on their way because Dingane had lit various fires along the Boers' route. After a few days, Pretorius discussed the idea of a Covenant, a prayer for God's help in overcoming the Zulu forces, with Sarel Cilliers. On 7 December 1838, on the banks of the Wasbank River, Sarel Cilliers offered the Covenant to God in prayer: "Here we stand before the Holy God of Heaven and Earth to make a vow to Him, that if He will protect us and deliver our enemy into our hands, we shall keep the day and date every year as a day of thanksgiving like a Sabbath, and that we shall build a house to His honour wherever it pleases Him, and that we will also tell our children that they should share in it with us as a memorial for future generations. For the honour of His name will be glorified by the fame and the honour of victory to Him." This prayer was repeated every evening until the night before the battle. The Covenant likely had a decisive impact on the campaign, as it bolstered the Boers' self-confidence and spiritual resilience.[73]

The Zulu forces (amabutho) also prepared themselves spiritually for the upcoming battle against the Boers. Special war doctors, known as izinyanga zempi, prepared war medicines (izintelezi) that were sprinkled over the warriors to

---

[72] Grobler, J. E. H. (2010). Afrikaner- en Zoeloeperspektiewe op die Slag van Bloedrivier, 16 Desember 1838. *Tydskrif vir Geesteswetenskappe*, *50*(3). pp.363-382, p.368
[73] Grobler, J. E. H. (2010). Afrikaner- en Zoeloeperspektiewe op die Slag van Bloedrivier, 16 Desember 1838. *Tydskrif vir Geesteswetenskappe*, *50*(3). pp.363-382, p.368

make them "invincible".[74] In their most significant ritual, the warriors gathered at the graves of their deceased kings, chanting praises, and beseeching the kings to assist them in their upcoming battle. To boost their bravery, Dingane ordered the amabutho (warriors) to recite the ancestral songs of his father, Senzangakhona, and perform a war dance at his grave.[75] The Zulu warriors also had to sharpen their assegais on the ancient sharpening stone of Senzangakona. Married Zulu women waved brooms back and forth and placed them on their husbands' sleeping mats in the evenings to ensure their safe return from battle. They also wore their leather skirts inside out until the campaign was over.[76] Now, Dingane ordered his commanders to halt the Boers' march to uMgungundlovu.

The Zulu army of approximately 10,000 to 12,000 warriors was organised by age into specific regiments (amabutho), each led by a hierarchy of commanders (indunas). Dingane's supreme commander was Umdunankulu Ndlela Ntuli, supported by commanders Nzobo kaSobadli (Dambuza) and Nzobo kaSobadli Ntombela.[77] The Zulu

---

[74] Grobler, J. E. H. (2010). Afrikaner- en Zoeloeperspektiewe op die Slag van Bloedrivier, 16 Desember 1838. *Tydskrif vir Geesteswetenskappe*, *50*(3). pp.363-382, p.369
[75] Grobler, J. E. H. (2010). Afrikaner- en Zoeloeperspektiewe op die Slag van Bloedrivier, 16 Desember 1838. *Tydskrif vir Geesteswetenskappe*, *50*(3). pp.363-382, p.369
[76] Grobler, J. E. H. (2010). Afrikaner- en Zoeloeperspektiewe op die Slag van Bloedrivier, 16 Desember 1838. *Tydskrif vir Geesteswetenskappe*, *50*(3). pp.363-382, p.369
[77] Grobler, J. E. H. (2010). Afrikaner- en Zoeloeperspektiewe op die Slag van Bloedrivier, 16 Desember 1838. *Tydskrif vir Geesteswetenskappe*, *50*(3). pp.363-382, p.368

strategy involved arranging the amabutho like the head and horns of a bull. The regiments forming the two horns were typically the younger amabutho, tasked with encircling the enemy to prevent their escape. In the middle, the head of the bull was the older, more experienced amabutho, whose role was to attack the enemy's main force.[78] Each regiment had unique shield colour patterns to distinguish them from one another. Zulu warriors were armed with throwing and stabbing assegais.[79] The younger amabutho were equipped with knobkerries, and their role was to finish off any remaining resistance from the enemy after victory was achieved. Additionally, there were the izindibi or mat carriers, too young to fight, who followed the main force from about a kilometre and were responsible for carrying food and other supplies. However, a new Zulu regiment, the Izitunyisa regiment, mounted on horses and armed with guns, would lead the upcoming battle against Pretorius's command.[80]

On 15 December 1838, when the Boers were positioned at a fork of the Buffalo River, known as Ncome to the Zulus, two of Hans de Lange's scouts reported that the Zulu main force was only about twenty kilometres from their camp. The scouts could clearly distinguish the various

---

[78] Grobler, J. E. H. (2010). Afrikaner- en Zoeloeperspektiewe op die Slag van Bloedrivier, 16 Desember 1838. *Tydskrif vir Geesteswetenskappe*, *50*(3). pp.363-382, p.368

[79] De Jong, R. C. (1979). Die Slag van Bloedrivier - 16 Desember 1838., *Scientia Militaria, South African Journal of Military Studies*, 9(4)., p.34

[80] Grobler, J. E. H. (2010). Afrikaner- en Zoeloeperspektiewe op die Slag van Bloedrivier, 16 Desember 1838. *Tydskrif vir Geesteswetenskappe*, *50*(3). pp.363-382, p.369

regiments of Zulu warriors.[81] Pretorius then rode out with 300 men to the location where the Zulus had been spotted. It appeared that the Zulus were advancing. Sarel Cilliers wanted to attack the Zulus at that point, but in a decision that likely saved the commando, Pretorius refused.[82] Meanwhile, on Pretorius's orders, "Rooi" Piet Moolman, with the approximately 150 men who remained behind set up a defensive laager. The laager was set up in an excellent strategic location.[83] To the south, a dry donga (ditch) of about fourteen feet (4.2m) deep protected the camp, connecting to the Ncome River and forming a seekoeigat (hippopotamus water hole) approximately 1400 yards long, which provided protection on the eastern side of the camp.[84] To the southwest, the wide Gelato Hill, later renamed "Vechtkop," hindered any attack from the west. This allowed the camp to be relatively open to attacks only from the north and, to a lesser extent, from the west, allowing the Boers to concentrate their defence in those directions.[85] By late afternoon on 15 December 1838, the Boer patrols still in the field were recalled to the camp with a loud cannon shot.

---

[81] Grobler, J. E. H. (2010). Afrikaner- en Zoeloeperspektiewe op die Slag van Bloedrivier, 16 Desember 1838. *Tydskrif vir Geesteswetenskappe*, *50*(3). pp.363-382, p.369-p.370

[82] Voigt, J. C. (1899). *Fifty Years of the History of the Republic in South Africa (1795-1845), Volume II*. E.P.Dutton &Co., p.95

[83] Grobler, J. E. H. (2010). Afrikaner- en Zoeloeperspektiewe op die Slag van Bloedrivier, 16 Desember 1838. *Tydskrif vir Geesteswetenskappe*, *50*(3). pp.363-382, p.370

[84] De Jong, R. C. (1979). Die Slag van Bloedrivier - 16 Desember 1838., *Scientia Militaria, South African Journal of Military Studies*, *9*(4)., p.30

[85] Grobler, J. E. H. (2010). Afrikaner- en Zoeloeperspektiewe op die Slag van Bloedrivier, 16 Desember 1838. *Tydskrif vir Geesteswetenskappe*, *50*(3). pp.363-382, p.370

Before daybreak on the morning of 16 December 1838, the Boers heard the Zulu army advancing to attack them.[86] The Zulus, led by Dingane's chief commander, Umdunankulu Ndlela Ntuli, assisted by Nzobo kaSobadli (Dambuza) and Nzobo kaSobadli Ntombela,[87] arrived from the east, crossing the plain beyond the Ncome River. The White Shield regiments, led by Nzobo kaSobadli Ntombela, took positions on the other side of the river, while the Black and Red Shields crossed the Ncome at the drifts and encircled the laager.[88] With daylight, the Boers could see their laager surrounded by thousands of Zulu warriors, a sight described by some Boers as intimidating, awe-inspiring and even beautiful.[89] At daybreak, the Red and Black Shields, under Nzobo kaSobadli (Dambuza), launched their initial mass assaults on the laager from the northwest and the north.[90] The Boers withheld their fire until the Zulus approached the wagon wall, then opened fire, causing havoc among the Zulu attackers. Some Zulu assailants managed to advance as close as ten meters from the laager but could not break through the Boer defences despite their fearless

---

[86] De Jong, R. C. (1979). DIE SLAG VAN BLOEDRIVIER - 16 DESEMBER 1838. *Scientia Militaria, South African Journal of Military Studies*, 9(4)., p.34

[87] Grobler, J. E. H. (2010). Afrikaner- en Zoeloeperspektiewe op die Slag van Bloedrivier, 16 Desember 1838. *Tydskrif vir Geesteswetenskappe*, 50(3). pp.363-382, p.368

[88] De Jong, R. C. (1979). Die Slag van Bloedrivier - 16 Desember 1838. *Scientia Militaria, South African Journal of Military Studies*, 9(4)., p.34

[89] Cory, G. E. (1926). *The Rise of South Africa, Vol.IV*. Longman's, Green & Co., p.76

[90] De Jong, R. C. (1979). Die Slag van Bloedrivier - 16 Desember 1838. *Scientia Militaria, South African Journal of Military Studies*, 9(4)., p.34

assaults.[91] The Zulu strategy was to exhaust the defenders through continuous assaults until the White Shield regiments under Ndhlela would come into action to finally break the laager's resistance.[92] It appeared that this strategy was beginning to succeed, but it was a tactical error to attack the laager in regiments rather than launching an overwhelming assault in unison. The Boer cannon fire effectively neutralised the advantage of the Zulus' overwhelming numbers.[93] The Zulus persisted with their tactics and launched three major assaults on the laagers.

When the Boers managed to repel the third attack after about two hours, Pretorius realised that he needed to change the course of the battle. If it continued in this manner, the Boers could run out of ammunition. He then ordered the main gate of the camp to be opened and personally led a mounted commando from the camp to attack the Zulus directly.[94] This move succeeded in engaging the White Shields, who had crossed the river at the northern drift to attack the laager. When the veteran regiments of the White Shields entered the battle prematurely, the Zulu generals' battle plan fell apart.[95] A Boer commando from the western

---

[91] Grobler, J. E. H. (2010). Afrikaner- en Zoeloeperspektiewe op die Slag van Bloedrivier, 16 Desember 1838. *Tydskrif vir Geesteswetenskappe*, *50*(3). pp.363-382, p.373
[92] De Jong, R. C. (1979). Die Slag van Bloedrivier - 16 Desember 1838. *Scientia Militaria, South African Journal of Military Studies*, 9(4)., p.34
[93] Cory, G. E. (1926). *The Rise of South Africa, Vol.IV*. Longman's, Green & Co., p.76
[94] Cory, G. E. (1926). *The Rise of South Africa, Vol.IV*. Longman's, Green & Co., p.76
[95] De Jong, R. C. (1979). Die Slag van Bloedrivier - 16 Desember 1838. *Scientia Militaria, South African Journal of Military Studies*, 9(4)., p.35

riverbank under Bart Pretorius halted the White Shields's advance. The deadly fire from the Boers created confusion among the dense masses of Zulu soldiers, causing them to flee. Some of those attempting to escape across the river were cut down by the dozens. Many Zulus who sought refuge in a donga became trapped, unable to move or climb out, and there, the short-range rifle fire of the Boers inflicted heavy casualties. The Boers then pursued the fleeing Zulus in mounted groups, which sealed the victory for the Boers.[96] Around 3,000 Zulu lay dead around the camp, in the donga, and along the riverbanks. Three Boers were wounded in the battle, including Pretorius himself, who suffered a wound in his left hand. Gerrit Raath sustained a more serious side wound but recovered, and Philip Fourie was wounded in the leg.[97]

In the meantime, on 4 December 1838, shortly after Pretorius and his commando departed for their campaign against Dingane, three British ships landed soldiers in Port Natal.[98] The British military, under the command of Major Samuel Charters and including Theophilus Shepstone as an interpreter with the Zulus, took possession of Port Natal. Governor Napier's objectives with this military occupation, as stated in his letter to State Secretary Glenelg on 16

---

[96] Grobler, J. E. H. (2010). Afrikaner- en Zoeloeperspektiewe op die Slag van Bloedrivier, 16 Desember 1838. *Tydskrif vir Geesteswetenskappe*, *50*(3). pp.363-382, p.374
[97] Grobler, J. E. H. (2010). Afrikaner- en Zoeloeperspektiewe op die Slag van Bloedrivier, 16 Desember 1838. *Tydskrif vir Geesteswetenskappe*, *50*(3). pp.363-382, p.376
[98] Walker, E. A. (1965). *The Great Trek* (5th ed.). Adam & Charles Black, London., p.185

October 1838, were to block the delivery of gunpowder and essential supplies to the Boers to "prevent aggression against the native tribes (the Zulus) by the Emigrant Farmers", and to prevent the Boers from establishing an independent government.[99] The occupation of the Port by Governor Napier was deeply unsettling to the Boers, but they stood alone. According to G.M. Theal, even the Cape Afrikaners supported the governor's taking possession of the Port, with the hope that Britain might not only occupy the area but permanently annex it to "provide for the safety and welfare of the Emigrants".[100] At the port, Major Charters seized a large quantity of ammunition belonging to the Boers from stores of English traders. This ammunition would only be returned if the Boers accepted the authority of Her Majesty's Government and agreed to use it solely for self-defence when under attack.[101] The Boers refused these terms. On 12 December 1838, Stephanus Maritz received a letter from Major Charters, informing Pretorius to stand down and not engage Dingane. Maritz, however, decided to withhold this information from Pretorius until after the expedition against Dingane. Instead, Maritz suggested to Charters that an impartial inquiry should investigate the reasons behind the British military presence in Natal.[102] On 16 December 1838,

---

[99] Theal, G. M. (1886). *Boers and Bantu: A History of the Wanderings and Wars of the Emigrant Farmers from their leaving the Cape Colony to the overthrow of Dingan.* Saul Solomon and Co., p.119
[100] Theal, G. M. (1886). *Boers and Bantu: A History of the Wanderings and Wars of the Emigrant Farmers from their leaving the Cape Colony to the overthrow of Dingan.* Saul Solomon and Co., p.119
[101] Cory, G. E. (1926). *The Rise of South Africa, Vol. IV.* Longman's, Green & Co., p.80
[102] Walker, E. A. (1965). *The Great Trek* (5th ed.). Adam & Charles Black, London., p.185

THE CREATION OF THE BOER IDENTITY

the very day that the Boers were fighting for their lives at Blood River, the British hoisted their flag at Port Natal.[103]

On Christmas Day of 1838, news of the commando's victory over Dingane reached the camps. People were initially hesitant to believe the news, but on 3 January 1839, when they received a written report from Andries Pretorius about the events at Blood River, they were overjoyed, and Pretorius's commando became known as the "Wenkommando" (Winning Commando).[104] Despite this triumph, the Wenkommando's mission was far from over. They had not yet recovered the Boers' cattle, and Dingane still possessed the firearms of Retief and his men, as well as those looted during the Bloukrans massacres. Pretorius now marched towards uMgungundlovu. When the commando reached uMgungundlovu, they found it abandoned and burnt down. On 21 December 1838, the Wenkommando set up camp near the Hill of Execution, KwaMatiwane, where Retief and his party were slain. They began the solemn task of gathering and burying the bones of their people who had been murdered there.[105] They identified the individuals by their clothing. In the leather pouch that Retief carried, Evert Potgieter discovered the title deed for the first Boer Republic

---

[103] Cory, G. E. (1926). *The Rise of South Africa, Vol. IV*. Longman's, Green & Co., p.79

[104] Grobler, J. E. H. (2010). Afrikaner- en Zoeloeperspektiewe op die Slag van Bloedrivier, 16 Desember 1838. *Tydskrif vir Geesteswetenskappe, 50*(3). pp.363-382, p.376

[105] Cory, G. E. (1926). *The Rise of South Africa, Vol. IV*. Longman's, Green & Co., p.78

THE BOER REPUBLICS

- the contract bearing Dingane's mark, granting the entire south of Natal to the Boers and their descendants.[106]

On the morning of 30 December 1838, a mounted commando of 250 men, led by Carel Landman with Hans de Lange as second-in-command, set out towards the White Umfolozi River. The war council of the Wenkommando decided that Pretorius, due to the burden of the assegai wound in his hand, couldn't lead the commando. The patrol aimed to locate Dingane and his forces and recover stolen Boer cattle.[107] After crossing a mountain pass and the river, suddenly, like at Italeni, between 7000 and 10000 of Dingane's soldiers appeared on the hills on both sides of the ravine. Zulu scouts had trailed the commando, and their army's leader had skilfully set up an ambush for the Boers. To the south of the commando, Zulu regiments formed a half-circle, blocking any escape, and to the north, large masses of Zulus converged on them. A skirmish broke out, lasting about half an hour when Landman told Hans de Lange that they should move up the hill to fight the Zulus from behind the large boulders. De Lange was outraged by this plan which would mean certain death because they would not be able to hold out against the overwhelming numbers of the Zulus for long. He then took charge of the battle and shouted:

---

[106] Cory, G. E. (1926). *The Rise of South Africa, Vol. IV*. Longman's, Green & Co., p.78
[107] Voigt, J. C. (1899). *Fifty Years of the History of the Republic in South Africa (1795-1845), Volume II*. E.P. Dutton &Co., p.106-p.107

THE CREATION OF THE BOER IDENTITY

"Forward, men, forward! He who loves me follows me!"[108] [109]

With his men closely behind, De Lange charged towards a thin part of the Zulu line where they were converging before them, firing from the saddle, causing heavy casualties among the Zulus, until they reached the open plain. As the battle continued, smaller groups of horsemen repeatedly broke off to attack the pursuing Zulus. These manoeuvres kept on for hours. The main body of the Zulu regiments then cut across the plain to attack the Boers who were now turning westwards to circle around the Zulus and get back to the river. The situation was now becoming a race to cross the river. When the Boers crossed the river, several horses became stuck in quicksand at the drifts, where a large number of warriors caught up with them. Hand-to-hand combat ensued at certain points as the Boers made their way across the river. Bart Pretorius's horse was killed under him, forcing him to fight on foot until he managed to seize a riderless horse moving through the stream, with which he eventually escaped. When they reached the other side, the main body of Boers headed for the laager, with a rear guard of about twenty-five to fifty Boers holding off the Zulus as much as possible. Halfway back to the laager from where they left the morning, a small detachment of Boers, sent by Pretorius, joined them to assist in their retreat. After a gruelling seven-hour running battle of almost constant

---

[108] This description of the Battle of the White Umfolozi is a condensed version of Voigt's account, which precisely reflects the memories of Commandant J.H. Visser, who participated in this battle and dictated it to him on 25 May 1881.
[109] Voigt, J. C. (1899). *Fifty Years of the History of the Republic in South Africa (1795-1845), Volume II*. E.P. Dutton &Co., p.109

fighting, the Zulus eventually broke off their attack. J.H. Visser remarked: "Were it not for Hans Dons (the nickname for Commandant Johan De Lange), we had all been killed that day."[110] During the Battle of the Wit Umfolozi, five Boers lost their lives: Gerrit van Staden, Barend Bester, Nicholas le Roux, Marthinus Goosen, and Johannes Oosthuizen. Alexander Bigger, an Englishman who had already lost his two sons in Natal, along with five of his Zulu followers, also fell on the side of the Boers.[111]

The Wenkommando stayed in their laager for another two days to allow their horses time to recover, after which they returned to the laagers at the Tugela. They reached the Boer laagers on 9 January 1839.[112] The Battle of Blood River did not break the Zulus' power; that would be done by the British when they put an end to an independent Zulu kingdom with the Battle of Ulundi on 4 July 1879. Blood River didn't even break Dingane's power; that would be done by Mpande with the Battle of Maqongqo on 29 January 1840. However, what Blood River did accomplish was delivering a clear message to Dingane that attacking the Boer laagers wasn't a good idea. After all the hardships they experienced in 1838, the victory at Blood River gave the Boers in Natal confidence and hope for the future, allowing them to dismantle their cramped, unhealthy laagers and spread out a

---

[110] Voigt, J. C. (1899). *Fifty Years of the History of the Republic in South Africa (1795-1845), Volume II*. E.P. Dutton &Co., p.110
[111] WikiTree. Project: Voortrekkers. Retrieved September 13, 2023, from https://www.wikitree.com/wiki/Project:Voortrekkers
[112] Cory, G. E. (1926). *The Rise of South Africa, Vol. IV*. Longman's, Green & Co., p.79

bit.[113] However, they couldn't be free to develop their new land as long as Dingane still possessed their cattle and other property and posed a threat from north of the Tugela. They also wouldn't be free to build their new state while British troops were in Port Natal.

The Volksraad, (Citizen Council) sent Carel Landman to engage in talks with Major Samuel Charters. On 14 January 1839, Landman met with Charters and explained to him that the Boers did not recognise British authority but desired amicable relations with the British government. He clarified to Charters that, based on their agreement with Dingane brokered by Piet Retief, the Boers now lawfully owned Natal, including Port Natal.[114] Despite efforts, the talks were unproductive, and Charters refused to return the Boers' ammunition. After the British troops had built a camp, which they called Fort Victoria, Major Charters returned to Cape Town, leaving Captain Jervis in command.[115] During his overland journey back to the Cape Colony, Charters passed through areas with Boer encampments. He later documented the following observations about the Boers in Natal: "...there existed every indication of squalid poverty and wretchedness;... families who, a short time previously, had been living in ease and comfort in the Colony, now reduced to poverty and misery." "They bore up against these calamities with wonderful firmness, however,... showed no

---

[113] Walker, E. A. (1965). *The Great Trek* (5th ed.). Adam & Charles Black, London., p.189

[114] Cory, G. E. (1926). *The Rise of South Africa, Vol. IV*. Longman's, Green & Co., p.79

[115] Cory, G. E. (1926). *The Rise of South Africa, Vol. IV*. Longman's, Green & Co., p.90

inclination to return (to the Cape colony)..." "All they now desired from it (the British government) was to leave them to their own resources, and not molest them again." "This spirit of dislike to the English sway was remarkably dominant amongst the women... who... rejected with scorn the idea of returning to the Colony."[116]

Meanwhile, Pretorius went to fetch his trek party that he had left at the Sandriver in Winburg in November 1838 before the campaign against Dingane. However, he first visited Henrik Potgieter in Potchefstroom. During his visit to Potgieter, he successfully resolved lingering tensions that arose after the Italeni debacle. He even secured a promise from Potgieter to collaborate with the Natalia Volksraad. Despite Potgieter's commitment to work with the Natalia Volksraad, their relationship did not substantially improve over the next few months. Potgieter was concerned about the presence of British troops in Port Natal, and he feared that a constitutional union of the regions could jeopardise the entire United Boer Republic if Britain were to annex Natal.[117] While at the Sandriver, Pretorius sent a certified copy of Retief's contract with Dingane in a letter to Sir Benjamin D'Urban on 24 February 1839, to demonstrate the Boers' peaceful intentions in Natal. In his letter, Pretorius wrote: "We also notice that the (British) government threatens us much, yet in the first place we know that all proclaim that

---

[116] Voigt, J. C. (1899). *Fifty Years of the History of the Republic in South Africa (1795-1845), Volume II*. E.P. Dutton &Co., p.130

[117] Storm, J.M.G. (1989). Die konvensie van Sandrivier as die afsluiting van die Groot Trek. *HTS Teologiese Studies / Theological Studies*, *45*(3), 680-695., p.685

every man should be free ... and we know very well that we are a freeborn people, and that we have a right to Natal, which was acquired not only by means of free purchase but for which we had to pay the price of suffering indescribable cruelty...".[118] Pretorius then, with his trek of 138 people, which included his wife, seven of his eight children, and twenty-three other families along with their belongings in sixty-eight wagons, settled in their new land.[119]

Piet Greyling, stepson of Piet Retief, took command of the Retief-laager and relocated it to the Pietermaritzburg area in July 1838. Initially, the Boers referred to the area as "Boschejemans Randt" due to the presence of San people in the surrounding hills. In October 1838, Greyling established the town and named it Pietermaritzburg, in honour of Piet Retief and Gerrit Maritz.[120] Greyling and his people laid out plots, cultivated gardens, and sowed farmland there.[121] They also constructed an extensive canal system from the town's main stream to supply water to the cultivated plots. In February 1839, the Volksraad, which also served as the municipal council for Pietermaritzburg, issued six regulations to the owners of the plots. Article four stipulated that plots had to be planted within two months of purchase, and Article five required houses to be built at the front of the plots, in

---

[118] Du Toit, A., & Giliomee, H. (1983). Afrikaner Political Thought. Volume 1: 1780-1850. University of California Press, p.216-p.217
[119] Botha, J. P. (2008). Ons Geskiedenis (1st ed.). J.P. Botha., p. 112
[120] Haswell, R. F., & Brann, R. W. (1984). Voortrekker Pieter Mauritz Burg. Contree: Journal for South African Urban and Regional History, 16, 16-19, p.16
[121] Jansen, E. G. (1938). *Die Voortrekkers in Natal.*, https://archive.org/details/VoortrekkersInNatal

line with each other.[122] Greyling specified that the plots should measure fifty by 150 feet. These measurements later became the standard for other Boer towns such as Weenen, Utrecht, and Lydenburg. Greyling might have been hasty in laying out the plots in Pietermaritzburg, as their lengths varied between 460 and 479 feet.[123] In March 1839, Andries Pretorius likely exaggerated to attract more Boers from the eastern Cape Colony to Natalia when he referred to Pieter Maritz Burgh as "a large, pleasant, water-rich village... with 300 beautiful plots already surveyed and planted... 50 miles from the Bay... and more beautiful than any town in the colony that I know of."[124]

After the Battle of Blood River, Dingane worked on rebuilding his forces for the ongoing war on the Boers. To get resources, he attempted to conquer the southern Swazi people of KwaNgwane but his Dlambedlu and Zinyosi regiments were defeated by the Swazis.[125] On 1 January 1839, Dingane asked his brother, Prince Mpande, to provide and lead his strongest Hlomendlini (home guards) regiment

---

[122] Haswell, R. F., & Brann, R. W. (1984). Voortrekker Pieter Mauritz Burg. Contree: Journal for South African Urban and Regional History, 16, 16-19, p.16
[123] Haswell, R. F., & Brann, R. W. (1984). Voortrekker Pieter Mauritz Burg. Contree: Journal for South African Urban and Regional History, 16, 16-19, p.17
[124] Haswell, R. F., & Brann, R. W. (1984). Voortrekker Pieter Mauritz Burg. Contree: Journal for South African Urban and Regional History, 16, 16-19, p.17
[125] Shamase, M. Z. (1999). *The reign of King Mpande and his relations with the Republic of Natalia and its successor, the British colony of Natal* [Doctoral dissertation, University of Zululand]., p.76

in the upcoming expeditions.[126] However, Mpande, tired of Dingane's executions and massacres, refused.[127] Frustrated by his army's defeat at Blood River and his failed Swazi campaigns, Dingane thought about forging closer ties with the British at Port Natal. On 23 February 1839, Dingane's representatives met with Captain Jervis at the port. When Jervis pushed for peace talks with the Boers, they told him that Dingane was open to any terms the British might dictate for peace with the Boers, but he hoped that the English would assist him in driving the Boers out of the country.[128] The Boers' Volksraad agreed to negotiations with Dingane but rejected British mediation.

On 26 March 1839, Pretorius met with Zulu delegates near present-day Durban to discuss peace terms. On 14 May 1839, they signed a peace agreement specifying the following conditions: the Zulus would return Boer horses, sheep, guns, and 19,000 cattle they had captured; free neighbouring tribes under their control; no Zulu or Boer could cross the Tugela without permission; and the Boers would help the Zulus in defensive wars.[129] The Volksraad ratified the deal on 24 May 1839. Following an earlier message from Dingane, the Boers left to collect their

---

[126] Shamase, M. Z. (1999). *The reign of King Mpande and his relations with the Republic of Natalia and its successor, the British colony of Natal* [Doctoral dissertation, University of Zululand]., p.76
[127] Maphalala, S. J. (1980). Zulu relations with the whites during the nineteenth century: A broad perspective. *Historia, 25*(1), 19-27., p.21
[128] Cory, G. E. (1926). *The Rise of South Africa, Vol. IV*. Longman's, Green & Co., p.87
[129] Walker, E. A. (1965). *The Great Trek* (5th ed.). Adam & Charles Black, London., p.195

belongings on the same day.[130] The Boers assembled a commando of 334 mounted men under Pretorius, and a small delegation, including William Cowie, J.A. van Niekerk, and J.P. Roscher, went ahead to Dingane's new place to take their belongings in possession.[131] However, the Boer delegation only received 1,300 cattle, 400 sheep, 52 guns, and 43 saddles, considerably less than the 19,300 cattle they had initially agreed on.[132] Cowie wasn't sure if Dingane fully understood how many cattle were expected from him.[133]

Dingane was furious when Mpande refused military service and decided to assassinate him.[134] Ndlela ka Sompisi Ntuli, Dingane's key general and Prime Minister, who was also the inkosi of the Ntuli clan, informed Prince Mpande of Dingane's plans to assassinate him. Ndlela also informed Mpanda of Dingane's initiative to build stronger ties with the British for support against the Boers and he advised Mpande to go to the Boers for military assistance to overthrow Dingane.[135] In September 1839, with 17,000 of his people and 25,000 cattle, Mpanda crossed the Tugela and

---

[130] Geyser, O. (1967). Die lastige bure op die Noordgrens. *Historia*, *12*(4), 225-233., p.231
[131] Voigt, J. C. (1899). *Fifty Years of the History of the Republic in South Africa (1795-1845), Volume II*. E.P. Dutton &Co., p.131
[132] Cory, G. E. (1926). *The Rise of South Africa, Vol. IV*. Longman's, Green & Co., p.89
[133] Walker, E. A. (1965). *The Great Trek* (5th ed.). Adam & Charles Black, London., p.197
[134] Shamase, M. Z. (1999). *The reign of King Mpande and his relations with the Republic of Natalia and its successor, the British colony of Natal* [Doctoral dissertation, University of Zululand]., p.76
[135] Shamase, M. Z. (1999). *The reign of King Mpande and his relations with the Republic of Natalia and its successor, the British colony of Natal* [Doctoral dissertation, University of Zululand]., p.76

established his Mahambehlula kraal on the banks of the Thongathi River, about thirty miles north of Port Natal.[136] The first Boer he met when he entered Natalia was Hans de Lange, who was hunting hippopotamus on the banks of the Tugela River. De Lange then informed the Volksraad of Mpande's presence in their territory and of his loyalty to the Boers.[137] The Boers recognised the strategic advantage of friendship and an alliance with Mpande in safeguarding against potential Zulu invasions from across the Tugela River.[138] The Volksraad met with Mpanda on 15 October 1839 and the alliance between him and the Boers was officially formed. Thereafter, on 21 October 1839, a Boer delegation under the landdrost (magistrate) of Congella, Frans Roos, visited Mpande's temporary kraal where Roos performed a ceremony to seal the alliance when he planted the tricolour of the young Republic of Natalia and declared Mpanda as the "Reigning Prince of the emigrant Zulus".[139]

The British government knew that the alliance between the Boers and Mpande would lead to war in Zululand. Nevertheless, in an apparent renunciation of their claim to Boer's allegiance to the British Crown, they

---

[136] Cory, G. E. (1926). *The Rise of South Africa, Vol. IV*. Longman's, Green & Co., p.98

[137] Shamase, M. Z. (1999). *The reign of King Mpande and his relations with the Republic of Natalia and its successor, the British colony of Natal* [Doctoral dissertation, University of Zululand]., p.100

[138] Shamase, M. Z. (1999). *The reign of King Mpande and his relations with the Republic of Natalia and its successor, the British colony of Natal* [Doctoral dissertation, University of Zululand]., p.100

[139] Geyser, O. (1967). Die lastige bure op die Noordgrens. *Historia, 12*(4), 225-233., p.231

withdrew their troops from Port Natal in December 1839.[140] The Union Jack was lowered on Christmas Day, and the British left Port Natal, ending their blockade of essential supplies, which caused great distress and deprivation among the Boers in Natal.[141] The Boers were finally free to establish their own Boer Republic based on their values of freedom, equality, and brotherhood.[142] Dingane, however, continued to pose an existential threat to the Boers, and the presence of his spies around Boer settlements increased the urgency of the Boers' preparations and the support they received from their brothers on the other side of the Drakensberg.[143] Mpande, whose support base continued to grow, also prepared his forces for the upcoming campaign against Dingane.[144] On 4 January 1840, the Volksraad instructed Pretorius to demand from Dingane the cattle agreed upon in their peace agreement, which now somehow doubled from 20,000 to 40,000. These instructions were given to Pretorius in a document containing twenty-two articles prescribing rules for a code of conduct, and it established, according to Boer tradition, a war council within the commando to which even Pretorius himself would be subjected to.[145] The Boer

---

[140] Cory, G. E. (1926). *The Rise of South Africa, Vol. IV*. Longman's, Green & Co., p.103

[141] Voigt, J. C. (1899). *Fifty Years of the History of the Republic in South Africa (1795-1845), Volume II*. E.P. Dutton &Co., p.137

[142] Cory, G. E. (1926). *The Rise of South Africa, Vol. IV*. Longman's, Green & Co., p.103

[143] Voigt, J. C. (1899). *Fifty Years of the History of the Republic in South Africa (1795-1845), Volume II*. E.P. Dutton &Co., p.138

[144] Cory, G. E. (1926). *The Rise of South Africa, Vol. IV*. Longman's, Green & Co., p.103

[145] Jansen, E. G. (1938). *Die Voortrekkers in Natal.*, https://archive.org/details/VoortrekkersInNatal

THE CREATION OF THE BOER IDENTITY

commando, consisting of 400 men and sixty wagons, left Pietermaritzburg on 14 January 1840, heading towards Dingane's new location at the Ivuna River. Mpande accompanied Pretorius in his commando, approaching Dingane from the northwest, while his own forces, an army of 10,000 men led by Nongalaza ka Nondela Mnyandu, approached Dingane from a southeastern direction.[146] On 21 January 1840, the commando crossed the Tugela River.

When Dingane learned about the alliance between Mpande and the Boers, he sent two unarmed emissaries, Dambuza Ntombela (known as Nzobo) and Sikhombazana, to Pretorius to negotiate a new peace treaty with the Boers.[147] Mpande accused Dambuza of being the mastermind behind Dingane's killings, including the massacres of Boer women and children at Bloukrans and Moordspruit, as well as the murders of Piet Retief and his men, and insisted that they be charged.[148] In response, Pretorius had the two men arrested. The Boers regularly sent out scouts and set up a defensive laager each night for secure overnight stays, much like during the Wen Commando. On 29 January 1840, they crossed the Buffalo River and set up laager on the banks of the Blood River, where they previously defeated Dingane. That same day, messengers from Mpande, approaching the laager under

---

[146] Jansen, E. G. (1938). *Die Voortrekkers in Natal.*, https://archive.org/details/VoortrekkersInNatal
[147] Shamase, M. Z. (1999). *The reign of King Mpande and his relations with the Republic of Natalia and its successor, the British colony of Natal* [Doctoral dissertation, University of Zululand]., p.101
[148] Shamase, M. Z. (1999). *The reign of King Mpande and his relations with the Republic of Natalia and its successor, the British colony of Natal* [Doctoral dissertation, University of Zululand]., p.101

a white flag with the letters VR for Volksraad to identify themselves, brought news that Mpande's army had skirmishes with the enemy and had now come face to face with Dingane's forces. Pretorius asked Mpande to hold his forces back until the commando could join up with them. The Boers would, however, have no part in the battle between Mpande's forces and that of Dingane, led by Ndlela ka Sompisi Ntuli, as the Battle of Maqongqo had already commenced.[149] In a fierce and bloody fight, two of Dingane's three regiments were wiped out,[150] and the other regiment defected to Nongalazana due to bitterness among the Zulu ranks.[151] On 31 January 1840, near the Black Mfolozi River, Dambuza and Sikhombazana appeared before a court-martial with Pretorius as judge and Mpande as prosecutor.[152] Mpande gave the following evidence in the court-martial: " It was the same Dambuza who urged the king to murder your Governor Retief and his men, as well as the women and children of your nation."[153] After Dumbuza admitted guilt, they were found guilty and sentenced to death. Although the two accused were tried and executed by a court and firing squad of the Boers, it is clear that Mpande himself, made the decisions in this case, as confirmed by his praises:

---

[149] Shamase, M. Z. (1999). *The reign of King Mpande and his relations with the Republic of Natalia and its successor, the British colony of Natal* [Doctoral dissertation, University of Zululand]., p.101

[150] Cory, G. E. (1926). *The Rise of South Africa, Vol. IV*. Longman's, Green & Co., p.107

[151] Maphalala, S. J. (1980). Zulu relations with the whites during the nineteenth century : A broad perspective. *Historia, 25*(1), 19-27., p.21

[152] Cory, G. E. (1926). *The Rise of South Africa, Vol. IV*. Longman's, Green & Co., p.108

[153] Voigt, J. C. (1899). *Fifty Years of the History of the Republic in South Africa (1795-1845), Volume II*. E.P. Dutton &Co., p.150

"Usongo lwensimbi yakoNdikidi,
[An iron coil of Ndikidi]
Elidli uDambuza beno Sikhombazana.
[That ate Dambuza and Sikhombazana]
lnzingelezi kaNdaba,
[The entanglement of Ndaba]
Emabal' azizinge,
[With multi-coloured appeal]"[154]

Pretorius received information that Dingane had fled to Swaziland. On 5 February 1840, a commando of 250 men under Commandant Lombaard crossed the White Umfolozi in pursuit of Dingane.[155] The commando reached the Pongola River on 8 February 1840 but learned that Dingane had fled with a small following across the Pongolo towards the Lebombo mountains in Swaziland five days earlier.[156] Dingane was later killed by the Swazis. By that time, the commando had lost several horses due to horse sickness in the area, and Lombard decided to return to the laager.[157] Meanwhile, on 5 February 1840, in accordance with Zulu tradition, Mpande was sworn in as the new Zulu king. In this Zulu ceremony, Mpande was sworn in as the king of the Zulus in the presence of Klwana Buthelezi and Maphitha ka

---

[154] Shamase, M. Z. (1999). *The reign of King Mpande and his relations with the Republic of Natalia and its successor, the British colony of Natal* [Doctoral dissertation, University of Zululand]., p.102-p.103

[155] Cory, G. E. (1926). *The Rise of South Africa, Vol. IV*. Longman's, Green & Co., p.109

[156] Jansen, E. G. (1938). *Die Voortrekkers in Natal.*, https://archive.org/details/VoortrekkersInNatal

[157] Cory, G. E. (1926). *The Rise of South Africa, Vol. IV*. Longman's, Green & Co., p.110

THE BOER REPUBLICS

Sojiyisa, the most powerful chiefs in Zululand (KwaZulu), who swore allegiance to Mpande.[158] On 10 February 1840, on the banks of the Black Umfolozi, in a Boer ceremony, Mpande took an oath before the Boers pledging that he would rule his kingdom in peace and a cordial relationship with the Boers as his southern neighbours. Pretorius expressed his satisfaction to Mpande concerning the conduct and bravery of Mpande's impi (army) and his people.[159] After a twenty-one-gun salute, Pretorius proclaimed Mpande king of the Zulus.

On 14 February 1840, the Boers raised the national flag of the Republic of Natalia in the presence of King Mpande and his headmen. Mpande acknowledged the borders of the Boer Republic of Natalia, from the Tugela River to the Umzimvubu River, as agreed upon between Piet Retief and Dingane and he accepted the vassal status of the area north of the Tugela River to the Black Mfolosi River.[160] Andries Pretorius issued a proclamation outlining the borders of the vassal territory of Natalia. According to this proclamation, the borders were: "All the land from the Tugela River to the Black Mfolozi River; that our boundary henceforth running from the sea along the Black Mfolozi River, where it passes through the Double Mountains, near its origin and then along the Rand Mountains, in a similar

---

[158] Shamase, M. Z. (1999). *The reign of King Mpande and his relations with the Republic of Natalia and its successor, the British colony of Natal* [Doctoral dissertation, University of Zululand]., p.103
[159] Jansen, E. G. (1938). *Die Voortrekkers in Natal.*,
https://archive.org/details/VoortrekkersInNatal
[160] Gie, S. F. (1932). Geskiedenis vir Suid-Afrika, II (2nd ed.). Pro Ecclesia-Drukkery, p.334

direction as the Drakensberg, including St. Lucia Bay, along with all coastal areas and harbours, already discovered or yet to be discovered, between the Umzimvubu River and the mouth of the Black Mfolozi River".[161] In acceptance of the terms of friendship and defence between himself and the Boers, Mpande said: "If one would do anything to your disfavour, you can only let me know and be assured that I will hurry to your assistance with my whole army and I will sacrifice my last man for you".[162] On the banks of the Klip River, the Boers received about 36,000 head of cattle as compensation for the losses they suffered at the hands of Dingane. When the commando arrived back in Pietermaritzburg, 14,000 cattle were given to the Boers of the highveld,[163] west of the Drakensberg and the remaining cattle were distributed among the Boers in Natalia. This, the third Boer commando against Dingane, was now called the Cattle Commando.

After the British military left Port Natal and peace was established with the new Zulu ruler to the north, the Boers achieved their goal of acquiring a piece of land where they could govern themselves. They began developing their state and society by improving their first constitution, Retief's Constitution, and expanding on it. The Volksraad was the supreme authority, but due to the Boers' resistance to

---

[161] Jansen, E. G. (1938). *Die Voortrekkers in Natal.*, https://archive.org/details/VoortrekkersInNatal
[162] Shamase, M. Z. (1999). *The reign of King Mpande and his relations with the Republic of Natalia and its successor, the British colony of Natal* [Doctoral dissertation, University of Zululand]., p.104
[163] Cory, G. E. (1926). *The Rise of South Africa, Vol. IV*. Longman's, Green & Co., p.112

THE BOER REPUBLICS

centralised power, there was no executive, which hampered the functioning of the state. The title of governor disappeared.[164] They established a radical form of self-governance. Elections were held annually, all Boer men above twenty-one could vote, and voters were also free to submit memoranda or appeals to the Volksraad.[165] This is significant considering that in England, at the time, even after the Great Reform Act of 1832, only 650 000 or about 18% of the total adult-male population in England and Wales, could vote. The framework of the Boers' self-rule contained all the principles of republicanism, including a free, independent class of citizens with property rights, as well as rights and responsibilities. According to Giliomee, these principles were already present among the Boers in the eastern frontier districts of the Cape long before the onset of the trek. The Boers' migration to the interior further bolstered these principles of freedom and independence within their culture. This highlighted the distinction between the Boers and the Cape Afrikaners, who were loyal to the British monarchy and were known by the British as the "loyal Cape Dutch."[166]

The Republic was divided into three landdrost (magistrate) districts, namely Pietermaritzburg, Weenen, and

---

[164] Muller, C.F.J. (1973). The Period of the Great Trek, 1834-1854. C.F.J. Muller (Ed.), Five Hundred Years. A History of South Africa (pp.146-182). (3rd ed.). Academia. ,p.168
[165] Giliomee, Hermann. Die Afrikaners (Afrikaans Edition). Tafelberg. Kindle Edition., p.163
[166] Giliomee, Hermann. Die Afrikaners (Afrikaans Edition). Tafelberg. Kindle Edition., p.163

THE CREATION OF THE BOER IDENTITY

Port Natal, with Pietermaritzburg as the capital.[167] local government, the old and tested institutions of landdrosts and heemraden, which had existed in the Cape frontier districts, were introduced.[168] They also implemented the British jury system. Farms were measured out and registered for the burghers (Boer citizens). The Boers retained their traditional commando military system. The head of the commandos was a commandant-general appointed by the Volksraad.[169] In 1840, this Volksraad abolished the position of commandant-general in peacetime.[170] Adult Boer men could be called upon for military service by their local field cornets to serve under their local commandant. After discussions between Andries Pretorius and Hendrik Potgieter in September 1840, the entire Boer territory, which included Natalia, Winburg, and Potchefstroom, was brought under the authority of the Volksraad of Natalia as a United Boer Republic.[171] The Boers west of the Drakensberg had representative seats in the Volksraad. In 1841, an Adjunct Raad (Deputy Council) of twelve members was established at Potchefstroom. Pretorius

---

[167] Gie, S. F. (1932). Geskiedenis vir Suid-Afrika, II (2nd ed.). Pro Ecclesia-Drukkery, p.334

[168] Muller, C.F.J. (1973). The Period of the Great Trek, 1834-1854. C.F.J. Muller (Ed.), Five Hundred Years. A History of South Africa (pp.146-182). (3rd ed.). Academia. ,p.168

[169] Giliomee, Hermann. Die Afrikaners (Afrikaans Edition). Tafelberg. Kindle Edition., p.162

[170] Giliomee, Hermann. Die Afrikaners (Afrikaans Edition). Tafelberg. Kindle Edition., p.162-p.163

[171] Muller, C.F.J. (1973). The Period of the Great Trek, 1834-1854. C.F.J. Muller (Ed.), Five Hundred Years. A History of South Africa (pp.146-182). (3rd ed.). Academia. ,p.168

was chief commandant for Natalia, and Potgieter was appointed chief commandant west of the Drakensberg.[172]

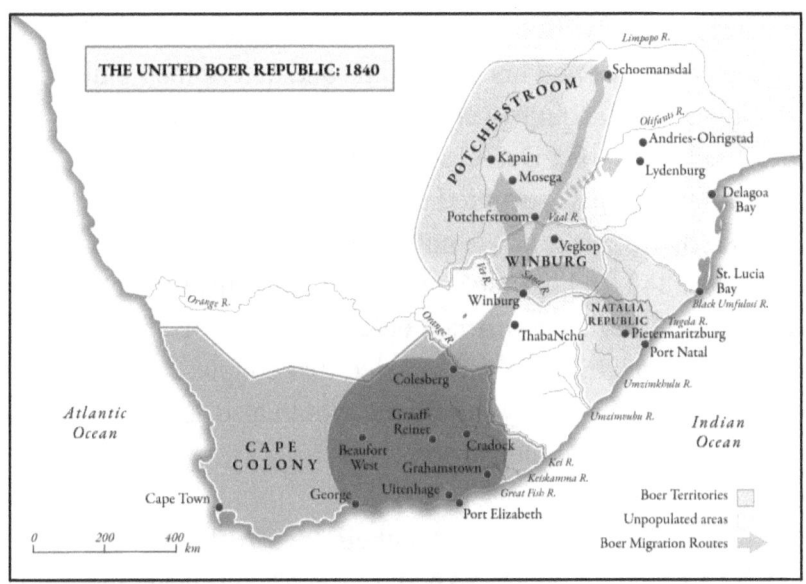

Map 4: The United Boer Republic under the Volksraad of Natalia

The Boers who survived could now enjoy the fruits of their sacrifices. They began to feel a sense of security and could leave their fortified laagers, which were already widely dispersed, to focus on their newly registered farms.[173] They could also construct more permanent structures. The town of Weenen (Weeping), named in memory of the Weenen massacres in February 1838, was planned in 1840 and consisted of 136 plots, each measuring 450 feet by 150

---

[172] Muller, C.F.J. (1973). The Period of the Great Trek, 1834-1854. C.F.J. Muller (Ed.), Five Hundred Years. A History of South Africa (pp.146-182). (3rd ed.). Academia. ,p.168

[173] Muller, C.F.J. (1973). The Period of the Great Trek, 1834-1854. C.F.J. Muller (Ed.), Five Hundred Years. A History of South Africa (pp.146-182). (3rd ed.). Academia. ,p.168

feet.[174] The Boers also built a church in Pietermaritzburg, as promised in their covenant with God before the Battle of Blood River. On 16 January 1841, after a commission, consisting of J.N. Boshoff, J.P. Zietsman, and Louwrens Badenhorst, verified his credentials and determined that his Presbyterian teachings were no different from what the Boers believed, Reverend Daniel Lindley, an American Presbyterian, was appointed as the first minister of the church in Pietermaritzburg.[175] He had been the Boers' preacher since January 1840. In his first Sunday service in the Church of the Covenant, Lindley confirmed elders and deacons, baptised twenty-seven children, and married two couples.[176] Lindley, who was well-loved by the Boers, would also serve the Boers in Winburg and Potchefstroom.

After Reverend W. Archbell, the Wesleyan minister stationed with Chief Moroko at Thaba N'Chu, visited the Boers in Natalia, he wrote an article for the Grahamstown Journal in September 1841 about their settlement: "The civil condition of the emigrants is much better than, from men in their circumstances, might have been looked for. They are settling down upon their farms without any regard to or fear of, the changes which from all we hear, must shortly take place. Their gardens, though well stocked with vegetables of every kind, and fruit trees of the second year, are not yet fenced. The farmers and their families are decently dressed,

---

[174] Voigt, J. C. (1899). *Fifty Years of the History of the Republic in South Africa (1795-1845), Volume II*. E.P. Dutton &Co., p.114
[175] Henning, E. E. (2014). *The cultural significance of the church of the vow in Pietermaritzburg* [Master's thesis, University of Pretoria]., p.70
[176] Henning, E. E. (2014). *The cultural significance of the church of the vow in Pietermaritzburg* [Master's thesis, University of Pretoria]., p.70

though articles of clothing are enormously expensive in Natal. They have built a large temporary church at the Umlazi, and a more permanent one at Bushmansrand (Pietermaritzburg) where the Rev. Mr. Lindley is now officiating." Regarding the black people living and working in Natalia, Reverend Archbell wrote the following in his article: The Natal natives "who are very numerous in villages among the Boers are a completely free people... The principles of freedom have been proclaimed throughout the whole migration...".[177] Many "agtertrekkers" (after trekkers - Boers who trekked after 1839) joined them from the Cape Colony, and trade between Natal and the Cape began to flourish.[178] In January 1840, the Volksraad formulated port regulations and appointed a harbour master for Port Natal.[179] As the community in Natalia developed, the Boers had to import administrators from the Cape who did not fully identify with the Boer cultural identity, which would result in internal clashes and weaken the Republic.

To ensure that their new republic could continue to exist freely and successfully, the Boers had to persuade the British government to abandon its policy of persecution towards them and recognise them as a free and independent people. On 4 September 1840, the Volksraad of Natalia, in a letter to Sir George Napier, the governor of the Cape Colony,

---

[177] Muller, C. F. J. (1946). *Die Britse Owerheid en die Groot Trek* [Doctoral dissertation, University of Stellenbosch]., p.429
[178] Muller, C.F.J. (1973). The Period of the Great Trek, 1834-1854. C.F.J. Muller (Ed.), Five Hundred Years. A History of South Africa (pp.146-182). (3rd ed.). Academia. ,p.168
[179] Voigt, J. C. (1899). *Fifty Years of the History of the Republic in South Africa (1795-1845), Volume II*. E.P. Dutton &Co., p.113

requested the British government to acknowledge them as a free and independent people. The request started as follows: "To submit to your Excellency, as the honoured representative of Her Majesty the Queen of England, that it may graciously please Her Majesty to acknowledge and declare us a free and independent people (a right so dearly purchased by our blood)".[180] In response to a letter from Napier on 2 November 1840, in which he requested more clarity on their proposal, the Volksraad, on 14 January 1841, outlined principles for the acknowledgement of their independence. Some of these principles were: "That we bind ourselves not to extend our borders any further, where this is detrimental to any of the surrounding tribes, nor to make any hostile movements against them, unless in self defence; "The Republic promises to give every encouragement to the spreading of the Gospel; "In the event of war between the British Government and any other power, the Republic is to be viewed as neutral; "The trade of British merchandise shall not be made subject to higher imposts than those of other countries; "The Republic binds itself not to aid the enemies of Great Britain nor to permit any of their vessels to enter the harbour; and generally, to live on friendly terms with the British Government and maintain peace with surrounding nations."[181]

Napier engaged in extensive correspondence with the Volksraad, but neither he nor the British Imperial

---

[180] Cory, G. E. (1926). *The Rise of South Africa, Vol. IV*. Longman's, Green & Co., p.116
[181] Cory, G. E. (1926). *The Rise of South Africa, Vol. IV*. Longman's, Green & Co., p.118-p.119

government had any intention of acknowledging the Boers as a free and independent people. On 10 June 1841 Napier wrote to the Volksraad that he "cannot enter into any negotiation or further negotiation with them until they, distinctly acknowledge their full and entire allegiance as British subjects to their sovereign, Her Majesty the Queen of England, and further declare their willingness to obey the lawful authority of the British Government."[182] State Secretary Russel confirmed Napier's stance. On 26 June 1841 Russel replied to Napier: "As matters now stand, the emigrant farmers must be informed that the Queen cannot acknowledge a portion of her own subjects as an independent Republic...".[183] In a memorandum in 1842, the succeeding British Secretary of State, Edward Stanley, again insisted on the Boers' loyalty to the British Crown: "it is clearly impossible to admit the claim of any portion of Her Majesty's subjects to cast off their allegiance, and establishing themselves on territory belonging to the Crown, to set up a claim to be treated as an independent state."[184] Responding to the question from Colonel Fox in the British House of Commons on 26 April 1842: "whether it was intended to recognise the independence of the Boers", Stanley answered: "it was quite impossible to accede to..."[185]

---

[182] Muller, C. F. J. (1946). *Die Britse Owerheid en die Groot Trek* [Doctoral dissertation, University of Stellenbosch]., p.310
[183] Muller, C. F. J. (1946). *Die Britse Owerheid en die Groot Trek* [Doctoral dissertation, University of Stellenbosch]., p.310
[184] Muller, C. F. J. (1946). *Die Britse Owerheid en die Groot Trek* [Doctoral dissertation, University of Stellenbosch]., p.311
[185] Muller, C. F. J. (1946). *Die Britse Owerheid en die Groot Trek* [Doctoral dissertation, University of Stellenbosch]., p.311

THE CREATION OF THE BOER IDENTITY

The British were not only unwilling to acknowledge the Boers as a free people, but they also, from various sources, including Governor Napier, British members of parliament, and English business interests, exerted pressure on the British Government to annex Natal. Governor Napier was probably the most active proponent for the annexation of Natal. On 22 June 1840 he wrote to Russel: "from the various accounts of the country proposed to be thus annexed to the British dominions, it (Natal) is without doubt the most fertile portion of southern Africa, and capable of being turned to advantage, not only for the purposes of pasturage, but also of agriculture."[186] In the same letter to Russel, he projected a scenario that might make it necessary for the British government to annex Natal: "…if Boers occupied areas of tribes south of Port Natal, "which must lead to bloody wars, and might prove fatal to the peace of this (Cape) colony."[187] On 6 December 1841, in another letter to Russel, he suggested that the British would develop Natal much better than the Boers could: "The farmers who are already in that country, possess neither sufficient enterprise nor capital to develop the resources of the country,... Their agricultural pursuits have hitherto been conducted on a most limited scale.[188] In the same letter, he again proposed that the British government should annex Natal: "to afford the native tribes of Africa the protection of the British arms against the

---

[186] Muller, C. F. J. (1946). *Die Britse Owerheid en die Groot Trek* [Doctoral dissertation, University of Stellenbosch]., p.266

[187] Muller, C. F. J. (1946). *Die Britse Owerheid en die Groot Trek* [Doctoral dissertation, University of Stellenbosch]., p.173

[188] Muller, C. F. J. (1946). *Die Britse Owerheid en die Groot Trek* [Doctoral dissertation, University of Stellenbosch]., p.266

aggressions of Her Majesty's subjects (the Boers)."[189] On 13 December 1842, Napier proposed in a letter to Stanley that the Transorangia (present-day Free State) should also be annexed. He wrote, "At present to check the unruly British Subjects (the Boers) who wander over Africa, is a matter of favour, but extend the nominal sovereignty of the Crown, and the obligation is one of right."[190]

English business interests and the media had substantial sway in promoting the annexation of Natal. On 27 March 1839, William Ward, a British Member of Parliament, presented a petition from English traders in the British Parliament for the annexation of Natal.[191] The "Natal Association" was established by English businessmen, and on 6 June 1839, its members had a meeting with the new Secretary of State, Lord Normanby, about the proposed colony in Natal.[192] On 10 June 1839, the Earl of Ripon presented a petition in the British House of Commons in which Liverpool traders requested that a colony be established in Natal.[193] On 11 June 1839, the British Imperial Government permitted members of the Natal Association to establish a committee of the Lower House "to inquire into the

---

[189] Muller, C. F. J. (1946). *Die Britse Owerheid en die Groot Trek* [Doctoral dissertation, University of Stellenbosch]., p.431
[190] Muller, C. F. J. (1946). *Die Britse Owerheid en die Groot Trek* [Doctoral dissertation, University of Stellenbosch]., p.216-p.217
[191] Muller, C. F. J. (1946). *Die Britse Owerheid en die Groot Trek* [Doctoral dissertation, University of Stellenbosch]., p.259
[192] Muller, C. F. J. (1946). *Die Britse Owerheid en die Groot Trek* [Doctoral dissertation, University of Stellenbosch]., p.259
[193] Muller, C. F. J. (1946). *Die Britse Owerheid en die Groot Trek* [Doctoral dissertation, University of Stellenbosch]., p.260

THE CREATION OF THE BOER IDENTITY

propriety of founding such a colony".[194] In a speech delivered in the British Parliament on 25 June 1839, Member of Parliament Ward made the following statement regarding Natal: "there is an absolute necessity that the Government should adopt some measures." "There has been a a re-migration, from the Cape of 5000 armed Boors (meaning Boers) of the old Dutch race, who have declared themselves independent of Great Britain."[195] In the same speech, Ward again urged the annexation of Natal: "We have had petitions presented from Glasgow, from Liverpool, from the merchants connected with the African trade in London, calling on us to deal with this question of Natal."[196]

The English media in Cape Town continuously propagated the persecution of the Boers. On 19 June 1839, The South African Commercial Advertiser wrote: "Revolt is Rebellion; and Rebellion is War." "We cannot, therefore, believe that Government is in possession of a formal Renunciation of Allegiance on the part of the Emigrants."[197] The newspaper attempted to influence the British government to act against the Boers. On 11 December 1839, it wrote: "And can it be supposed for an instant, that she (the British Empire) will... permit a handful of Boers... to defy her power...?" "Can Great Britain permit any portion of her

---

[194] Muller, C. F. J. (1946). *Die Britse Owerheid en die Groot Trek* [Doctoral dissertation, University of Stellenbosch]., p.260
[195] Muller, C. F. J. (1946). *Die Britse Owerheid en die Groot Trek* [Doctoral dissertation, University of Stellenbosch]., p.324
[196] Muller, C. F. J. (1946). *Die Britse Owerheid en die Groot Trek* [Doctoral dissertation, University of Stellenbosch]., p.260
[197] Muller, C. F. J. (1946). *Die Britse Owerheid en die Groot Trek* [Doctoral dissertation, University of Stellenbosch]., p.325

subjects to lay waste, by their own authority, any portion of a country which she had solemnly bound herself to protect against lawless violence on the part of the subjects of all other states?"[198] On 16 November 1842, the South African Commercial Advertiser demanded from the British government: "to represent the power of the British empire among a numerous and hardy host of rebels in their own stronghold (Natalia)." "British supremacy must be re-established; this revolt must be suppressed; and Port Natal secured."[199]

The dire state of Britain's financial situation temporarily prevented the British government from annexing Natal. In a letter to Napier on 5 September 1840, State Secretary Russel expressed his reluctance to incur large expenses: "I should be very apprehensive that a forcible occupation by a force of 1,200 or 1,500 men would in all probability lead to fresh contests and new difficulties.... l am... not prepared to expend large funds to conquer the territory from the Emigrant farmers."[200] When Napier requested financial support from the Imperial government on 5 November 1840, to cover expenses for protecting the Cape's eastern border, Russell refused to provide Imperial funds and instructed Napier to use colonial funds for that

---

[198] Muller, C. F. J. (1946). *Die Britse Owerheid en die Groot Trek* [Doctoral dissertation, University of Stellenbosch]., p.326
[199] Muller, C. F. J. (1946). *Die Britse Owerheid en die Groot Trek* [Doctoral dissertation, University of Stellenbosch]., p.314
[200] Muller, C. F. J. (1946). *Die Britse Owerheid en die Groot Trek* [Doctoral dissertation, University of Stellenbosch]., p.177

purpose.[201] Governor Napier highlighted the poor financial situation of the Cape Colony to Secretary Russell on 16 June 1841, stating: "The Civil Establishment of this (Cape) Colony has been reduced to the lowest level possible..."[202] On 14 August 1841, Napier wrote to Russell that the Cape government did not even have sufficient funds to cover current expenses.[203]

When the Treasury restrained its spending, the British government considered Africa unimportant and financially not worth the effort compared to other regions. In 1840, the British Permanent Under-Secretary of State for the Colonies, Sir James Stephen, wrote that "even if our material resources were far more ample than they at present are it would be very bad policy to employ in Africa that part of them which is available for colonisation." "In North America and in Australia, we have vacant continents to occupy, and every shilling well expended there may be made to yield a large and secure return."[204] On 31 January 1842, in response to Napier's pleas for the annexation of Natal, Stephen wrote in a memorandum: "Territory in South Africa is not worth the having; as a part of the foreign Dominions of the Crown, and... our true policy, if it had not become impracticable, would be to abandon all the colony excepting the seaport

---

[201] Muller, C. F. J. (1946). *Die Britse Owerheid en die Groot Trek* [Doctoral dissertation, University of Stellenbosch]., p.151
[202] Muller, C. F. J. (1946). *Die Britse Owerheid en die Groot Trek* [Doctoral dissertation, University of Stellenbosch]., p.150
[203] Muller, C. F. J. (1946). *Die Britse Owerheid en die Groot Trek* [Doctoral dissertation, University of Stellenbosch]., p.150
[204] Muller, C. F. J. (1946). *Die Britse Owerheid en die Groot Trek* [Doctoral dissertation, University of Stellenbosch]., p.178

towns, and the immediate neighbourhood on which they depend for food. ... and that to make a new settlement at Port Natal, when there is not even an accessible port or a safe roadstead, would be merely to throw away so much money, and to multiply our relations and responsibilities towards barbarous tribes, from which nothing could ever come..."[205]

While the official policy was not to annex Natal, the British government did not recognise the Boer Republic and insisted that the Boers were British subjects who had no right to create an independent state. In a letter to Russel on 22 June 1841, Napier wrote that, although he agreed in principle that the British Empire should not further expand its foreign possessions, the addition of Natal was "inevitable and compelled by circumstances." Napier informed Russel that the Boers were not discouraged, and the longer they remained in possession of Natal, the more challenging its annexation would be later on.[206] Napier and the British Imperial government consistently exerted pressure on the Boers in Natal by threatening annexation. The Boers in Natal were divided on how to respond to the ongoing military threat from the British government. On one side were those who, due to Britain's global prestige and reputation, believed they should not dare to oppose or provoke Britain and on the other side were those who believed that the Volksraad should act in the interest of the Republic, regardless of the British

---

[205] Muller, C. F. J. (1946). *Die Britse Owerheid en die Groot Trek* [Doctoral dissertation, University of Stellenbosch]., p.178
[206] Cory, G. E. (1926). *The Rise of South Africa, Vol. IV*. Longman's, Green & Co., p.117

government's response. The British government would use various incidents as pretext for annexing Natal.

The Boers no longer faced external threats from invading forces, but they encountered challenges along the southern border of the Republic. Persistent livestock thefts by the San people and the Bhaca tribe who lived near the Umzimvubu River against the Drakensberg, led by Chief Ncaphayi, were a concern. The Bhacas posed not only a threat to the local Boer community but also conducted raids and cattle thefts among the Pondos, under Chief Faku's leadership. Chief Faku even sought "permission" from the Boers to form an alliance with the Hlangweni tribe, led by Chief Fodo, to launch an attack on the Bacas.[207] Efforts were made by the Boers early on to establish positive relations with Chief Faku. In 1838, when British agent Gideon Joubert visited the Boers in Natal on Governor Napier's orders, L. Badenhorst, a member of the Volksraad, showed him a letter sent to Faku and two letters from Faku's Wesleyan missionary Jenkins — one to Badenhorst himself and the other to Field Cornet Cobi (William Cowie). Joubert inferred from these letters that the Boers maintained "the strongest friendship with that people (the Pondos), so that I found the Boers had no other enemies (aside from Dingaan)".[208] Upon Major Charters' return to Natal through Pondoland after he left in January 1839, he discovered that one of the Boers' first actions upon arriving in Natal was to establish contact with

---

[207] Voigt, J. C. (1899). *Fifty Years of the History of the Republic in South Africa (1795-1845), Volume II*. E.P.Dutton &Co., p.180
[208] Jansen, E. G. (1938). *Die Voortrekkers in Natal.*,
https://archive.org/details/VoortrekkersInNatal

Faku and assure him of their goodwill and peaceful intentions.[209] However, Charters advised Faku to have nothing to do with the Boers as "they were in their present position contrary to the authority of Her Majesty's Government."[210]

Commandant-General Pretorius, acting on the Volksraad's orders, dispatched a commando of two hundred and sixty men under Commandant Lombard on 19 December 1840, to retrieve the Boers' cattle from Ncaphayi. In this operation, thirty Bhacas were killed, and the Boers seized 3000 cattle. On 23 December 1840, missionary Garner informed the superintendent of the Wesleyan Society that a Boer commando had attacked the Bhacas, stating, "If the (British) Government do not in some way interfere, Ncaphayi and Faku will soon be destroyed."[211] In response, the missionaries sent a letter, signed with Faku's mark, to the British colonial government on 5 January 1841, in which Faku pleaded for protection against "the fire that he feared was coming from Natal, as he was a friend of the English."[212] In the same letter, the missionaries told Napier that all the land between the Umzimvubu and Umzimkulu rivers, the entire southern part of Natalia, belonged to Faku.[213] Despite

---

[209] Cory, G. E. (1926). *The Rise of South Africa, Vol. IV*. Longman's, Green & Co., p.90
[210] Cory, G. E. (1926). *The Rise of South Africa, Vol. IV*. Longman's, Green & Co., p.91
[211] Muller, C. F. J. (1946). *Die Britse Owerheid en die Groot Trek* [Doctoral dissertation, University of Stellenbosch]., p.426
[212] Muller, C. F. J. (1946). *Die Britse Owerheid en die Groot Trek* [Doctoral dissertation, University of Stellenbosch]., p.426-p.427
[213] Voigt, J. C. (1899). *Fifty Years of the History of the Republic in South Africa (1795-1845), Volume II*. E.P.Dutton &Co., p.181

the Boers not posing any threat to Faku, Napier within days dispatched British troops under Captain T.C. Smith to take a position in the Umgazi valley to protect the Pondos against the Boers. On 22 January 1841, Napier explained his actions to Secretary Russell: "...but when Your Lordship considers that unless this system of aggression is put a stop to and unless the tribes of unoffending natives are protected from such murderous attacks, they will be driven down upon our frontier (the Cape colony) and thereby cause a further and more dreadful sacrifice of human life for our protection, I feel confident that the present expenditure will not be deemed unnecessary, but on the contrary that it will prove an eventual saving."[214] In response to Napier's actions, the Volksraad, on 7 April 1841, sent a letter to Napier informing him of their friendly relations with Faku and expressing confusion about his request for protection against the Boers. In this letter, the Volksraad also told Napier: "Finally, we can assure Your Excellency that neither Ncaphayi nor Faku nor anyone else, need fear the slightest offence from us, if they will only let us alone."

The period of peace Natal following the destruction of Dingaan, led to an influx of refugees, primarily Zulus, into the new republic. While the Boers in the eastern Cape had always faced a labour shortage, the issue now was an excess of workers. The large number of refugees entering Natal also posed a threat to the Boers' safety. To address this, the Volksraad ordered that farmers could not accommodate more

---

[214] Muller, C. F. J. (1946). *Die Britse Owerheid en die Groot Trek* [Doctoral dissertation, University of Stellenbosch]., p.175

than five refugee families as labourers on their farms.[215] On 2 August 1841, the Volksraad determined that all non-employed Zulu refugees within the Boer republic should be relocated to the south of the country, between the Mthamvuna and Umzimvubu Rivers. This extensive tract of land provided sufficient grazing for their cattle, with abundant water and firewood. While living there, the refugees were protected from their persecutors by the Boers and, importantly, they could rule themselves.[216] Napier, who considered this southern part of Natalia as land belonging to the Pondo chief, Faku, was angered by the Boers' decision "to thrust masses of Natal natives down into Faku's country without leave of that chief" which will lead to "warfare and bloodshed".[217] On 2 December 1841, Napier issued a proclamation declaring that the Boers had no right to be recognised as an independent people or state, and he declared his intention to occupy Natal by military force.[218] Napier, in a letter to Russel on 6 December 1841, argued that the occupation of Natal was necessary "to afford the native tribes of Africa the protection of the British arms against the aggressions of Her Majesty's subjects (the Boers)."[219]

---

[215] Muller, C.F.J. (1969). The Period of the Great Trek, 1834-1854. C.F.J. Muller (Ed.), Five Hundred Years. A History of South Africa (pp.122-156). Academia., p.171
[216] Shamase, M. Z. (1999). *The reign of King Mpande and his relations with the Republic of Natalia and its successor, the British colony of Natal* [Doctoral dissertation, University of Zululand]., p.112
[217] Walker, E. A. (1965). *The Great Trek* (5th ed.). Adam & Charles Black, London., p.260
[218] Du Toit, A., & Giliomee, H. (1983). *Afrikaner Political Thought. Volume 1: 1780-1850*. University of California Press, p220
[219] Muller, C. F. J. (1946). *Die Britse Owerheid en die Groot Trek* [Doctoral dissertation, University of Stellenbosch]., p.431

Napier aimed to block foreign trade at Port Natal to prevent the Boer government from generating revenue through tariffs or importing weapons and ammunition. In his view, according to a letter from him to Secretary Russell on 25 July 1842, the only way to prevent foreign trading ships, "whether Dutch or American", from engaging in trade with the Boers was to annex Natal.[220] When the American merchant ship Levant, led by Captain Holmes, engaged in limited trade at Natal in August 1841, English business interests in the Cape remarked that the Americans found in Port Natal "a most convenient harbour for their vessels; of all denominations, trading to the East".[221] Shortly before Captain Smith arrived in Port Natal, the Dutch trading vessel Brazilie, commanded by Captain Reus, visited Port Natal between 26 March and 24 April 1842, which caused suspicions in certain British circles. Some believed that the Dutch government or even the French, using Dutch merchant ships, aimed to undermine British supremacy in southeast Africa.[222] However, James Stephen, the British permanent under-secretary of colonies, questioned how American ships in Port Natal, situated over 1000 miles from the Cape, could harm British business interests.[223] The British government was aware that the Netherlands posed no threat to them. If the

---

[220] Muller, C.F.J. (1969). The Period of the Great Trek, 1834-1854. C.F.J. Muller (Ed.), Five Hundred Years. A History of South Africa (pp.122-156). Academia., p.278

[221] Muller, C. F. J. (1946). *Die Britse Owerheid en die Groot Trek* [Doctoral dissertation, University of Stellenbosch]., p.264

[222] Muller, C.F.J. (1969). The Period of the Great Trek, 1834-1854. C.F.J. Muller (Ed.), Five Hundred Years. A History of South Africa (pp.122-156). Academia. ,p.171

[223] Muller, C. F. J. (1946). *Die Britse Owerheid en die Groot Trek* [Doctoral dissertation, University of Stellenbosch]., p.270

Boers anticipated any support from the Dutch government, the Dutch response to the Brazilie's visit unequivocally indicated their disapproval of any support for the Boers and affirmed their support of Britain: "... disloyal communications... have been repelled with all the indignation that was to be expected from a power in close alliance and amity with her Brittanic Majesty; and that the king of Holland and his Ministers have taken every possible step to mark their entire disapproval of the unjustifiable use of their name ..."[224] The Dutch government, later, upon the British government's request, provided complete cargo lists of Dutch ships heading to Delagoa Bay to prevent the supply of weapons and ammunition to the Boers. The British government therefore possessed detailed information about Dutch ships before they even left Dutch harbours.[225]

In March 1842, the Cape governor, Napier, sent British troops to occupy Port Natal. On 1 April 1842, Captain T. C. Smith, with a small force of about 255 soldiers, crossed the Umzimvubu River into Natalia. By 2 May 1842, Smith reached Van Rooyen's farm, fifteen miles from Port Natal, where he declined to accept a protest from Commandant Jan Meyer on behalf of the Volksraad because he was "...on the

---

[224] Cubbin, A. E. (1992). An exposition of the clash of Anglo-Voortrekker interests at Port Natal leading to the military conflict of 23-24 May 1842. *Historia, 37*(2), 48-69., p.49
[225] Muller, C.F.J. (1969). The Period of the Great Trek, 1834-1854. C.F.J. Muller (Ed.), Five Hundred Years. A History of South Africa (pp.122-156). Academia., p.289

Queen's Territory".[226] Smith proceeded to set up a camp on the northwest side of Durban Bay. Despite attempts by the Boers to communicate, on 4 May 1842 Smith refused to meet a Boer delegation, consisting of Jan Meyer, Ferreira, and Edmund Morewood.[227] Later, Smith marched through Congella, where he posted Napier's Proclamation of 2 December 1841. On 7 May 1842, Commandant General Pretorius, acting on orders of the Volksraad, set up laager at Congella, about five kilometres south of the British camp. Following Volksraad's instructions not to shoot first, Pretorius, along with twenty-five Boers, replaced Napier's proclamation with a notice of the Volksraad.[228] On 14 May 1842, Smith wrote to Napier: "I shall avoid collision as long as I prudently can (for such I apprehend to be Your Excellency's wish) and endeavour if possible to make it their own act instead of our own".[229] In this letter, he referred to the Boers as "ignorant people" who, being farmers, would neither be able nor willing to stay away from their homes for an extended period. He labelled the commandant general

---

[226] Cubbin, A. E. (1992). An exposition of the clash of Anglo-Voortrekker interests at Port Natal leading to the military conflict of 23-24 May 1842. *Historia, 37*(2), 48-69., p.63

[227] Cubbin, A. E. (1992). An exposition of the clash of Anglo-Voortrekker interests at Port Natal leading to the military conflict of 23-24 May 1842. *Historia, 37*(2), 48-69., p.65

[228] Cubbin, A. E. (1992). An exposition of the clash of Anglo-Voortrekker interests at Port Natal leading to the military conflict of 23-24 May 1842. *Historia, 37*(2), 48-69., p.65

[229] Cubbin, A. E. (1992). An exposition of the clash of Anglo-Voortrekker interests at Port Natal leading to the military conflict of 23-24 May 1842. *Historia, 37*(2), 48-69., p.67

(Pretorius) as a "rank coward" and he had "not the least doubt" of the result of his expedition.[230]

On 16 May 1842, the Volksraad convened in Congella instead of Pietermaritzburg. Here, Karel Landman asked the Boers assembled there if they wished to become British subjects. They vehemently rejected this idea and demanded the withdrawal of British troops from Port Natal.[231] The Volksraad then instructed Pretorius to order Smith to leave their territory immediately. On 17 May 1842, Pretorius informed Smith that he had until noon to depart Natalia because he dishonoured the Boers' sovereignty, laws, and flag, removed official notices, and broke into the Boers' magazine.[232] In response to this ultimatum, Smith claimed that the Boers were British subjects and demanded they "abandon the hostile attitude".[233] On 22 May 1842, the Mazeppa arrived in the harbour, and Smith sent Lieutenant Irwin with twenty-five men to unload a cannon and British supplies. The Boers, however, still took no action against the British invasion. The next day, Stephanus Maritz of the Volksraad delivered a letter from Pretorius to Smith which

---

[230] Cubbin, A. E. (1992). An exposition of the clash of Anglo-Voortrekker interests at Port Natal leading to the military conflict of 23-24 May 1842. *Historia, 37*(2), 48-69., p.67
[231] Cubbin, A. E. (1992). An exposition of the clash of Anglo-Voortrekker interests at Port Natal leading to the military conflict of 23-24 May 1842. *Historia, 37*(2), 48-69., p.67
[232] Cubbin, A. E. (1992). An exposition of the clash of Anglo-Voortrekker interests at Port Natal leading to the military conflict of 23-24 May 1842. *Historia, 37*(2), 48-69., p.67
[233] Cubbin, A. E. (1992). An exposition of the clash of Anglo-Voortrekker interests at Port Natal leading to the military conflict of 23-24 May 1842. *Historia, 37*(2), 48-69., p.68

stated: "I must finally enjoin you, in the name of the Government, and at the instance of the public generally, without delay to break up your camp, to pay us the expenses occasioned by you, and to quit our territory; and warning you for the last time that on your responsibility, and that of your Government, will be charged the bloodshed and other undesirable and hurtful consequences of acts to which we shall be obliged to have recourse in defence of our liberty". Smith responded that he was under the orders of his "Sovereign" and warned the Boers about the consequences of any "rebellious conduct".[234] Thirty minutes later, the Boers confiscated Smith's military cattle, leaving them without draft oxen and meat.[235] For Smith, this meant war.

At 11 o'clock on the night of 23 May 1842, Smith set out to launch an attack on the Boer laager at Congella. To surprise the Boers, he decided to avoid the dense bushes that separated the two camps (which is now Durban's central business district) and take a detour along the beach.[236] Smith also attached a howitzer to a longboat from the Mazeppa to position it directly opposite Congella, from where it could

---

[234] Cubbin, A. E. (1992). An exposition of the clash of Anglo-Voortrekker interests at Port Natal leading to the military conflict of 23-24 May 1842. *Historia, 37*(2), 48-69., p.69
[235] Cubbin, A. E. (1992). An exposition of the clash of Anglo-Voortrekker interests at Port Natal leading to the military conflict of 23-24 May 1842. *Historia, 37*(2), 48-69., p.69
[236] Saks, D. (2004). The Real "First Anglo-Boer War": The Siege of Port Natal, 1842. *The South African Military History Society, Military History Journal, 13*(1)., Retrieved June 13, 2023, from https://samilitaryhistory.org/vol131ds.html

provide supporting fire once the attack began.[237] Although Pretorius did not expect an attack through a beach march, he nonetheless positioned a group of elderly Boer rifle marksmen, including Pieter Joubert, behind sand dunes on the beach.[238] Around one o'clock that night, Smith signalled for the longboat to bombard the Boer laager. However, due to low tide, the boat ran aground on a sandbank and was not in position. Smith ordered his troops to continue their advance, but when they were within a distance of 100 meters, the small group of Boers opened fire. This skirmish lasted only a few minutes before Smith, as he mentioned in his report, deemed it "expedient to retire".[239] He hastily returned to the camp to organise their defence.

Smith's men, bravely, began to retreat in an orderly manner, but when the few Boer defenders received reinforcements, they left their cannons behind and hastily followed Smith back to their camp. Some soldiers were driven into the sea, and at least two drowned. By half-past three in the morning, the Boers attacked the British camp. The total British losses were reported as thirty-four killed,

---

[237] Saks, D. (2004). The Real "First Anglo-Boer War": The Siege of Port Natal, 1842. *The South African Military History Society, Military History Journal*, *13*(1)., Retrieved June 13, 2023, from https://samilitaryhistory.org/vol131ds.html
[238] Saks, D. (2004). The Real "First Anglo-Boer War": The Siege of Port Natal, 1842. *The South African Military History Society, Military History Journal*, *13*(1)., Retrieved June 13, 2023, from https://samilitaryhistory.org/vol131ds.html
[239] Saks, D. (2004). The Real "First Anglo-Boer War": The Siege of Port Natal, 1842. *The South African Military History Society, Military History Journal*, *13*(1)., Retrieved June 13, 2023, from https://samilitaryhistory.org/vol131ds.html

sixty-three wounded, and six missing.[240] At the end of the battle, the Boers lost Pieter Greyling, Johannes Greyling, a Strydom, and a Hattingh, who were killed, and J. Prinsloo, P. Nel, T. Schutte, Klaas Dekker, Stefanus Bothma, Jan Landman, and J. Vermaak were wounded.[241] The young Pieter Greyling was shot from a store near the Point where English "Uitlanders," including the Boers' trusted Field Cornet William Cowie, without the Boers' knowledge, had barricaded the building and were secretly supporting the British troops.[242] On 24 and 25 May 1842, the wounded British soldiers were treated in the Boer laager by the American medical missionary, Reverend Dr. Adams, and then sent back to the British camp for further treatment by their own doctor. The Boers also brought the British dead to their camp so they could have a proper funeral.[243] The Boers, now engaging in a type of warfare they were entirely unfamiliar with, besieged and bombarded the British camp, primarily using the cannons the British had left behind on the beach.[244] In desperation, Smith sought assistance from the Zulu king, but Mpande shrewdly responded: "No, you are now fighting for the upper hand, and whichever gains must

---

[240] Voigt, J. C. (1899). *Fifty Years of the History of the Republic in South Africa (1795-1845), Volume II*. E.P.Dutton &Co., p.230

[241] Voigt, J. C. (1899). *Fifty Years of the History of the Republic in South Africa (1795-1845), Volume II*. E.P.Dutton &Co., p.232, p.244

[242] Voigt, J. C. (1899). *Fifty Years of the History of the Republic in South Africa (1795-1845), Volume II*. E.P.Dutton &Co., p.230

[243] Voigt, J. C. (1899). *Fifty Years of the History of the Republic in South Africa (1795-1845), Volume II*. E.P.Dutton &Co., p.230

[244] Saks, D. (2004). The Real "First Anglo-Boer War": The Siege of Port Natal, 1842. *The South African Military History Society, Military History Journal, 13*(1)., Retrieved June 13, 2023, from https://samilitaryhistory.org/vol131ds.html

be my master."[245] On 26 May 1842, Richard ('Dick') King, a local Englishman, accompanied by his Zulu servant, Ndongeni, embarked on an epic ten-day journey to seek aid in Grahamstown for the besieged British forces.

Lieutenant Colonel A. J. Cloete was sent from Cape Town to relieve Smith. Napier issued his instructions, which he attached to his letter to the new Secretary of State, Lord Stanley, on 13 June 1842, to Lieutenant-Colonel A. J. Cloete. These instructions outlined the primary goal of his expedition to Natal: "the re-establishment of the British influence at Port Natal; secure possession of Natal and subdue any rebellions manifestations in that quarter."[246] The mouthpiece of the evangelical philanthropists at the Cape, the South African Commercial Advertiser, endorsed the British military intervention against the Boers in Natal in a report on 25 June 1842: "The contest in which we are at present engaged with the Emigrant Boers is expressly in defence of the Natives. We follow them for no other reason than to prevent bloodshed and extermination - both of which have marked the course of these men since the time they left the colony."[247] On the afternoon of 24 June 1842, the Port Elizabeth schooner, the Conch, anchored in Port Natal with a

---

[245] Shamase, M. Z. (1999). *The reign of King Mpande and his relations with the Republic of Natalia and its successor, the British colony of Natal* [Doctoral dissertation, University of Zululand]., p.159
[246] Muller, C.F.J. (1969). The Period of the Great Trek, 1834-1854. C.F.J. Muller (Ed.), Five Hundred Years. A History of South Africa (pp.122-156). Academia., p.314
[247] Muller, C.F.J. (1969). The Period of the Great Trek, 1834-1854. C.F.J. Muller (Ed.), Five Hundred Years. A History of South Africa (pp.122-156). Academia., p.434

hundred soldiers on board. To deceive the Boers, soldiers hid in the hold while those on deck were dressed in civilian clothes, presenting the Conch as an innocent trading vessel.[248] The following morning, the frigate Southampton, equipped with fifty cannons, arrived in Port Natal with 800 men under the command of Colonel Cloete.[249] Under the cover of the Southampton's cannons, several boatloads of soldiers landed, forcing the Boers to retreat. Pretorius fell back a few miles inland, near the present-day Pinetown, where he set up a laager. At approximately four o'clock, Colonel Cloete lifted the siege on Captain Smith's camp.[250] Cloete refused to negotiate with Pretorius until the Boers surrendered, and he offered protection to all Boers who would swear allegiance. Not a single Boer accepted his offer.[251]

Cloete then called on the surrounding Zulus, in exchange for a reward, to seize cattle and horses from the Boers and bring them to him.[252] This resulted in a spade of farm attacks on the Boers, during which three elderly Boers, Dirk van Rooyen, Theunis Oosthuizen, and Cornelis van

---

[248] Cory, G. E. (1926). *The Rise of South Africa, Vol. IV*. Longman's, Green & Co., p.151
[249] Saks, D. (2004). The Real "First Anglo-Boer War": The Siege of Port Natal, 1842. *The South African Military History Society, Military History Journal, 13*(1)., Retrieved June 13, 2023, from https://samilitaryhistory.org/vol131ds.html
[250] Voigt, J. C. (1899). *Fifty Years of the History of the Republic in South Africa (1795-1845), Volume II*. E.P.Dutton &Co., p.250
[251] Walker, E. A. (1965). *The Great Trek* (5th ed.). Adam & Charles Black, London., p.280
[252] Walker, E. A. (1965). *The Great Trek* (5th ed.). Adam & Charles Black, London., p.280

Schalkwyk, were murdered in cold blood and the Boer women were stripped naked and driven across the veld. They were later saved by Bart Pretorius.[253] When Pretorius objected, Cloete replied: "You and your unfortunate, misguided people brought it about by your acts of determined hostilities towards Her Majesty's government and troops."[254] Cloete received emissaries from King Mpande and put the Zulu king under the impression that the British occupation of Port Natal meant the defeat of the Boers, after which Mpande offered to attack the Boers.[255] Upon receiving messages that Mpande was mobilising his impis to attack Pietermaritzburg, Pretorius had no choice but to send his men home to protect their families and property. The total annihilation of the Boers in Natal was now a real danger. Pretorius and the commando's War Council immediately sent two messengers, Van Aardt and S. Maritz, to Port Natal to discuss terms for a cessation of hostilities.[256] Cloete demanded that the Boers submit to Her Majesty's government, stating, "refusing which the emigrant farmers must await all the evils they will have brought upon themselves."[257] In return, the British Government promised that all private property would be

---

[253] Voigt, J. C. (1899). *Fifty Years of the History of the Republic in South Africa (1795-1845), Volume II*. E.P.Dutton &Co., p.251

[254] Shamase, M. Z. (1999). *The reign of King Mpande and his relations with the Republic of Natalia and its successor, the British colony of Natal* [Doctoral dissertation, University of Zululand]., p.117

[255] Shamase, M. Z. (1999). *The reign of King Mpande and his relations with the Republic of Natalia and its successor, the British colony of Natal* [Doctoral dissertation, University of Zululand]., p.118

[256] Cory, G. E. (1926). *The Rise of South Africa, Vol. IV*. Longman's, Green & Co., p.161

[257] Cory, G. E. (1926). *The Rise of South Africa, Vol. IV*. Longman's, Green & Co., p.161-p.162

respected, farmers could return undisturbed to their places with their horses and guns, and "protection will be afforded against attacks by the Zulus".[258]

The Volksraad asked Cloete to meet in Pietermaritzburg. On 15 July 1842, on the advice of Andries Pretorius and Carel Landman, and amidst vehement protests from a portion of the Boers, the Volksraad accepted Cloete's terms and formally tendered its submission. The surrender was especially unacceptable to the Boers from the other side of the Drakensberg who had come to assist in the fighting. In a letter to Napier on 3 July 1842, Cloete expressed his remorse for the strategy they employed against the Boers: "If England will not put down the Boers by her own legitimate means, it was better to abandon the project altogether, and submit even to the insult we have received, than adopt the degrading process of enlisting the savage in our cause, or call upon the Zulu assegais to commit all the atrocities of indiscriminate bloodshed and spoliation."[259] Colonel Cloete also knew that his force was not strong enough to defeat the Boers militarily. He counted on the assumption that the Boers, when facing an existential threat from Mpande's impi on their widely dispersed and isolated farms, would not resist. On 6 July 1842, in a private letter to Sir Benjamin D'Urban, who still resided in the Cape, he wrote: "Without the cooperation of a large body of Boers..., I see no chance,

---

[258] Cory, G. E. (1926). *The Rise of South Africa, Vol. IV*. Longman's, Green & Co., p.162
[259] Shamase, M. Z. (1999). *The reign of King Mpande and his relations with the Republic of Natalia and its successor, the British colony of Natal* [Doctoral dissertation, University of Zululand]., p.118

in their present strength, and determination to resist; of successfully taking the offensive against them, without more than risking the small body of troops confided to me... I need to tell you that a British soldier is equipped so as totally to unfit him to enter the Bush at all, but more particularly against such opponents; and confidentially speaking, our men do not like the Bush."[260] On 21 July 1842, Colonel Cloete left Natal, leaving Smith, who had now been promoted to major, with a force of 361 officers and men, along with four large guns, in control of Natal.

The Boers of Natal now found themselves in a period of confusion, and many began to leave the country. There was discord among the Boers; Pretorius resigned as commandant-general, and Gert Rudolph replaced him. According to the agreement reached with Colonel Cloete on 15 July 1842, the Volksraad continued to govern the area, excluding the surroundings of Port Natal. However, they couldn't make decisions without Major Smith's approval. This uncomfortable situation persisted for a year until England sent an envoy to discuss the administration of the area with the Boers. In December 1842, the British colonial secretary, Lord Stanley, annexed Natal for England, and on 12 May 1843, Napier declared the area a British colony.[261] Napier appointed Advocate Henry Cloete, the brother of Colonel A.J. Cloete, as the commissioner to Natal.[262] Cloete

---

[260] Muller, C. F. J. (1946). *Die Britse Owerheid en die Groot Trek* [Doctoral dissertation, University of Stellenbosch]., p.227-p.228
[261] Botha, J. P. (2008). Ons Geskiedenis (1st ed.). J.P. Botha., p.118
[262] Rautenbach, T. C. (2021). Sir George Napier en die Natalse Voortrekkers, 1838-1844. *Historia, 34*(2), p.22-p.31., p.30

arrived in Natal on 5 June 1843 and addressed the people in Pietermaritzburg on 9 June 1843. Due to resistance among the Boers, the meeting with the Volksraad to discuss the terms of annexation only took place two months later, in August 1843. It was the Boer women, particularly, who passionately confronted Cloete about Natalia's annexation. They told him that, for freedom, they would rather "walk barefoot over the Drakensberg" than live under British rule. Cloete was disturbed by the women's anger and later wrote: "It was a disgrace to their husbands to allow them such freedom."[263] The mouthpiece of the Cape Afrikaners, De Zuid Afrikaan, fully supported Napier's policy toward the Boers in Natal. In 1843, the publication described Henry Cloete's mission in Natal as a remarkable proof of British "kindness and goodwill," expected to significantly contribute "to create a deep and sincere feeling of love and respect toward Her Majesty's Government in the hearts of every Dutch Colonist."[264]

During this time, three groups of people arrived in Natalia, which escalated the potential for conflict. Firstly, the Zulu king Mpande, who had strengthened his army, orchestrated the murder of his half-brother Gqugqu, who had claims to the Zulu throne. This murder caused unrest in Zululand, leading Gqugqu's mother, Mawa, along with several chiefs and a large following of approximately 50,000 Zulus and numerous cattle, to migrate southward across the

---

[263] Giliomee, Hermann. Die Afrikaners (Afrikaans Edition). Tafelberg. Kindle Edition., p.166-p.167
[264] Scholtz, J. D. P. (1939). *Die Afrikaner en sy Taal*. Nasionale Pers., p.53

Tugela River.[265] The sudden increase of Zulus in Natalia caused significant unease among the Boers. Since they were not allowed by the English authorities to establish self-defence commandos, many Boers abandoned their farms and moved to Pietermaritzburg.[266] Secondly, a large group of armed Boer representatives from Winburg and Potchefstroom, including Commandants Jan Mocke, Greyling, Jan Kock, and J. P. Delport, arrived in Pietermaritzburg.[267] This display of force by the Boers aimed to deter the Zulus who had crossed the Tugela from attacking the Natal Boers, to lift the resisting spirit of the Boers in Natal, to show Cloete that the Natal Boers were not standing alone, and to ensure the exclusion of the Boer republic west of the Drakensberg from British annexation.[268] The third group was the arrival of British reinforcements in Port Natal. In early August 1843, on the assurance of the Boers that he would be safe, Cloete travelled alone to Pietermaritzburg, but he had long ago arranged for reinforcements. When HMS Thunderbolt arrived with an additional 550 soldiers at Port Natal, Major Smith was supposed to hurry to Pietermaritzburg before the Volksraad was in session.[269] However, when the reinforcements arrived without mounted

---

[265] Shamase, M. Z. (1999). *The reign of King Mpande and his relations with the Republic of Natalia and its successor, the British colony of Natal* [Doctoral dissertation, University of Zululand]., p.84
[266] Jansen, E. G. (1938). *Die Voortrekkers in Natal.*, https://archive.org/details/VoortrekkersInNatal
[267] Voigt, J. C. (1899). *Fifty Years of the History of the Republic in South Africa (1795-1845), Volume II.* E.P.Dutton &Co., p.265
[268] Voigt, J. C. (1899). *Fifty Years of the History of the Republic in South Africa (1795-1845), Volume II.* E.P.Dutton &Co., p.266
[269] Walker, E. A. (1965). *The Great Trek* (5th ed.). Adam & Charles Black, London., p.310

troops, essential for military action against the Boers, Smith refused to advance to Pietermaritzburg, leaving Cloete furious.

The Deputy Council of Potchefstroom was absent during the surrender of the Natal Council on 15 July 1842. Therefore, according to the Natalia constitution, the surrender agreement with Colonel Cloete, made without their consent, was technically illegal because they were part of the Volksraad. They knew that the majority of Natal Volksraad members would accept the terms of the British government, but they wished to participate in the process to protect the interests of the Boers of Winburg and Potchefstroom. Five Potchefstroomers - F.G. Wolmarans, P.F. Strydom, P. du Preez, H. van der Merwe, and H. van Staden - were sworn in as members of the Volksraad to discuss the proclamation of 12 May 1843, with Cloete.[270] Their primary concern was to understand the legal implications of the proclamation for the Winburg-Potchefstroom territories of the Boer Republic. When Cloete assured them that the Drakensberg Mountains would be the border of the new British colony and thus not affect the inland areas, they withdrew from the Natal Volksraad and also did not sign the surrender document on 8 August 1843.[271] On 9 April 1844, the Potchefstroom Burgerraad re-established the United Boer Republic and

---

[270] Storm, J.M.G. (1989). Die konvensie van Sandrivier as die afsluiting van die Groot Trek. *HTS Teologiese Studies / Theological Studies*, *45*(3), 680-695., p.687-p.688

[271] Storm, J.M.G. (1989). Die konvensie van Sandrivier as die afsluiting van die Groot Trek. *HTS Teologiese Studies / Theological Studies*, *45*(3), 680-695., p.687-p.688

drafted a constitution, known as the Thirty-Three Articles.[272] The next day, on 10 April 1844, the Potchefstroom Burgerraad, in a letter signed by J.D. van Coller as President and twenty-three others, including Andries Potgieter, informed the Natal Volksraad that they did not recognise any agreements made with Cloete. In the letter, they declared that they are not willing "to enter into any negotiations whatever with Her Majesty" and that they "consider ourselves free and independent and will proceed with our government."[273]

When the Boers in Natal at first behaved defiantly against Cloete and refused to accept British authority, Governor Napier became so enraged that he personally, in his own handwriting, designed a military plan to forcibly subdue all resistant Boers.[274] His strategy involved a pincer movement by attacking the Boers from two sides. Firstly, reinforcements, including 150 mounted soldiers, would be sent to Natal to strengthen the existing troop presence. According to Napier's plan, the indigenous tribes on the southern border of Natal would support his forces in their attack on the Boers. At the same time, he planned to attack the Boers from the west by crossing Philippolis, Modderrivier, and the Drakensberg. For this force, he intended to enlist the Griqua captains, Andries Waterboer and Adam Kok II, to recruit as many fighters as possible,

---

[272] Storm, J.M.G. (1989). Die konvensie van Sandrivier as die afsluiting van die Groot Trek. *HTS Teologiese Studies / Theological Studies, 45*(3), 680-695., p.688
[273] Cory, G. E. (1926). *The Rise of South Africa, Vol. IV*. Longman's, Green & Co., p.198-p.199
[274] Rautenbach, T. C. (2021). Sir George Napier en die Natalse Voortrekkers, 1838-1844. *Historia, 34*(2), p.22-p.31., p.30

which would then be reinforced by British infantry.[275] Napier anticipated that some Boers might escape this pincer movement, but he calculated that the Zulus would intercept them and kill every man, woman, and child.[276] This was the reason he had already sent reinforcements with the Thunderbolt to Natal. Napier was willing to make an example of these people to prevent any future uprising against British authority. Fortunately, on 8 August 1843, the Boers accepted Cloete's conditions, rendering Napier's plan unnecessary.[277] In an attempt to make the Boers more receptive to British authority, Napier sent a minister from the Dutch Reformed Church, Abraham Faure, from the Cape to influence the Boers in Natal. However, when Faure proposed a toast to Queen Victoria as the sovereign power in southern Africa, it upset the Boers.[278] Faure did not complete his tour among the Boers in Natal, as the congregation of Weenen preferred to bring a Dutch minister from Delagoa Bay.[279]

In early October 1843, Cloete visited Mpande at his Nodwengu headquarters. The Zulu king regarded the increase in Zulu refugees in Natal, which the British did nothing to prevent, as a significant concern because it undermined his authority in Zululand. The drastic decline in cattle herds in

---

[275] Rautenbach, T. C. (2021). Sir George Napier en die Natalse Voortrekkers, 1838-1844. *Historia, 34*(2), p.22-p.31., p.30
[276] Rautenbach, T. C. (2021). Sir George Napier en die Natalse Voortrekkers, 1838-1844. *Historia, 34*(2), p.22-p.31., p.30
[277] Rautenbach, T. C. (2021). Sir George Napier en die Natalse Voortrekkers, 1838-1844. *Historia, 34*(2), p.22-p.31., p.30
[278] Giliomee, Hermann. Die Afrikaners (Afrikaans Edition). Tafelberg. Kindle Edition., p.205
[279] Rautenbach, T. C. (2021). Sir George Napier en die Natalse Voortrekkers, 1838-1844. *Historia, 34*(2), p.22-p.31., p.31

Zululand as a result of this uncontrolled migration further weakened his authority.[280] Cloete and Mpande agreed that the Zulu refugees in Natal could stay, but the cattle they had taken would be returned to Mpande.[281] By 1845, there were approximately 75,000 Zulus between the Tugela and Mzimkhulu rivers, and this number increased to 305,000 by 1872.[282] During this meeting, Cloete focused on securing St. Lucia Bay for the British. He was aware that Mpande had previously granted the bay to the Boers as a reward for their assistance in the war against Dingane. Cloete argued: "As long as the Emigrant farmers beyond the Drakensberg continue in an insane struggle for independence, and (I regret to think) are encouraged by a few wicked and desperate characters who are still allowed to reside within this territory, and as long as they indulge in hopes of being provided with ammunition and other necessities... by keeping open some communication with the sea, it will be impossible to expect that the inhabitants of this colony will be entirely free from the contamination and excitement prevailing around them".[283] Cloete requested Mpande to transfer St. Lucia Bay to the British, arguing that Mpande would benefit because

---

[280] Shamase, M. Z. (1999). *The reign of King Mpande and his relations with the Republic of Natalia and its successor, the British colony of Natal* [Doctoral dissertation, University of Zululand]., p.123
[281] Shamase, M. Z. (1999). *The reign of King Mpande and his relations with the Republic of Natalia and its successor, the British colony of Natal* [Doctoral dissertation, University of Zululand]., p.123
[282] Shamase, M. Z. (1999). *The reign of King Mpande and his relations with the Republic of Natalia and its successor, the British colony of Natal* [Doctoral dissertation, University of Zululand]., p.85
[283] Shamase, M. Z. (1999). *The reign of King Mpande and his relations with the Republic of Natalia and its successor, the British colony of Natal* [Doctoral dissertation, University of Zululand]., p.121

THE CREATION OF THE BOER IDENTITY

England would keep all other European powers away from this bay. According to a later statement by an eyewitness, D.C. Uys, Mpande refused this request.[284] Four years later, Mpande once again ceded the area to the Boers.

During this time, many Boers migrated, and by the end of 1843, only about five hundred families remained in Natal. Most of the Natal Boers relocated to the Winburg district and Boer communities north of the Vaal River. A group of Boers, consisting of seventy families led by Andries Spies, Hans de Lange, and Petrus Lafras Uys, negotiated with King Mpande over the Kliprivier area, situated between the Tugela River and the Buffalo River. Mpande welcomed the Boers in the region as a buffer between his kingdom and the British, and he dispatched some of his headmen to the Boers to establish the border between the Boers and the Zulus.[285] After Mpande confirmed that this area was not part of Britain's annexation, the Boers purchased the land in April 1847 from the Zulu king for 1000 Rixdollars.[286] When British Lieutenant-Governor West learned of the Boers' land transaction with King Mpande, he sent copies of Sir Peregrine Maitland's proclamation of 21 August 1845, to Spies. This proclamation confirmed the Buffalo River as the northern boundary of the Natal colony, an extension of the

---

[284] Shamase, M. Z. (1999). *The reign of King Mpande and his relations with the Republic of Natalia and its successor, the British colony of Natal* [Doctoral dissertation, University of Zululand]., p.121

[285] Shamase, M. Z. (1999). *The reign of King Mpande and his relations with the Republic of Natalia and its successor, the British colony of Natal* [Doctoral dissertation, University of Zululand]., p.127

[286] Markram, W. J. (2001). *Die lewe en werk van Petrus Lafras Uys, 1797-1838* [Doctoral dissertation, University of Stellenbosch]., p.311

former Boer Republic of Natalia, which had the Tugela River as the northern boundary. West requested Spies to distribute these copies among the Kliprivier Boers, but Spies refused and returned them unopened to West.[287] He stated that they acquired the land from Mpande and said that they would rather live under the Zulu king than under the British.[288]

Andries Pretorius tried his best to persuade the Boers not to leave Natal. However, no stable government was established for Natal. The Volksraad continued to function, but they couldn't make autonomous decisions. As a result, uncertainty and unrest persisted. In August 1844, a new Volksraad was elected, but its members refused to swear allegiance to the British crown. Major Smith then disbanded the Volksraad and reinstated the old one.[289] However, Smith prevented the first decisions they took, using a commando led by D. Pretorius, a blacksmith, to remove incoming refugees from their farms.[290] The Volksraad made several recommendations to the governor, but they were ignored. In August 1845, the borders of Natal were established by proclamation. In December 1845, Martin West, former civil commissioner of Albany, arrived in Natal with several officials to establish the new administration under British

---

[287] Markram, W. J. (2001). *Die lewe en werk van Petrus Lafras Uys, 1797-1838* [Doctoral dissertation, University of Stellenbosch]., p.311
[288] Shamase, M. Z. (1999). *The reign of King Mpande and his relations with the Republic of Natalia and its successor, the British colony of Natal* [Doctoral dissertation, University of Zululand]., p.133
[289] Jansen, E. G. (1938). *Die Voortrekkers in Natal.*, https://archive.org/details/VoortrekkersInNatal
[290] Cory, G. E. (1926). *The Rise of South Africa, Vol. IV*. Longman's, Green & Co., p.201

rule.[291] The influx of refugees continued unchecked, and widespread cattle theft occurred. Crime escalated to the point that even Pretorius and his family had to flee their farm,[292] His complaints about cattle theft, arson, and insecurity were ignored by the British authorities, as evidenced in correspondence between Pretorius and Lieutenant-Governor West.[293]

The second Trek, from Natal into the interior, occurred because the conditions in Natal had become largely similar to those in the eastern Cape at the beginning of the Great Trek. The British authority didn't allow the Boers to govern themselves or to defend themselves against crime and attacks. At the same time, they were unwilling to bear the expenses for an effective administration and for the security of the residents. There were rumours that Mpande was planning an invasion of Natal. When the Boers in the Kliprivier area began to leave even with their sown crops still in the fields, most of the remaining Boers south of the Tugela followed suit. Under British rule, the lives of the Boers in Natal were unsafe,[294] and they concluded that there was no other solution but to migrate again. In a final attempt to improve conditions in Natal, the Boers sent Pretorius to meet the Cape governor, Pottinger, in Grahamstown. Pottinger,

---

[291] Jansen, E. G. (1938). *Die Voortrekkers in Natal.*, https://archive.org/details/VoortrekkersInNatal
[292] Steyn, J.C. 2016 *Afrikanerjoernaal. 'n Vervolgverhaal in 365 episodes*. Pretoria: FAK., p.119
[293] Jansen, E. G. (1938). *Die Voortrekkers in Natal.*, https://archive.org/details/VoortrekkersInNatal
[294] Giliomee, Hermann. Die Afrikaners (Afrikaans Edition). Tafelberg. Kindle Edition., p.169

however, refused to receive him. At his return from Grahamstown, Pretorius found about 400 of the remaining Boers, including his own family, in a laager at Doornkop, the same place where they had stood ten years ago when they entered Natal. Due to swollen rivers, they had to stay there for weeks before they could trek over the Drakensberg again. When Pretorius found his family, his wife was lying ill in a wagon, and his youngest daughter was leading the oxen, although she was severely injured by one of them.[295]

The new governor of the Cape, Sir Harry Smith, rushed to Natal to prevent Pretorius and the remaining Boers from leaving Natal. He found Pretorius and his trek in pouring rain just over the Drakensberg. In his usual dramatic style, Governor Smith commented on this exodus: "I was almost paralysed to witness the whole of the population, with few exceptions, 'trekking' [sic]. Rains on this side of the mountains are tropical... and [these] families were exposed to a state of misery which I never before saw equalled."[296] Because the Tugela was flooded, the governor stayed with Pretorius for a few days.[297] Due to the respect Governor Smith had earned among the Boers for his decisive actions during the Sixth Frontier War from 1834 to 1836 when he served as the military commander in the Cape, he was convinced that he could persuade the Boers to be loyal to British authority. He also believed that the majority of Boers

---

[295] G. M. Theal (1888). *History of the Emigrant Boers in South Africa.* (2nd ed.). Swan Sonnenschein, Lowrey & Co., p.244
[296] Giliomee, Hermann. Die Afrikaners (Afrikaans Edition). Tafelberg. Kindle Edition., p.170
[297] G. M. Theal (1888). *History of the Emigrant Boers in South Africa.* (2nd ed.). Swan Sonnenschein, Lowrey & Co., p.244

preferred being under British rule. During his journey through the Transorangia, Winburg, and Natal, he was warmly welcomed by the Boers. He received numerous requests, including from twenty-seven families in Winburg, to annex the Transorangia under the British flag. However, he confused the Cape trekboers, who were loyal British subjects, with the Boers,[298] and he didn't consider that the vast majority of Winburg Boers did not meet him on his trip. When Andries Pretorius refused his appointment to the Natal Land Council, and the Boers in Natal declined to return to their farms, Smith found it incomprehensible. He referred to Pretorius as the "arch-rebel who disregarded Her Majesty's sovereignty."[299] Smith then threatened Pretorius that Britain would annex the Transorangia and the area north of the Vaal River as British territories. In February 1848, Pretorius declared that he would proclaim the Boer territories in the interior as an independent state and was willing to achieve independence through any means—petitions, negotiations, or military force.[300]

---

[298] The trekboers of this era were farmers from the northern regions of the Cape Colony who, solely for material reasons such as better pastures and water for their herds, migrated to southern Transorangia (later the Free State). They did not participate in the Great Trek due to influences such as propaganda from the Dutch Reformed Church, the media, and regulations of the British government in the Cape. These trekboers, like the so-called Cape Afrikaners from the western districts of the Cape Colony, were not Boers because they did not experience the shared history and shared trauma that shaped Boer identity. They did not develop the Boers' spirit of independence and became loyal British subjects.
[299] Jansen, E. G. (1938). *Die Voortrekkers in Natal.*, https://archive.org/details/VoortrekkersInNatal
[300] Giliomee, Hermann. Die Afrikaners (Afrikaans Edition). Tafelberg. Kindle Edition., p.170

THE BOER REPUBLICS

The Boers who settled across the Vaal River described the territory they claimed in 1840. The territory they described closely resembled the land that Mzilikazi had conquered and occupied before they drove him out of the region. The delineation of their territory was formalised in the Act of Union of the areas west and east of the Drakensberg, accepted on 16 October 1840, during a public meeting in Potchefstroom.[301] From 1839, farms were registered, and a list of farm registrations was maintained.[302] In 1843, Potgieter sent a commission of eighty Winburgers and Potchefstromers to Delagoa Bay to negotiate trade possibilities with the Portuguese. Despite the challenging journey, with flooded rivers and the threat of the tsetse fly, the group returned to the Magaliesberg by the end of August 1844.[303] Based on this expedition, the Burgerraad instructed Potgieter to organise a relocation closer to the Portuguese harbour. The recent annexation of Natal and the threat posed by Britain's "Cape of Good Hope Punishment Act" on their independence, certainly played a key role in the decision of these Boers to move because Ohrigstad falls outside the jurisdiction of this Act. By August 1845, more than 1,000 Boers, approximately three hundred families, had already settled in the new area, which they named Andries Ohrigstad.[304] Paul Kruger's father, Casper, and his uncle Gert

---

[301] Bergh, J. S. (1992). Die vestiging van die Voortrekkers noord van die Vaalrivier tot 1840. *Historia, 37*(2), pp.39-47., p.42
[302] Bergh, J. S. (1992). Die vestiging van die Voortrekkers noord van die Vaalrivier tot 1840. *Historia, 37*(2), pp.39-47., p.44
[303] Botha, J. P. (2008). Ons Geskiedenis (1st ed.). J.P. Botha., p.123-p.124
[304] Botha, J. P. (2008). Ons Geskiedenis (1st ed.). J.P. Botha., p.125

also participated in the trek to Ohrigstad, but they returned to the Potchefstroom district early on.

While the Boers were in Ohrigstad, Swazi King Mswati II launched an attack on King Mpande's Zulu outposts, seizing all the cattle in the process.[305] Mpande, seeking to avoid conflict with the Boers, informed them of his intention to take military action against the Swazis. Potgieter explained to Mpande that there was a friendly relationship between the Boers and Swazis but assured him of Boer neutrality in the Zulu-Swazi conflict. Potgieter emphasised that the Boers would find the killing of Swazi women and children unacceptable.[306] However, the Swazi king then approached the Boers for support against the Zulus. On 26 July 1846, Mswati and the Boers signed a defence treaty forming an alliance against the Zulus.[307] According to the terms of the treaty, the Boers committed to supporting the Swazis in their war against the Zulus in exchange for a substantial piece of land in the eastern highveld (now Mpumalanga). This area stretched from the Olifants River in the north to the Crocodile River in the south. In July 1847, Mpande deployed his isaNgqu, iNkonkoni, uDlokwe, and uNokhenke regiments against the Swazis, but they had to

---

[305] Shamase, M. Z. (1999). *The reign of King Mpande and his relations with the Republic of Natalia and its successor, the British colony of Natal* [Doctoral dissertation, University of Zululand]., p.123

[306] Shamase, M. Z. (1999). *The reign of King Mpande and his relations with the Republic of Natalia and its successor, the British colony of Natal* [Doctoral dissertation, University of Zululand]., p.123

[307] Shamase, M. Z. (1999). *The reign of King Mpande and his relations with the Republic of Natalia and its successor, the British colony of Natal* [Doctoral dissertation, University of Zululand]., p.85

withdraw without achieving success. Thanks to the Boers' alliance with Mswati, the total annihilation of the Swazi people was ultimately prevented.[308]

In contrast to the Boers' declared policy of occupying only uninhabited land, some of the land in this region was already occupied. The Ndzundza had permanently settled between the Steelpoort and Dwarsrivier since 1839, where the Boers found them in a wretched condition after being nearly destroyed by devastating attacks from Mzilikazi.[309] The Pedi and various smaller tribes also inhabited the area.[310] The Boers initially approached Mabhogo, the Chief of the Ndzundza, regarding land purchase, but Mabhogo referred them to the Swazis who had already conquered the land.[311] After the land transaction with Swazi King Mswati II on 26 July 1846, the Boers did not recognise any land rights of the other tribes in the area and simply occupied the land permanently inhabited by these tribes. There was no separate land agreement with the Ndzundza. However, in a letter to Sir Harry Smith on 15 May 1848, Andries Potgieter mentioned that the Boers had a peace treaty with Mabhogo, in terms of which the Boers would protect them against

---

[308] Shamase, M. Z. (1999). *The reign of King Mpande and his relations with the Republic of Natalia and its successor, the British colony of Natal* [Doctoral dissertation, University of Zululand]., p.85
[309] Van Jaarsveld, F. A. (1985), . Die Ndzundza-Ndebele en die Blankes in Transvaal 1845-1883 [Master's Thesis, Rhodes Universiteit]., p.26
[310] Van Jaarsveld, F. A. (1985), . Die Ndzundza-Ndebele en die Blankes in Transvaal 1845-1883 [Master's Thesis, Rhodes Universiteit]., p.27
[311] Van Jaarsveld, F. A. (1985), . Die Ndzundza-Ndebele en die Blankes in Transvaal 1845-1883 [Master's Thesis, Rhodes Universiteit]., p.29

THE CREATION OF THE BOER IDENTITY

attacks from hostile tribes.[312] The Swazis also offered to destroy the Ndzundza, but the Boers rejected the offer. In 1861, a Swazi captain told the landdrost of Lydenburg that "the name of Mapoch (Mabhogo) would probably not have been mentioned again," indicating that the Ndzundza would no longer have existed if the Boers had not prevented the Swazis from exterminating them.[313]

The Ohrigstad settlement struggled due to challenges in trading through the Portuguese harbour, the difficult route to Delagoa Bay, and the constant threat of malaria. Andries Potgieter then led an expedition northward with 230 men. During this expedition, they again clashed with Mzilikazi in the far north, and they also identified a suitable site for a new settlement at Soutpansberg. In early 1848, Potgieter and his followers established a new settlement, Schoemansdal, at Soutpansberg.[314] Meanwhile, the Boers who remained in Ohrigstad under the leadership of Jacobus Burger were struck by a malaria epidemic in 1848, claiming more than a hundred lives. They then moved southward to a higher-altitude area, where on 20 September 1849, they established a new settlement named Leidenburg.[315] In 1856, the Boers proclaimed the Republic of Lydenburg on the land they acquired from the Swazi king. In Soutpansberg, Potgieter and

---

[312] Van Jaarsveld, F. A. (1985), . Die Ndzundza-Ndebele en die Blankes in Transvaal 1845-1883 [Master's Thesis, Rhodes Universiteit]., p.31
[313] Van Jaarsveld, F. A. (1985), . Die Ndzundza-Ndebele en die Blankes in Transvaal 1845-1883 [Master's Thesis, Rhodes Universiteit]., p.30
[314] Botha, J. P. (2008). Ons Geskiedenis (1st ed.). J.P. Botha., p.130-p.131
[315] Botha, J. P. (2008). Ons Geskiedenis (1st ed.). J.P. Botha., p.130-p.131

Mzilikazi reconciled. Mzilikazi acknowledged Boer authority and ownership of the land he relinquished during their 1837 battle. Mzilikazi sought military aid from Potgieter because he was threatened by Tswana clans from present-day Botswana, who were armed with guns and ammunition supplied by English traders and the missionary David Livingstone. The Boers then entered into a Treaty of Peace and Friendship with the Ndebele. The treaty was signed in Schoemansdal on 8 January 1853, three weeks after Potgieter's death, by his son, Piet, who succeeded him as commandant-general, and by Marap, Mzilikazi's representative.

Transorangia, situated between the Orange River and the Vaal River in what is now the Free State province of South Africa, was characterised by diverse populations, with the potential for conflicts over land. In the northern region, between the Vet and Vaal Rivers and the Drakensberg to the west, was Winburg, which belonged to the Boers after Hendrik Potgieter acquired the land from Chief Makwana of the Batuanga. The Boers in Winburg were in union with their compatriots north of the Vaal River. The southern part of Transorangia included various Griqua and Bantu states and reserves. Nicolaas Waterboer of Griqualand West had a treaty with the Cape government. Adam Kok, leader of the Griqua people in Philippolis, claimed authority over the area from the Orange River to the Modder River also had a treaty with the British. South of Kok's territory was the Batlapin reserve at Betlindie. On the west of the Caledon River, there were mission reserves for Bantu and Coloured groups at Beersheba, Thaba Nchu, Platberg, Mekuatling, Merumetsu, and Imparani.³¹⁶ Further west, the Basuto were settled around Thaba Bosigo, and the territory of Sikonyela extended farther west. English settlers and Cape trekboers under Michiel Oberholzer also established themselves in the area. The Cape trekboers' move to Transorangia was based on material considerations only. They were still loyal British subjects and advocated for the annexation of Transorangia by the British government.³¹⁷

Towards the end of 1835, British State Secretary, Glenelg, instituted a treaty system to regulate relations between Britain and the various population groups in southern Africa. He appointed Andries Stockenström as the lieutenant governor of the eastern districts of the Cape Colony and tasked him with negotiating treaties with various tribes. Stockenström outlined the objectives of the treaty system: "our objects ought to be these, ...the safety of the Colony against future inroads... Secondly, the improvement of the Kaffir nation, and its maintenance as an independent ally."³¹⁸ The British government compensated the Chiefs, often with a fixed income, in exchange that they prevent attacks on the Colony. Most treaties included provisions for mutual military assistance in case of an attack. The British government entered into treaties with nearly all surrounding tribes, including Mzilikazi, who had previously caused large-scale, violent upheaval in the central highland of southern

---

[316] Walker, E. A. (1922). *Historical Atlas of South Africa*. Humphrey Milford Oxford University Press., p.17
[317] Botha, J. P. (2008). Ons Geskiedenis (1st ed.). J.P. Botha., p.132
[318] Du Toit, A., & Giliomee, H. (1983). *Afrikaner Political Thought. Volume 1: 1780-1850*. University of California Press., p.174

Africa during the Mfecane period. Through these treaties, the British government effectively acknowledged the independence of these nations and affirmed their right to their land. However, this policy of recognition and collaboration with indigenous tribes sharply contrasted with the British approach towards the Boers. The British refused to recognise the Boers as an independent people and pursued them, annexing their lands. The Boers would later, after the annexation of the second Boer territory, Winburg, officially express their disapproval of this unequal treatment by the British government in a memorandum to Governor Smith.[319]

In 1844, an incident occurred between the Boers and the Griquas, during which Hendrik Potgieter highlighted the Boers' approach to interactions with other African tribes. Griqua Captain Adam Kok arrested a Boer, Hermanus van Staden, on charges of murdering an Englishman. Despite the Boers' demand for Van Staden's trial in Winburg, Kok sent him to Colesberg in the Cape Colony. As tensions escalated between the Boers and the Griquas, Andries Potgieter personally went to Phillipolis to improve relations with the Griquas. However, Kok made it clear to Potgieter that, according to his treaty with the British government, the Boers were considered British subjects, and thus he did not recognise the Boers as an independent people with any authority. Van Staden was acquitted in the Colesberg court,

---

[319] Memorandum by Pretorius dated 18 July 1848, signed by 900 Boer commandants and field cornets; Du Toit, A., & Giliomee, H. (1983). Afrikaner Political Thought. Volume 1: 1780-1850. University of California Press, p.223-p.225

THE CREATION OF THE BOER IDENTITY

resolving the problem.[320] Afterwards, Potgieter attempted to establish a communication channel for dispute resolution in a letter to Kok. In this letter, he outlined the Boers' policy on relations with other communities, based on equality and non-interference. He emphasised that the leadership of both communities should retain full authority within their respective territories.[321] Potgieter wrote: "We are emigrants together with you and are regarded as such and regard ourselves as emigrants who together with you dwell in the same strange land, and we desire to be regarded as neither more nor less than your fellow emigrants (*both the Griquas and the Boers left the Cape to govern themselves*), inhabitants of the country, enjoying the same privileges with you." "It is by no means the intention of the Head Commandant and his council to bring any native chief under their laws and authority, but to leave each one to exercise his own authority." "But in the case of any crime committed by a Boer against a native, the native shall complain to the leader of the Boers and when a crime is committed by a native against a Boer, the Boer shall complain to a ruler of the natives."[322]

When Governor Smith met Pretorius at Doornkop during the latter's departure from Natal, he promised Pretorius that he would postpone declaring the Transorangia as British Sovereignty until Pretorius provided evidence that

---

[320] Gie, S. F. (1932). *Geskiedenis vir Suid-Afrika, II* (2nd ed.). Pro Ecclesia-Drukkery, p.344
[321] Du Toit, A., & Giliomee, H. (1983). *Afrikaner Political Thought. Volume 1: 1780-1850*. University of California Press., p.141
[322] Du Toit, A., & Giliomee, H. (1983). *Afrikaner Political Thought. Volume 1: 1780-1850*. University of California Press., p.173

most Boers opposed British rule. However, Smith, without further consultation, published the proclamation of the Orange River Sovereignty on 3 February 1848, thereby also annexing the Boer land of Winburg which they legally acquired from Chief Makwana of the Batuanga. In reaction, Pretorius responded to Smith with a manifesto signed by nine hundred Boers:

"We all, the undersigned Commandants and Field Comets... perceive... that you threaten us with a war of military power; which appears to us very unjust to constrain us on lands which we have justly bartered from the natives..."

"To them (the natives) are acknowledged and secured the lands they have inherited; to them are allowed the privileges of self-government and their own laws; but as soon as we are on the same lands, which we have justly obtained from them, these privileges are immediately taken from us, so that we may justly say that we do not even share equally with the coloured tribes..."

"We repeat again, as well to Your Excellency as to the world, that had we perchance been coloured, it might perhaps be possible, but now we find it impossible, because we are white African Boers. We speak not loosely; we speak not in hatred; because we were oppressed by the British authority..."

"And now do we arrive at the great Mirror of Natal... How did we obtain possession of that country — unjustly or easily? No; we obtained it justly from a Sovereign power; and subsequently it cost us the blood of dearest wives and children, and we will never refrain from exclaiming it before the great Creator and the world."

"With tearful eyes are we obliged to look back on our churches, and dearly-bought land... Where are then the former proprietors of the land (Natalia)? Here they are wandering in the wilderness of South Africa." "But should you now drive us deeper into the wilderness, will you thereby make us better? "

"Oh, these hardships you will never eradicate from the heart of an African Boer, neither with promises nor with threats; you will cause a further flight and dissatisfaction, but never a silent submission. And thus we have severely suffered; we have silently left our motherland under all these hardships; for liberty we sacrificed all!"

"But we wish to entreat Your Excellency to leave us unmolested and without further interference, on those grounds which we have justly obtained from the legal proprietors, and thus we shall exclaim to the world and our Creator, (who we know looks down upon us from on high, and to Him alone we owe all gratitude and reverence), that we have not yet been totally extirpated."[323]

The motivation behind Smith's annexation of Transorangia is unclear. Officially, he claimed it was to protect indigenous populations from potential attacks and mistreatment by the Boers. In a letter to British Secretary Grey, Smith wrote: "I was moved to that act (proclamation of the Orange River Sovereignty) by the desire to establish amicable relationship with the native chiefs, to uphold them in their hereditary rights and to protect them from aggression (from the Boers),...".[324] However, this official explanation

---

[323] Du Toit, A., & Giliomee, H. (1983). *Afrikaner Political Thought. Volume 1: 1780-1850*. University of California Press., p.223-p.225
[324] Muller, C. F. J. (1946). *Die Britse Owerheid en die Groot Trek* [Doctoral dissertation, University of Stellenbosch]., p.500

contradicts the on-the-ground reality that Smith himself acknowledged in a letter to Grey on 10 February 1848, at the time of the proclamation of the Sovereignty. In this letter, Smith described the relationships between the Boers and other tribes as positive, stating: "...throughout my journey among the emigrants (the Boers) I saw no appearance of slaves - much less any traffic in them - which has been erroneously alleged to exist..." "The Boers and natives, as far as my observations went, are everywhere on the best terms."[325] In February 1848, Andries Pretorius recognised the necessity of using force in their resistance against the British government. He declared that the Boer territories in the interior would be an independent state, expressing readiness to achieve independence through any means — petitions, negotiations, or military force.[326] Pretorius addressed Boers on both sides of the Vaal River, emphasising that freedom could not be attained through trekking or fleeing but only through struggle. He issued a general call for mobilisation for a Freedom War against the British government, but faced opposition, especially from Boers north of the Vaal River, including Andries Potgieter. They rejected any engagement with the British government, refusing both negotiation and confrontation. Disheartened by the Boers' response, Pretorius retired to his farm, Rust der Ouden (Rest of the Elders) in the Magaliesberg.

---

[325] Muller, C. F. J. (1946). *Die Britse Owerheid en die Groot Trek* [Doctoral dissertation, University of Stellenbosch]., p.496
[326] Giliomee, Hermann. Die Afrikaners (Afrikaans Edition). Tafelberg. Kindle Edition., p.170

When Governor Smith learned of Pretorius' efforts to mobilise the Boers, he issued a manifesto on 29 May 1848 to explain the annexation of Transorangia. Smith believed the annexation was justified because four out of five Boers supported it. In the manifesto, he stated: "some evil-minded persons, prone to wickedness, to mischief and to evil ways, have been in the Territory beyond the Orange River, over which I have proclaimed the Sovereignty of Her Majesty, have been calling meetings to pervert the true spirit and meaning of my Proclamation..." " — I deem it my duty to publish an explanation of the motives which have induced me to establish a Government over deluded, disappointed and dissatisfied men, who have expatriated themselves from the Land of their Fathers — from the homes which reared them — and from their relations and friends."[327] The annexation became a reality for the Boers in the Winburg territory when, on 22 May 1848, Smith replaced the Boer landdros W. Jacobs with an English magistrate, T.J. Biddulph.[328] The Winburg Boers then appealed to Andries Pretorius to lead them in a struggle against the British government.[329] During this time, Pretorius's wife, Christina (born De Wit), was seriously ill. Despite her condition, she insisted that he serve his people: "I am very sick, and life is something you cannot give me. They ask for your help. Go to your people and see what you can do for them while the matter is urgent".[330]

---

[327] Cory, G. E. (1926). *The Rise of South Africa, Vol. IV*. Longman's, Green & Co., p.138-p.139
[328] Cory, G. E. (1926). *The Rise of South Africa, Vol. IV*. Longman's, Green & Co., p.143
[329] Botha, J. P. (2008). Ons Geskiedenis (1st ed.). J.P. Botha., p.134
[330] Steyn, J.C. 2016 *Afrikanerjoernaal. 'n Vervolgverhaal in 365 episodes*. Pretoria: FAK., p.121

THE BOER REPUBLICS

When Pretorius left his wife in June 1848 to liberate Winburg, it was the last time he would ever see her.

Approximately 120 Boers from Winburg, under the leadership of Landdrost Jacobs, gathered on the farm of a Boer named Vermeulen to discuss a plan of action. After also discussing the matter with Pretorius, they decided to officially inform Biddulph about the Boers' position on his appointment. Landdrost Jacobs then sent a letter, signed by himself and Heemraden A. Cronje, G. P. Brits, P. M. Bester, and F. J. Bezuidenhout, to Biddulph with the message: "To the magistrate who has arrived at Winburg, it is hereby, in the name of the United Public, and according to a memorial already sent to the governor (Smith), made known that we will not acknowledge you as magistrate in any way, we remain (in our positions) in the name of the Public."[331] On 23 June 1848, Biddulph left Winburg and went to Bloemfontein, where the British Resident, Major Henry Warden, was stationed. Pretorius arrived at Winburg on 12 July 1848, with a force of five hundred men. More Boers joined him at Winburg, and then, with a force of about a thousand men, he proceeded to Bloemfontein, where on 17 July 1848, they set up laager about two miles from the town. Major Warden accepted an ultimatum from Pretorius, requiring his troops and all inhabitants of Bloemfontein to leave the town within three days. Pretorius allowed them to take all their belongings, both public and private, with them and arranged

---

[331] Cory, G. E. (1926). *The Rise of South Africa, Vol. IV*. Longman's, Green & Co., p.145-p.146

THE CREATION OF THE BOER IDENTITY

the necessary wagons for their relocation.[332] Pretorius, through Major Warden, requested a meeting with Smith, but Smith refused to "negotiate with a rebel" and pledged to "...protect Her Majesty's loyal emigrant subjects (probably the Cape trekboers) from insult and to suppress rebellion with Her Majesty's cannon and soldiers..."[333] Smith placed a reward of £1000, later increased to £2000, for the capture of Pretorius. On 26 July 1848, Harry Smith wrote to Secretary Grey: "It shall very soon be shown whose authority is paramount, that of Her Majesty of England, or of this rebel."[334]

On 2 August 1848, Major Warden, on behalf of Governor Smith, requested military assistance from the Basotho king Moshesh, Batlokwa Chief Sikonyela, Koranna leader Gert Taaibosch, and the Griqua Chiefs Jan Bloem, Adam Kok, and Andries Waterboer.[335] Governor Smith led his contingent across the Orange River into the Orange River Sovereignty on 26 August 1848. The contingent comprised about 1,200 men, three cannons, and 177 wagons carrying supplies for thirty days. Adam Kok and Andries Waterboer joined Smith's forces across the Orange River with 250 Griqua troops.[336] Cape trekboers under Commandants Pieter

---

[332] Cory, G. E. (1926). *The Rise of South Africa, Vol. IV*. Longman's, Green & Co., p.150
[333] Cory, G. E. (1926). *The Rise of South Africa, Vol. IV*. Longman's, Green & Co., p.153
[334] Muller, C. F. J. (1946). *Die Britse Owerheid en die Groot Trek* [Doctoral dissertation, University of Stellenbosch]., p.319
[335] Cory, G. E. (1926). *The Rise of South Africa, Vol. IV*. Longman's, Green & Co., p.153
[336] Cory, G. E. (1926). *The Rise of South Africa, Vol. IV*. Longman's, Green & Co., p.156

Erasmus and J. T. Snyman also joined Smith's army to protect the supply wagons.[337] Pretorius devised a strategy to ambush Smith on flat terrain with two rows of low hills on the farm Boomplaats near Jagersfontein. Smith reached Boomplaats on 29 August 1848, at 11:00 in the morning and advanced toward the hills. As Lieutenant Salis' Cape Corps troop, accompanied by Smith and his staff, reached the second hill on their right, they encountered the first group of Boers, who prematurely opened fire on them. Pretorius' plan was to wait until the entire British column was within firing range.[338] During this initial skirmish, Smith was narrowly missed by a bullet, and three Khoi-Khoi soldiers of the Cape Corps were killed. Lieutenant Salis, who lay wounded on the ground, was approached by two Boers. He feared they would kill him and called out that he had a wife and two children at home. The Boers let him go, and he was later taken for treatment to a hospital tent in the rear.

Smith instructed Lieutenant Dynely of the Royal Artillery to position the cannons and fire upon the Boer forces. When the Boers sought shelter behind rocks on the hill, Captain Murray's Rifle Brigade stormed the hill. During this assault, Murray was severely wounded, and he died later that night. Many of Murray's men were also wounded or killed on the slope, and before they reached the hill's summit, the Boers had already retreated and regrouped on the next

---

[337] G. M. Theal (1888). *History of the Emigrant Boers in South Africa.* (2nd ed.). Swan Sonnenschein, Lowrey & Co., p.254
[338] G. M. Theal (1888). *History of the Emigrant Boers in South Africa.* (2nd ed.). Swan Sonnenschein, Lowrey & Co., p.257

hill.[339] A small group of Boers, led by Commandant Jan Kock, then rushed across the plain to attack the British wagons and supplies. The Cape Corps was sent to engage Kock, and after intense fighting, they forced Kock to withdraw to the main Boer commando. The British 91st, supported by the Rifle Brigade and the 45th, was then deployed to break the Boers' defensive line. Smith personally selected gun positions, and the second hill was stormed similarly to the first. The Boers retreated again and took up a third position on the slopes overlooking the high ridge neck for their final stand. The Cape Corps and the Griquas then launched a mounted attack on the Boers, but they were repelled. Smith, leading with the infantry, stormed the Boer positions with his entire force. The Boers were dislodged from their positions and fled across the plain.[340]

The defeat at Boomplaats was a significant setback in the Boers' pursuit of independence. After the battle, Smith, an experienced military officer, described the encounter in a letter to the Secretary of State as "one of the most severe skirmishes that he had ever witnessed."[341] The British suffered twenty-four men killed and thirty-nine wounded, while nine Boers were killed and five wounded. A young Boer, Thomas Dreyer, was captured during the conflict. He was later charged with "armed resistance against his lawful sovereign," the Queen of England, and was executed by a

---

[339] G. M. Theal (1888). *History of the Emigrant Boers in South Africa.* (2nd ed.). Swan Sonnenschein, Lowrey & Co., p.258
[340] G. M. Theal (1888). *History of the Emigrant Boers in South Africa.* (2nd ed.). Swan Sonnenschein, Lowrey & Co., p.259
[341] G. M. Theal (1888). *History of the Emigrant Boers in South Africa.* (2nd ed.). Swan Sonnenschein, Lowrey & Co., p.259

firing squad on 3 September 1848. Pretorius considered Dreyer's execution a "crying scandalous act".[342] Smith has now increased the reward for the capture of Pretorius to £2,000 and he issued rewards of £500 each for the capture of Andries Spies, Jan Krynauw, and Louw Pretorius. He confiscated the farms of Jan Krynauw, Louw Pretorius, Frederick Otto, Jan Jacobs, Philip van Coller, Jan Viljoen, and Adrian Stander and he also imposed fines as follows: Ocker Jacobus van Schalkwyk £200, Pieter Louw and Jan Botes each £150, Christoffel Snyman £100, and Roelof Grobbelaar £50.[343] In a letter dated 10 September 1848, Smith declared to British Secretary Grey that he successfully subdued "these turbulent Boers" in time, preventing the emergence of "a mass of white barbarians" on the northern border of the Cape Colony.[344] In a letter to Smith on 29 August 1848, Pretorius blamed Smith for the bloodshed because he was unwilling to talk. He also warned Smith: "I further consider it my duty to tell Your Excellency that we would rather go into the wilderness of southern Africa and fight to the death than to find ourselves here under Her Majesty's authority, and if you did not want to reach a fair settlement with us, that all further disasters will then be your responsibility, ..."[345] The Cape newspaper, De Zuid Afrikaan, the mouthpiece for the Cape Afrikaners, approved of Harry

---

[342] Steyn, J.C. 2016 *Afrikanerjoernaal. 'n Vervolgverhaal in 365 episodes*. Pretoria: FAK., p.120
[343] G. M. Theal (1888). *History of the Emigrant Boers in South Africa*. (2nd ed.). Swan Sonnenschein, Lowrey & Co., p.261-p.262
[344] Muller, C. F. J. (1946). *Die Britse Owerheid en die Groot Trek* [Doctoral dissertation, University of Stellenbosch]., p.208-p.209
[345] G. M. Theal (1888). *History of the Emigrant Boers in South Africa*. (2nd ed.). Swan Sonnenschein, Lowrey & Co., p.260

Smith's annexation of the Transorangia territory. After the Battle of Boomplaats, De Zuid Afrikaan appealed to the British government to use "conciliatory measures" to show the exiled Boers "the great privilege of being subjects of the British Crown".[346]

Shortly after Smith declared the Orange River Sovereignty, there was a significant change in British policy regarding its relationships with the various population groups in southern Africa. The influence of evangelical Christians on the British government in London began to decline sharply. The London Missionary Society faced a lack of funds, and its leader in southern Africa, Dr. Phillip, encountered personal obstacles that hindered his work.[347] The military and financial impact of the Eighth Xhosa War (1850-1853) on the eastern border of the Cape Colony, conflicts with the Basotho Chief, Moshesh, and the threat posed by the Boers north of the Vaal River led the British government to alter its policies towards both the indigenous tribes and the Boers. The border wars and Moshesh's military successes against Britain convinced British politicians that the work of missionaries among the black tribes was unsuccessful and could bear no fruit. Fifteen years after Piet Retief condemned the missionaries for becoming involved in politics against the Boers, the British government itself condemned the missionaries for their political

---

[346] Scholtz, J. D. P. (1939). *Die Afrikaner en sy Taal*. Nasionale Pers., p.53
[347] Muller, C. F. J. (1946). *Die Britse Owerheid en die Groot Trek* [Doctoral dissertation, University of Stellenbosch]., p.467

involvement.³⁴⁸ After a visit to the Orange River Sovereignty, the Scottish minister of the Dutch Reformed Church, Dr W. Robertson, wrote in a private letter to Sir Harry Smith: "It would, in every respect, be better if the missionaries were not made the medium of communication between the government and the native chiefs."³⁴⁹ In September 1852, Governor Cathcart wrote that in "long and elaborate treatises on political subjects" received from indigenous tribal leaders, it is evident that the missionaries were not only the translators of the letters but also the authors. Cathcart considered the letters drafted by the missionaries on behalf of tribal leaders as "political fraud" and declared that he would henceforth ignore written communication from tribal leaders.³⁵⁰

The Eighth Xhosa War in British Kaffraria, on the eastern border of the Cape Colony, posed the most challenging frontier conflict yet for the Cape government. The frontier war was complicated even more when the Khoi-Khoi of the Kat River settlement in the eastern Cape rebelled. Cape Governor Smith had to withdraw troops from the Orange River Sovereignty to assist in the eastern Cape. Meanwhile, Moshesh began arming himself with guns and ammunition, and he threatened tribes that were friendly to the British government and settlers in the Orange River Sovereignty. According to a letter from Smith to State

---

[348] Muller, C. F. J. (1946). *Die Britse Owerheid en die Groot Trek* [Doctoral dissertation, University of Stellenbosch]., p.477
[349] Muller, C. F. J. (1946). *Die Britse Owerheid en die Groot Trek* [Doctoral dissertation, University of Stellenbosch]., p.478
[350] Muller, C. F. J. (1946). *Die Britse Owerheid en die Groot Trek* [Doctoral dissertation, University of Stellenbosch]., p.488

Secretary Grey on 5 November 1851, Moshesh sent messages to Xhosa leaders Kreli and Sandili "on a weekly basis," encouraging them to hostilities against the British government.[351] On 25 June 1851, Major Warden, the British Resident in Bloemfontein, issued an ultimatum to Moshesh, demanding compensation of 6000 cattle and 300 horses for tribes aligned to the British government and Sovereignty farmers who suffered losses from Basotho attacks.[352] Moshesh, a shrewd politician, did not comply with the demand and urged the Boers in the Sovereignty not to support the British forces in the conflict. The Boers then visited Moshesh at Thaba Boshigo, and a peace treaty between the Boers and Moshesh was signed on 3 September 1851, by Moshesh and his sons Molapo, Masupha, and Nehemiah, and for the Boers by G. F. Linde and Jan Vermaak.[353] On 25 August 1851, 137 Boers in Winburg signed a document requesting Andries Pretorius to accept the position of Administrator-General of the Winburg district. The Boers then ignored Warden's call to support the British forces against Moshesh, and a British force under Major Warden was humiliated by Moshesh on 30 June 1851, during the Battle of Viervoet.

These events in southern Africa significantly changed the perspectives of British politicians. In 1851, Secretary

---

[351] Muller, C. F. J. (1946). *Die Britse Owerheid en die Groot Trek* [Doctoral dissertation, University of Stellenbosch]., p.370

[352] De Wet, N. C. (1998). *Blank-Swart-Verhoudinge soos weerspieël in die Vrystaatse Historiografie, 1800-1910* [Doctoral dissertation, Universiteit van die Oranje Vrystaat]., p.75

[353] G. M. Theal (1888). *History of the Emigrant Boers in South Africa.* (2nd ed.). Swan Sonnenschein, Lowrey & Co., p.261-p.293

Grey described the Eighth Xhosa War in the British Parliament as "a most unprovoked outbreak," condemning the Xhosas' actions as "the barbarous proceedings of those savages".[354] In a speech in the British Parliament in June 1849, Molesworth portrayed the indigenous tribes as "rapacious and warlike savages, whom the Colonial Office, one time mistook for peaceful and harmless shepherds."[355] Adderly stated that British policies toward the indigenous tribes "had utterly and entirely failed".[356] Former State Secretary Gladstone remarked that the Aborigines Committee's policy of treaties with the tribes "proved a total failure and the fact was that the wars in that colony since that period had been more bloody, costly and ruinous than they had ever been before."[357] In April 1851, Secretary Grey wrote in a private memorandum: "...the kaffers are altogether unable to understand a policy of justice; and attribute all our measureas founded upon this principle to weakness - That it is idle to expect them to be restrained by any such motives as respect for treaties and a sense of justice, and that nothing but a display of force can keep them in order."[358] Even John Fairbairn, the Editor of the South African Commercial Advertiser, who consistently advocated for the persecution of the Boers, seemed to have gained different insights and now

---

[354] Muller, C. F. J. (1946). *Die Britse Owerheid en die Groot Trek* [Doctoral dissertation, University of Stellenbosch]., p.482
[355] Muller, C. F. J. (1946). *Die Britse Owerheid en die Groot Trek* [Doctoral dissertation, University of Stellenbosch]., p.474
[356] Muller, C. F. J. (1946). *Die Britse Owerheid en die Groot Trek* [Doctoral dissertation, University of Stellenbosch]., p.483
[357] Muller, C. F. J. (1946). *Die Britse Owerheid en die Groot Trek* [Doctoral dissertation, University of Stellenbosch]., p.483
[358] Muller, C. F. J. (1946). *Die Britse Owerheid en die Groot Trek* [Doctoral dissertation, University of Stellenbosch]., p.485

wrote: "It is now clear that the destruction of Mzilikazi and the overthrow of Dingane were steps in the Providential Scheme of tranquilising Southern Africa."[359]

On 15 April 1851, an interesting debate took place in the British House of Commons. Colonel Thompson made a statement: "Gunpowder, everybody knew, was explosive and so were Kaffirs."[360] According to Vernon Smith, experience proved to the British authorities: "that they could not have peace with the Kaffirs."[361] Sir George Napier, the former governor of the Cape, who was responsible for most treaties with the indigenous tribes and who pursued an aggressive policy of persecuting the Boers to "protect the indigenous tribes from the Boers," has now undergone a complete change in his view of the political situation in the Cape. During the parliamentary debate on 15 April 1851, he said: "... I will venture to say, that those treaties made by Sir A. Stockenström were never once infringed by the colonists, by the Government, by Dutchmen, or by Englishmen, the whole time I was there; but they were infringed by the Kaffirs over and over again. The moment it occurs to a savage that it is his interest to do so and so, treaties may go to the wind."[362] Napier further stated that the tribes must be completely defeated so that they do not think the British government is

---

[359] Giliomee, Hermann. Die Afrikaners (Afrikaans Edition). Tafelberg. Kindle Edition., p.172
[360] Muller, C. F. J. (1946). *Die Britse Owerheid en die Groot Trek* [Doctoral dissertation, University of Stellenbosch]., p.370
[361] Muller, C. F. J. (1946). *Die Britse Owerheid en die Groot Trek* [Doctoral dissertation, University of Stellenbosch]., p.362
[362] Muller, C. F. J. (1946). *Die Britse Owerheid en die Groot Trek* [Doctoral dissertation, University of Stellenbosch]., p.484

afraid of them. They must be compelled to plead for peace.[363] The British media then began advocating for self-governance in the Cape, which could relieve the Imperial Government of a significant burden in southern Africa. On 20 December 1851, The Times in London wrote: "We are wasting our blood and our millions because we will not give the Cape a constitution."[364]

After the setback at Boomplaats, the Boers north of the Vaal River, residing in various areas, experienced an increase in numbers as many Boers from Natal and now also the Orange River Sovereignty joined them. Several meetings were held in the region to establish unity, some of which were attended by both Andries Pretorius and Hendrik Potgieter. In May 1848, at Derdepoort near present-day Pretoria, the Boers decided to form a United Bond of all Boers north of the Vaal River, under a representative Volksraad (Citizen Council).[365] In January 1851, the Volksraad appointed four commandant generals: Potgieter for Zoutpansberg, Pretorius for Magaliesberg and Potchefstroom, W.F. Joubert for Lydenburg, and J.A. Enslin for Marico.[366] These four commandant generals operated under the authority of the Volksraad. Following the British

---

[363] Muller, C. F. J. (1946). *Die Britse Owerheid en die Groot Trek* [Doctoral dissertation, University of Stellenbosch]., p.484
[364] Muller, C. F. J. (1946). *Die Britse Owerheid en die Groot Trek* [Doctoral dissertation, University of Stellenbosch]., p.199
[365] Storm, J.M.G. (1989). Die konvensie van Sandrivier as die afsluiting van die Groot Trek. *HTS Teologiese Studies / Theological Studies, 45*(3), 680-695., p.689
[366] Storm, J.M.G. (1989). Die konvensie van Sandrivier as die afsluiting van die Groot Trek. *HTS Teologiese Studies / Theological Studies, 45*(3), 680-695., p.689

defeat at Viervoet, Pretorius received a letter from the Boers of Winburg in the Orange River Sovereignty, requesting his assistance to free them from British rule.[367] Pretorius responded immediately, and on 8 September 1851, this request and the situation in the Sovereignty were discussed during a meeting of the Boers' War Council and at a large public assembly at Magaliesberg. The war council decided to send Pretorius, along with F.G. Wolmarans and J.H. Grobbelaar, to negotiate with the British government.[368] The next day, on 9 September 1851, Pretorius wrote to the British Resident of the Sovereignty, Major Warden, requesting negotiations.

The Dutch Reformed Church minister, Andrew Murray (junior), appointed by Smith as the minister for Bloemfontein and Winburg, visited the Boers in Potchefstroom a few weeks later to discuss matters related to Sovereignty with Pretorius and other Boer leaders. The British government was concerned that they might get involved in Sovereignty affairs. The Boers clarified to Murray that they were not interested in meddling in Sovereignty matters but were serious about negotiating a treaty with England to secure Boer independence.[369] On 4 October 1851, Pretorius wrote to Warden, informing him that

---

[367] Storm, J.M.G. (1989). Die konvensie van Sandrivier as die afsluiting van die Groot Trek. *HTS Teologiese Studies / Theological Studies*, *45*(3), 680-695., p.690

[368] Storm, J.M.G. (1989). Die konvensie van Sandrivier as die afsluiting van die Groot Trek. *HTS Teologiese Studies / Theological Studies*, *45*(3), 680-695., p.690

[369] G. M. Theal (1888). *History of the Emigrant Boers in South Africa.* (2nd ed.). Swan Sonnenschein, Lowrey & Co., p.294

he, along with Wolmarans and Grobbelaar, had been tasked by the Boer War Council to enter into a peace treaty with England, that would acknowledge Boer independence. Major Warden then explained to the Cape governor, Sir Harry Smith, that the Sovereignty would now be determined by Pretorius's actions and recommended negotiating with him.[370] Smith accepted Warden's proposals and informed him that assistant commissioners with broad powers, Major W. S. Hogge and Mr. C. Mostyn Owen, would travel to the Sovereignty as soon as possible to handle the matter. When the assistant commissioners arrived in Bloemfontein on 27 November 1851, the Sovereignty was in chaos. The British government now considered it a better option to ally with the Boers to better defend the extensive borders of British territories. On 16 January 1852, the assistant commissioners met the Boer delegation at P.A. Venter's farm near the Sand River. The next day, on 17 January 1852, the Sand River Convention was signed, with the British government finally acknowledging the Boers' independence and their territory north of the Vaal River. At last, the British government acknowledged the Boers as an independent people with the right to renounce their British allegiance. Pretorius wanted to include the Boers in the Sovereignty (Winburg) in the agreement, demanding the return of all land previously belonging to the Boers, but Britain was not ready to cede territory in the Sovereignty. On 16 March 1852, a large gathering of Boers in Rustenburg unanimously ratified the Sand River Convention, marking the establishment of the

---

[370] G. M. Theal (1888). *History of the Emigrant Boers in South Africa.* (2nd ed.). Swan Sonnenschein, Lowrey & Co., p.295

Boer Republic, from September 1853 known as the South African Republic (Z.A.R.).[371]

After Sir Harry Smith fell out of favour with the British government in London and was recalled, Lieutenant-General George Cathcart was sent to the Cape to end the border war in British Kaffraria.[372] On 12 October 1852, Cathcart proposed to the Secretary of State that the Orange River Sovereignty be handed over to the Boers: "An acknowledged foreign state would be far more easily... and economically controlled... and would form a more secure barrier against barbarians from outside, than can ever be accomplished by British political interference and British governance without an expensive military establishment for its support."[373] However, Cathcart first needed to restore British prestige in southern Africa, which was damaged during the Battle of Viervoet. Cathcart attacked Moshesh with a force of 2,500 British troops, but he was defeated at Berea on 20 December 1852.[374] Moshesh, however, sought peace first to provide Cathcart with an honourable way out of the war. After the Battle of Berea, British politicians were persuaded to relinquish the Sovereignty. Molesworth declared in the British Parliament: "...(the Sovereignty) is

---

[371] Storm, J.M.G. (1989). Die konvensie van Sandrivier as die afsluiting van die Groot Trek. *HTS Teologiese Studies / Theological Studies, 45*(3), 680-695., p.691

[372] Muller, C. F. J. (1981). *500 Years - A History of South Africa* (3rd ed.). Academica., p.178

[373] Muller, C. F. J. (1946). *Die Britse Owerheid en die Groot Trek* [Doctoral dissertation, University of Stellenbosch]., p.214

[374] Muller, C. F. J. (1981). *500 Years - A History of South Africa* (3rd ed.). Academica., p.179

inhabited by disaffected Boers and hostile savages, and exposed to the incursions of the fiercest barbarians on the face of the earth; and which can only be retained by means of a large and increasing expenditure... wars, fierce and costly, are certain to occur periodically in the Orange River territory, as long as we retain possession of it."[375] The British government now preferred to see the Boers handle the challenges in the Sovereignty and the border disputes with Moshesh. On 4 March 1852, Lord Desart, the British under-secretary for colonies, wrote: "I am satisfied that by a judicious policy of conciliation towards the Boers, our difficulties at the Cape would comparatively speaking, disappear." If the Boers were considered allies, "the Caffer would no longer appear such a formidable enemy."[376]

Despite the significant number of English settlers who established themselves in the Orange River Sovereignty and the loyal Dutch-Afrikaans trekboers advocating for British retention of the Sovereignty, the British government decided to negotiate the transfer of the Sovereignty with the Boers. Dutch Reformed preacher, Murray, even travelled to London to plead in the British Parliament for the preservation of the Orange River Sovereignty by Britain.[377] Britain had already issued a royal proclamation on 30 January 1854, "abandoning and renouncing all dominion and sovereignty

---

[375] Muller, C. F. J. (1946). *Die Britse Owerheid en die Groot Trek* [Doctoral dissertation, University of Stellenbosch]., p.215
[376] Muller, C. F. J. (1946). *Die Britse Owerheid en die Groot Trek* [Doctoral dissertation, University of Stellenbosch]., p.372-p.373
[377] G. M. Theal (1888). *History of the Emigrant Boers in South Africa.* (2nd ed.). Swan Sonnenschein, Lowrey & Co., p.350

over the Orange River territory."[378] On 23 February 1854, Sir George Clerk and Boer representatives signed the Bloemfontein Convention, acknowledging Britain's recognition of the political independence of the area between the Orange and Vaal Rivers. This act formally established the Republic of the Orange Free State. In Cape Town, citizens were dismayed by the British government's relinquishment of the Orange River Sovereignty. In February 1854, they sent a petition to the British government stating: "But above all, for the honour of the British nation and the good faith of Great Britain to revoke the Convention."[379] Others, like the English historian and author J.A. Froude, believed that the British government dishonourably shifted the difficulties in the Sovereignty onto the Boers: "On abandoning the Orange Free State, we bequeathed as a legacy an unsettled border dispute with the Basutos. We were tired of fighting with them ourselves, and we left the President and Volksraad at Bloemfontein to arrange the differences as they could."[380]

---

[378] G. M. Theal (1888). *History of the Emigrant Boers in South Africa.* (2nd ed.). Swan Sonnenschein, Lowrey & Co., p.359
[379] Muller, C. F. J. (1946). *Die Britse Owerheid en die Groot Trek* [Doctoral dissertation, University of Stellenbosch]., p.333
[380] De Wet, N. C. (1998). *Blank-Swart-Verhoudinge soos weerspieël in die Vrystaatse Historiografie, 1800-1910* [Doctoral dissertation, Universiteit van die Oranje Vrystaat]., p.87

THE BOER REPUBLICS

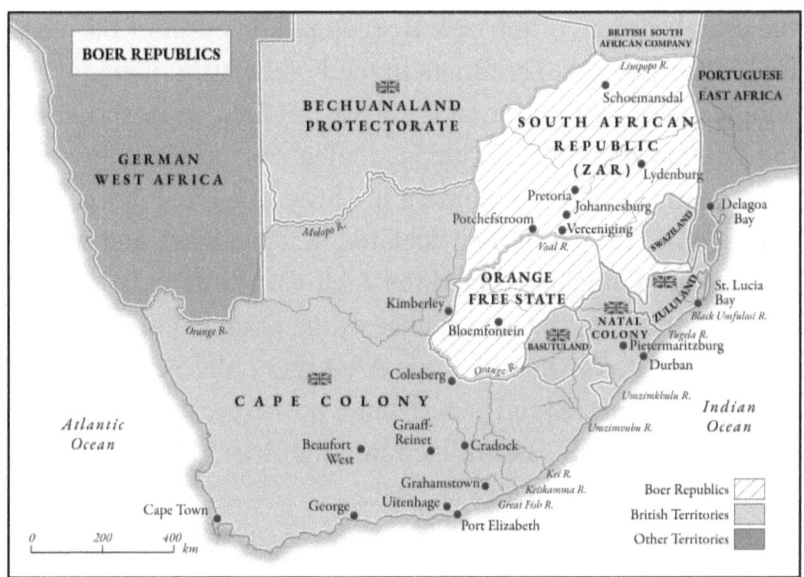

Map 5: The Boer Republics

The Bloemfontein Convention, after two decades, brought an end to the Boers' Great Trek. The Boer republics, the South African Republic (ZAR), and the Republic of the Orange Free State (OFS), now symbolised and protected the rights and freedoms of the Boers. Unfortunately, the last two prominent Voortrekker leaders of the Boers, Hendrik Potgieter and Andries Pretorius, passed away before they could witness the independence of the Orange Free State. Potgieter died on 16 December 1852, the Boers' Day of the Vow, and Pretorius died seven months later on 23 July 1853. In his final message to his people, Pretorius beseeched them to remain united, urging them to resolve any discord early and to remain faithful to each other and to God.[381] However,

---

[381] G. M. Theal (1888). *History of the Emigrant Boers in South Africa.* (2nd ed.). Swan Sonnenschein, Lowrey & Co., p.344-p.345

the establishment of the new Boer Republic north of the Vaal took several years. The Boers in the Potchefstroom area adopted the Constitution of the ZAR in 1856, while those in the Zoutpansberg district pledged allegiance in 1858. Pretoria became the seat of government in 1860. The Lydenburg Boers, who had previously declared independence and later united with Utrecht, adopted the ZAR Constitution in 1860.[382] Initially, the governance of the Orange Free State was mostly dominated by Cape Afrikaners like Sir John Brand (Johannes Brand). Over time, however, some leaders, such as F.W. Reitz, assimilated into the Boer identity and aligned themselves with the ZAR.

---

[382] Walker, E. A. (1922). *Historical Atlas of South Africa*. Humphrey Milford Oxford University Press., p.19

Epilogue

During the century when the Boer identity was formed, the unique circumstances and experiences that shaped their character and culture effectively equipped them to handle the challenges and persecution of the subsequent era. This not only allowed them to cope but also contributed to further developing and strengthening the Boer identity. Although the Boers were already a unique cultural entity before leaving the Cape Colony, the Great Trek further developed and strengthened their Boer identity. The shared history and shared trauma during the Great Trek had a significant impact on the development of Boer identity among the Boer people. Their struggle for survival as a group, facing attacks by large indigenous forces and enduring ongoing persecution by the British authorities, confirmed their unique identity. From the initial confrontations with Mzilikazi's attacks, the Boers learned that they could only overcome challenges as a united cultural group. The distinction between the Boers and the Dutch-Afrikaans population in the western districts of the Cape Colony, known as the Cape Afrikaners, those who did not participate in the Great Trek, became more apparent with the unfolding of the Great Trek.

THE CREATION OF THE BOER IDENTITY

It is, however, crucial to distinguish between national and cultural identity. Despite sacrificing everything for self-determination and freedom, the Boers were not nationalists. They regarded their Boer identity as a cohesive cultural entity transcending borders. Piet Retief, the first overarching leader of the Boers, attempted to improve conditions in the Cape Colony to encourage the Boers to stay in the Cape. Only in 1847, four years after the annexation of Natalia, did Andries Pretorius and Sarel Cilliers leave Natal. They were willing to accept and live under a British government, but the British authorities were not willing to consider their interests or recognise and respect their cultural Boer identity.

Bibliography

Baten, Joerg and Fourie, Johan, (2015), Numeracy of Africans, Asians, and Europeans during the early modern period: new evidence from Cape Colony court registers, Economic History Review, 68, issue 2, p. 632-656

Bergh, J. S. (1992). Die vestiging van die Voortrekkers noord van die Vaalrivier tot 1840. Historia, 37(2), pp.39-47.

Bezuidenhout, J. P. (1985). Forte en Verdedigingswerke op die Kaapse Oosgrens 1806-1836. Scientia Militaria, South African Journal of Military Studies, 15(4), 23-45.

Botha, J. P. (2008). Ons Geskiedenis (1st ed.). J.P. Botha.

Britannica, T. Editors of Encyclopaedia (2022, Oktober 3). Napoleontiese Oorloë. Encyclopedia Britannica. (https://www.britannica.com/event/Napoleonic-Wars

Cilliers, D. H. (1951). Die Eerste Verhoudinge Tussen Boer en Brit. Koersjoernaal, 19(3)

Claasen, J. W. (1994) Skotse predikante en die geestelike bearbeiding van die Voortrekkers. HTS Teologiese Studies/Theological Studies, 50.3.

Cory, G. E. (1921). The Rise of South Africa, Vol.I. Longmans, Green & Co.

Cory, G. E. (1926). The Rise of South Africa, Vol.IV. Longman's, Green & Co.

Cubbin, A. E. (1988). The English alliance with the Voortrekkers against the Zoeloes during March and April 1838. Historia, 33(2), 63-73.

Cubbin, A. E. (1992). An exposition of the clash of Anglo-Voortrekker interests at Port Natal leading to the military conflict of 23-24 May 1842. Historia, 37(2), 48-69.

De Jong, R. C. (1979). Die Slag van Bloedrivier - 16 Desember 1838. Scientia Militaria, South African Journal of Military Studies, 9(4).

De Kiewiet, C. W. (1957). A History of South Africa, Social & Economic. Oxford University Press.

De Klerk, P. (2002). 1652 - Die begin van kolonialisme in Suid-Afrika? Historia, 47(2), 739-764

De Villiers, J. (2012). Colonel John Graham of Fintry and the Fourth Cape Eastern Frontier War, 1811-1812. Scientia Militaria - South African Journal of Military Studies, 31(2).

De Wet, J. (1888). Beknopte geschiedenis van de Nederduitsche Hervormde Kerk van de Kaap de Goede Hoop sedert de stichting der volkplanting in 1652 tot 1804. J.C. Juta & Co.

De Wet, N. C. (1998). Blank-Swart-Verhoudinge soos weerspieël in die Vrystaatse Historiografie, 1800-1910 [Doctoral dissertation, Universiteit van die Oranje Vrystaat].

Dieter and Johan Fourie, (2010), A history with evidence: Income inequality in the Dutch Cape Colony, No 184, Working Papers, Economic Research Southern Africa

Du Plessis, J. S. (1952) Jan Van Riebeeck — 'N Biografiese Skets En Enkele Karaktereienskappe. Koers, vol. 19, no. 4, 1952, pp. 129-143.

Du Toit, A., & Giliomee, H. (1983). Afrikaner Political Thought. Volume 1: 1780-1850. University of California Press

Duvenhage, G. D. J. (1963). Wanneer het die Trichardt-trek begin? Historia, 8(2), 100-103.

Emanuelson, O. E. (1927). A History of Native Education in Natal between 1835-1927., Master's Thesis, University of KwaZoeloe-Natal.

Erasmus, L. J. (1972). Die Tweede Britse Verowering van die Kaap, 1806 [Master's Thesis, Potchefstroomse Universiteit vir Christelike Hoer Onderwys].

Fourie, J. & von Fintel, D. (2010) The Fruit of the Vine? An Augmented Endowments-Inequality Hypothesis and the Rise of an Elite in the Cape Colony. WIDER Working Paper 2010/112. Helsinki: UNU-WIDER.

Fourie, J., The remarkable wealth of the Dutch Cape Colony: measurements from eighteenth-century probate inventories, Economic History Review, 66, 2 (2013), pp. 419-448

Fourie, Johan and Uys, Jolandi, (2011), A survey and comparison of luxury item ownership in the eighteenth century Dutch Cape Colony, No 14/2011, Working Papers, Stellenbosch University, Department of Economics

Fourie, Johan and van Zanden, Jan Luiten, (2012), GDP in the Dutch Cape Colony: The national accounts of a slave-based society, No 04/2012, Working Papers, Stellenbosch University, Department of Economics

Fourie, Johan, (2011), Slaves as capital investment in the Dutch Cape Colony, 1652-1795, No 21/2011, Working Papers, Stellenbosch University, Department of Economics

Fourie, Johan, (2013), The quantitative Cape: Notes from a new Historiography of the Dutch Cape Colony, No 371, Working Papers, Economic Research Southern Africa

Gabriels, B. (1999). 'n Vergelyking tussen die verengelsingsbeleid na die Tweede Britse besetting van die Kaap aan die begin van die 19de eeu en die verengelsingsbeleid na die oorname van die ANC-regering in 1994 in Suid-Afrika [Master's Thesis, Stellenbosch Universiteit].

Geyser, O. (1967). Die lastige bure op die Noordgrens. Historia, 12(4), 225-233.

Gie, S. F. (1932). Geskiedenis vir Suid-Afrika, II (2nd ed.). Pro Ecclesia-Drukkery.

Giliomee, H. B. (1971). Die Kaap tydens die Eerste Britse Bewind, 1795-1803 [Doctoral dissertation, University of Stellenbosch],

Giliomee, H. B. (1973). Die Kaapse samelewing teen die einde van die kompanjiesbewind. Historia, 18(1), 2-17.

Giliomee, Hermann. Die Afrikaners (Afrikaans Edition). Tafelberg. Kindle Edition.

Godlonton, R. (1879). Case of the colonists (2nd ed.). Richards, Slater & Co.

Grebe, H. P. (1999). Oosgrensafrikaans : 'n te eksklusiewe begrip? Literator, Vol. 20(no.1), pp.51-66.

Grobler, J. E. H. (2010). Afrikaner- en Zoeloeperspektiewe op die Slag van Bloedrivier, 16 Desember 1838. Tydskrif vir Geesteswetenskappe, 50(3). pp.363-382.

Grobler, J. (2011). The Retief Massacre of 6 February 1838 revisited. Historia, 56(2), pp.113-132.

Grönum, W. (1987). Die Mfecane: Oorsprong, Ontplooiing an Invloed op die Tswana [Master's thesis, North-West University].

Haswell, R. F., & Brann, R. W. (1984). Voortrekker Pieter Mauritz Burg. Contree: Journal for South African Urban and Regional History, 16, 16-19.

Hattingh, J. L. (1988). Kaapse Notariële stukke waarin slawe van Vryburgers en amptenare vermeld word (1658 - 1730). Kronos: Journal of Cape History, 14(1), 43-65.

Heese, H. F. (2019). Cape Melting Pot, The role and status of the mixed population at the Cape 1652-1795, as translated by Delia Robertson from Groep Sonder Grense

Henning, E. E. (2014). The cultural significance of the church of the vow in Pietermaritzburg [Master's thesis, University of Pretoria].

Historical Publications Southern Africa (n.d.). The Diary of the Rev. F. Owen, Missionary with Dingaan, together with the accounts of Zoeloe affairs by the interpreters, Messrs.

Hully and Kirkman. Retrieved October 4, 2023, from https://hipsa.org.za/publication/the-diary-of-the-rev-f-owen-missionary-with-dingaan-together-with-the-accounts-of-Zoeloe-affairs-by-the-interpreters-messrs-hully-and-kirkman/

Hollfelder, N., Erasmus, J.C., Hammaren, R. et al. Patterns of African and Asian admixture in the Afrikaner population of South Africa. BMC Biol 18, 16 (2020).

Hugo, M. (1988). Piet Retief in die Suid-Afrikaanse geskiedskrywing. South African Journal of Cultural History, 2(2), 108-126.

Jansen, E. G. (1938). Die Voortrekkers in Natal., https://archive.org/details/VoortrekkersInNatal

Johan Fourie and Dieter von Fintel, (2010), The dynamics of inequality in a newly settled, pre-industrial society: the case of the Cape Colony, Cliometrica, Journal of Historical Economics and Econometric History, 4, (3), 229-267

Kapp, P. (2002). Die VOC-tydperk en die ontwikkeling van identiteitsbewussyne aan die Kaap. Historia, 47(2), 709-738., p720 (Prof. Kapp refers to a statement in his doctoral thesis by A. Biewenga)

Kotze C.R., Edited by Muller, C. F. (1984). 500 Years, A History of South Africa (4th ed.). Academica.

Kotze, C. R. (2021). Reaksie van die Afrikaners op die owerheidsbeleid teenoor hulle, 1806-1828: II. Historia

Lambert, T. (2021, March 14). A History of the Population of England. Retrieved June 12, 2023, from https://localhistories.org/a-history-of-the-population-of-england/

Le Roux, P. E. (1946). Die geskiedenis van die burgerkommando's in die Kaapkolonie (1652-1878) [Doctoral dissertation, University of Stellenbosch].

Leftwich, A. (1976). Colonialism and the constitution of Cape society under the Dutch East India Company. Doctoral dissertation, University of York.

Maphalala, S. J. (1980). Zulu relations with the whites during the nineteenth century : A broad perspective. Historia, 25(1), 19-27.

Markram, W. J. (1992). Stephanus Petrus Erasmus: Grensboerpionier en Voortrekker, 1788-1847 [Master's thesis, University of Stellenbosch].

Markram, W. J. (2001). Die lewe en werk van Petrus Lafras Uys, 1797-1838 [Doctoral dissertation, University of Stellenbosch].

Meintjes, K. (n.d.). The Massacre at Zuurberg. Eggsa.org. Retrieved September 17, 2023, from https://www.eggsa.org/articles/Zuurberg_intro.htm

Muller, C. F. J. (1946). Die Britse Owerheid en die Groot Trek [Doctoral dissertation, University of Stellenbosch].

Muller, C. F. J. (1971). Andries Pretorius se grondverkopings in Graaffreinet, 1837 tot 1838: 'n hersiening van dr. G.S. Preller se gevolgtrekkings. Historia, 16(1), 2-8.

Muller, C. F. J. (1981). 500 Years - A History of South Africa (3rd ed.). Academica

Muller, C. F. J. (1987). Die oorsprong van die Groot Trek (2nd ed.). Tafelberg Uitgewers.

Nel, H. F. (1967). Die Britse verowering van die Kaap in 1795 [Masters' Thesis, University of Cape Town]

Oberholzer, J.. (1989). Die Voortrekkerideaal - Natal of Transvaal?. HTS Teologiese Studies / Theological Studies. 45. 10.4102/hts.v45i3.2316.

Olga Witmer, Germans, the Dutch East India Company, and Early Colonial South Africa., German Historical Institute London Blog, 15/09/2020, https://ghil.hypotheses.org/23.

Olivier, G. C. (1968). Die vestiging van die eerste vryburgers aan die Kaap die Goeie Hoop. Historia, 13(3), 146-175.

Patterson, S. (1957). The Last Trek: A study of the Boer people and the Afrikaner Nation. Routledge & Keagan Paul Ltd., London.

Penn, N. (1995). The Northern Cape frontier zone, 1700 - c.1815. (Doctoral thesis). University of Cape Town, Faculty of Humanities, Department of Historical Studies.

Ploeger, J. (2012). In diens van die Kompanjie. Scientia Militaria - South African Journal of Military Studies

Pont, A. D., (1978). Die herderlijken brief van die Sinode van 1837. HTS Teologiese Studies/Theological Studies. (34)(4), 91-105.

Rautenbach, T. C. (2021). Sir George Napier en die Natalse Voortrekkers, 1838-1844. Historia, 34(2), p.22-p.31.

Retief, J. (2015)., The Voortrekker and the Ndebele, Part One: Attacks at the Vaal River and Liebenbergskoppie, 21 and 23 August 1836, Military History Journal, 16(6)., https://www.samilitaryhistory.org/vol166jr.html

Retief, J. (2016). The Voortrekker and the Ndebele, Part Two: The Battle of Vegkop, 20 October 1836. Military History Journal, 17(1)., https://www.samilitaryhistory.org/vol171jr.html

Roux, P. E. (1946). Die geskiedenis van die burgerkommando's in die Kaapkolonie (1652-1878) [Doctoral dissertation, Universiteit Stellenbosch].

Saks, D. (2004). The Real "First Anglo-Boer War": The Siege of Port Natal, 1842. The South African Military History Society, Military History Journal, 13(1)., Retrieved June 13, 2023, from https://samilitaryhistory.org/vol131ds.html

Scholtz, J. D. P. (1939). Die Afrikaner en sy Taal. Nasionale Pers.

Schutte, G.J., (2002) Neerlands India. De wereld van de VOC: calvinistisch en multi-cultureel, Historia 47(1), Mei 2002

Shamase, M. Z. (1999). The reign of King Mpande and his relations with the Republic of Natalia and its successor,

the British colony of Natal [Doctoral dissertation, University of Zoeloeland].
Smith, K. W. (1974). From frontier to midlands - A history of the Graaff-Reinet District, 1786-1910 [Doctoral dissertation, Rhodes University]
Steyn, J.C. 2016., Afrikanerjoernaal. 'n Vervolgverhaal in 365 episodes. Pretoria: FAK
Storm, J.M.G. (1989). Die konvensie van Sandrivier as die afsluiting van die Groot Trek. HTS Teologiese Studies / Theological Studies, 45(3), 680-695.
Strauss, P. (2015). Die Kaapse NG Kerk en die Groot Trek: 'n evaluering. Stellenbosch Theological Journal, 1(1), 273-289.
The South African Military History Society (n.d.). South African Military History Society Eastern Cape Branch Newsletter / Nuusbrief August/ August 2013: Great Trek Anniversary: Military encounters of the Voortrekkers 4. http://samilitaryhistory.org/13/p13augne.html
Theal, G. M. (1886). Boers and Bantu: A History of the Wanderings and Wars of the Emigrant Farmers from their leaving the Cape Colony to the overthrow of Dingan. Saul Solomon and Co.
Theal G. M. (1888). History of the Emigrant Boers in South Africa. (2nd ed.). Swan Sonnenschein, Lowrey & Co.
Theal, G. M. (1913). Willem Adriaan van der Dtel and other Historical Sketches. Thomas Maskew Miller, Publisher.
Theal, G. M. (1916). The story of Nations - South Africa (8th ed., p. 24). T. Fisher Unwin Ltd.
Uys, I.S. (1979). The Battle of Italeni. The South African Military History Society, Military History Journal, 4(5)., The Battle of Italeni - Military History Society - Journal (samilitaryhistory.org)
Van Aswegen, H. J. (1994). Die Mfecane. Werklikheid of mite? Historia, 39(1), 19-32.

Van Boven, M. W. (2006). "Memory of the World - Archives of the Dutch East India Company: Nomination Form - VOC Archives Appendix 2".

Van der Merwe, J. P. (1926). Die Kaap onder die Bataafse Republiek 1803-1806. Swets & Zeilinger, Amsterdam.

Van der Merwe, P. J. (1937). Die Noordwaartse beweging van die Boere voor die Groot Trek (1770-1842) [Doctoral dissertation, Rijksuniversiteit, Leyden].

Van der Merwe, P. J. (1995). The Migrant Farmer in the History of the Cape Colony 1657-1842. Ohio University Press

Van Jaarsveld, F. A. (1963). Anthropo-geographical aspects of the Great Trek: 1836-1863. Historia, 8(2), 93-99.

Van Jaarsveld, F. A. (1985). Die Ndzundza-Ndebele en die Blankes in Transvaal 1845-1883 [Master's Thesis, Rhodes Universiteit].

Van Zyl M.C., Edited by Muller, C. F. J. (1984). 500 Years, A History of South Africa (4th ed.). Academica

Van Zyl, M. C. (1986). Die Slag van Vegkop. Historia, 31(2).

Visagie, J. C. (1980). Louis Jacobus Nel: 'n voortrekkerleier uit die tweede linie. Journal of Cape History, 3(1), 52-89.

Visagie, J. C. (1988). Jan en Breggie Pretorius van die Tregardttrek. Journal of Cape History, 13(1), 14-22.

Visagie, J. C. (1990). Minder bekende Voortrekkerleiers. Historia, 35(1), 39-57.

Visagie, J. C. (1992). 'n Besoek aan Mzilikazi in 1830. Historia, 37(1), 9-23.

Visagie, J. C. (1993). Verset teen die burgermilisieplan van 1835. Historical Association of South Africa (HASA), 38(2).

Visagie, J. C. (1996). Die fyn onderskeid tussen die Voortrekkers en die trekboere. Historia, 41(2).

Voigt, J. C. (1969). Fifty years of the history of the Republic in South Africa 1795 - 1845, Volume 1. New York, Negro Universities Press

Voigt, J. C. (1899). Fifty Years of the History of the Republic in South Africa 1795-1845, Volume II. E.P. Dutton & Co.

Vrey, W.J.H., (1968), Blanke besetting en bevolkingsgroei van die Republiek van Suid-Afrika vanaf 1652 tot 1960, Doctoral dissertation, University of the Orange Free State,Bloemfontein.

Walker, E. A. (1965). The Great Trek (5th ed.). Adam & Charles Black, London.

WikiTree. (2023, March 18). Project: Voortrekkers. Retrieved September 13, 2023, from https://www.wikitree.com/wiki/Project:Voortrekkers

Zukowski, A. (1992). Polish relations with and settlement in South Africa (circa 1500-1835). Historia, 37(1).

www.ingramcontent.com/pod-product-compliance
Lightning Source LLC
Chambersburg PA
CBHW031405290426
44110CB00011B/268